I TELL IT LIKE IT IS! Volume One

Copyright © 2025 by John Kuhn

First Edition: October 2025

ISBN (Hardcover): 978-1-969988-00-4

ISBN (Paperback): 978-1-969988-01-1

Published by: Self-Published

Charleston, South Carolina, USA

Printed in the United States of America

10 9 8 7 6 5 4 3 2 1

Contents

3

FOREWORD

Dear Reader: John Kuhn here. My first statement to you: These American authors (Female Author Ayn Rand of New York City); and transcendentalist authors (Ralph Waldo Emerson and Henry David Thoreau from Massachusetts) are the bedrock of American thought.

Dagny Taggart

The greatest heroine (and my hero) in all of literature (because she is always true to herself) is Dagny Taggart in *Atlas Shrugged*, by Ayn Rand.

(Dagny was the ultimate in being herself and always doing her best, no matter what the cost).

Dagny SHOULD BE the rock star of our age. She is my rock star!

The next two American writers I learned in my **high school** classroom (American boarding high school, Culver Military Academy and Culver Girls Academy) when I learned the greatest of all American Thinking came from two 19th Century brilliant transcendentalist American writers, my two favorite Transcendentalists: Henry David Thoreau and Ralph Waldo Emerson (Both, Concord, Massachusetts, 1830s to 1850s):

To be yourself in a world that is constantly trying to make you something else is the greatest accomplishment.
Ralph Waldo Emerson, *Essays*, 1841.

Rather than love, than money, than fame, give me truth.

Again, I believe you will be able to live a valuable and fulfilling life, with self-esteem, if you follow this message from Henry David Thoreau, *Walden*, 1854.

This above all: To thine own self be true.

Hamlet, Act 1, scene 3, 78–82.

This, by Shakespeare, is what I lived my life by, ever since I was born. You will see that I live my life by this philosophy in every chapter of this autobiography. (By the way, no true writer can resist Shakespeare, so we don't even try!)

Shout outs by the author, John Kuhn:

Because this is a trilogy, a shout out to one of the best, William Manchester and Paul Reid's *Churchill* biography!

Because it is in homage to one of the funniest books ever written, a shout out to

John Kennedy Toole for *A Confederacy of Dunces*!

John Kuhn, Charleston, June 2025.

ACKNOWLEDGEMENTS FROM THE AUTHOR:

First, I want to thank my "with it" 94-Year-Old Aunt Vreneli Kuhn Wilson (born Christmas Day, 1931) who is still "with it" in every single possible way! How do I know that? Because in January 2025 I delivered a hard copy of the first 89 pages of my Manuscript to her, and, unbeknownst to me, she read every word and proofread it for me (that is what you get when you **send written work to a 1st Grade teacher – lol!).**

Two weeks later she calls me and says, "John, I read your book. This is the funniest book on farming I have ever read! But, I want to go though it on the phone with you and correct some of your tenses and punctuation." Then, we spent 2 hours on the telephone going through every page she found errors, and I corrected them with her! How cool is that?

Now, when I say that my Aunt Vreneli has still "with it" in every way, I was even more astounded, two hours into the phone call, when she says, "You know John, I have been thinking my own youth growing up on our little California dairy when your father (Fritz Kuhn, Jr.) and I were milking all the cows on our own father's dairy every single day, from age 4 to age 14.

The more I think about it, I believe that you have got Homogenized mixed up with Pasteurized!" She said, "All though the Chapter titled **American Farmers Will Not Eat their own Food In the Grocery Stores – they know better!**

you have confused the process that creates Homogenized Milk with the process that creates Pasteurized Milk." This is from my 94-Year-Old Aunt Vreneli Kuhn Wilson!

Vreneli said: "Homogenization is a natural, God-given, process in milk where over time, the milk will separate by weight, which will help you make cheese instead of skim milk. Which is a good thing. But, Pasteurization is a human intervention in the milk process, where we often ruin the milk by heating it, to make it last longer on the shelf." She said, "Everything you say in the book is correct, but you need to change 'Homogenization' to 'Pasteurization' because it is the human intervention process of Pasteurization that ruins most milk in the USA and makes so many people sick to their stomach. But, God's Homogenization does not do that."

Of course, Vreneli is correct, so I had to go through all that Chapter and change Homogenization to Pasteurization. That way you, dear reader, are buying milk that God made with all the female animals (including humans) and not heated up and ruined by human beings in our Pasteurization plants.

Just so you know, my Aunt Vreneli Kuhn Wilson has written her own children's books; but, her most recent and longest book, switched gears entirely, and is about my grandfather, Fritz Kuhn, Sr, and her perspective of growing up on the same Dairy Farm in California with my dad (her brother), Fritz Kuhn, Jr.

I will not spoil my first chapter, for you, dear reader. YOU will have to read Chapter One (three pages from now – you are so close to starting my story!) of this book to see all the birthday coincidences in my Kuhn Family and they are shockingly cool!

Vreneli's most recent book, *The Pheasant In the Tree – The Wisdom of Fritz,* was invaluable to me in understanding my family history and growing up on Dairy Farm on the Mexican Border. This book also does a better job than most farming books in the United States of helping you understand working the land before tractors, entirely by hand and oxen and horses.

When Vreneli, and all Americans who grew up on farms from 1650 to 1950, grew up on their farms, horses, mules, and oxen did ALL the work of a tractor. **Unimaginable, even to me – not to mention the rest of 21st Century America who do not grow up on farms**. In her book, Vreneli even tells you where eggs come from (because you may not know) and she tells you how a Swiss person will never cheat with numbers, not even in counting eggs!!! We Swiss follow numbers religiously, no matter where they take you! Why do you think Zurich, Switzerland, had one of the top Engineering Colleges in this world (right up there with MIT!)

PROLOGUE BY THE AUTHOR

Because, I, author John Kuhn, am writing this book (and not my Swiss *mechanical-brain* father), I can blame my English ancestry mother, Madeline Hall Kuhn for the literary side of me. This paragraph is intentionally "British humor" tongue-in-cheek about my mother, because, truthfully, my mother has been my inspiration for everything in my whole life. **I owe my whole world to my Mother. No matter how many Harry Potter shots I take at her in this book! Lol!**

Truthfully, I was fortunate to be born with both left-brain logical and right-brain artistic: From Swiss engineering type father (Que up Zurich's most famous European Engineering University) to my English Literature type mother: My mother's home country, England, has two of the top European Literature Universities in the world: Cue up Cambridge University and Oxford University in England!

As you will see throughout this whole book, I cannot help myself **when it comes to my propensity for Music AND Movie Triva**. Thus, I will start with movie AND the soundtrack, for *"Chariots of Fire,"* before we even get to the book, itself! And, you will see, Dear Reader, that **I promise to humor you with this musicology and movie making magic in every single chapter of this book:**

Cambridge University is the English University where one of my all-time Top 10 Movies was set and filmed: *"Chariots of Fire"* in 1981. Not surprisingly, it comes with the best soundtrack of the year, Vangelis's avant-garde soundtrack, *"Chariots of Fire,"* which was the first to go to number one in the USA without any words, and many of us Americans hummed all of the time.

Cambridge University is also where, in the 2014 famous movie, "*The Theory of Everything*," actor Eddie Redmayne and Actress Felicity Jones go Punting on the River Cam in front of many of Cambridge's gorgeous gothic buildings.

Oh, I get a pun on this one when it comes to "punting" because in the United States punting means punting an American Football and not Punting on a boat in a river where you will sink. But, in England that means "punting in a small boat on a river." Plus, I will take you on a double pun with "punting" in American Football being quite different than "punting" in European football: European football is not football at all in America – it is decidedly "Soccer" to us Americans!) But, you Europeans do think we are crazy to call American football, "football" when there is almost no feet used at all in our football – except, ironically the "punting" part of American football, which is the only time our feet are used in American football. Thus, you want to call pushing yourself around on a little boat, "Punting?" Then we Americans can call our big outdoor gladiator game, "Football" As Shakespeare said in Henry V: "Once more unto the breach, dear friends, once more." There, I quoted all of our favorite playwright, on both sides of the pond! Lol!

Oxford University was used to film almost every Harry Potter film, especially Christ Church College staircase and Great Hall, which became the "Great Hall" in the books; New College's stunningly beautiful "Cloisters" were used all the time; Oxford's Divinity School; and, Bodleian Library, which was also used as the Harry Potter Library. Dear Reader, **I will treat you to all manner of Harry Potter mischief in this very book you are reading, being as Harry Potter and I share the same birthday**!

NOW FOR "SHOUT OUTS" TO ALL WHO HELPED ME,

SIGNIFICANTLY:

First, I want to personally thank my very young paralegal, Michaella Mayfield Powell, for just getting me to start writing my autobiography. She knew I could write, and she knew I would write funny. Everyone needs enormous encouragement when they are sitting on the fence about becoming an Author. If it were not for 21-Year-Old Michaella, this book would never have started!

I also want to thank my law office "cleaning guy," Vince French for being my # 1 Cheerleader and Reader! I needed someone who "got me" and was super-on-board with every word I wrote – and kept encouraging my manuscript to be funnier than before. Vince especially loves all the humanized farming stories.

Next I want to thank my incredible friend, Britney Franklin, who for the past 3 years listened to me week after week, be sooooooo excited about what I was writing and listening to some of the stories as I was writing them and encouraging me every page of the way! Britney, you are the best listener ever! And, the best supportive "Cancer Zodiac Sign" ever! Thank you, Britney!

Last, but not least, I could not have written these 260 pages without my two young paralegals who encouraged me IN EVERY SINGLE WAY: Kamryn Vance and Mercury Hipp.

Kamryn Vance is the fastest reader I have ever seen in my life – so shout out to Ohio State University for that! Kamryn was helpful every week the past year, when I wanted a chapter read on a Monday Morning (oh yes, pun intended

– with Lindsey Buckingham of Fleetwood Mac on his song "*Monday Morning*") after writing at my law firm desk on many weekends!

Mercury Hipp is top 10 smartest people I have met at any time in my whole life and I am SOOOOOOO fortunate to have her as our Paralegal! Shout out to Hollins University there! And, thank you, Mercury, for helping me analyze every single chapter, "every which way but loose!" (Now, I believe that is a pun with a famous movie, right? Oh yes! That is actor Clint Eastwood's comedy from 1978 and **one of the first movies I ever saw**: "*Every Which Way But Loose*. I love all Clint Eastwood movies, from "***The Good, The Bad and the Ugly***," to "***Cry Macho***."   And, being a farmer from the confirmed countryside in California, I loved that County Western movie (gone mainstream, because of Eddie Rabbitt's Number One County Music song that went with it, as well, "*Every Which Way But Loose*." Mercury Hipp has helped me analyze every single word of this book "every which way but loose," so that you, Dear Reader, have a better book in your hands than we would have had without Ms. Mercury!

JOHN KUHN'S PRE-POSTSCRIPT

(you see, I am still endeavoring to invent new words for our English Dictionary!)

Shout out to The Beatles' song, *"Got to Get You Into My Life,"* for, in some weird way, helping me finish Volume One and get back to the Publisher! That song always makes me think of dating my wife as undergraduates at Vanderbilt University, so that is where that is coming from! I cannot do this Trilogy without her and she helps me with many mental roadblocks! ☺

DEDICATION TO MY WIFE

I want to dedicate Volume One to my wife, Augusta Porcher Kuhn ("Shea") because, without Shea making sure that I had non-stop days blocked out, and her covering our clients, for almost the entire two years of 2024 and 2025, there is no way I would have even remotely finished this first 250 pages. **From the bottom of my heart, I thank you, Shea!**

JOHN KUHN STATEMENT TO THE READER

I am not going to teach you how to play
– although that comes with it –
I am going to teach you how to Live!

Author John Kuhn

CHAPTER 1

CHICAGO IS COLD

I was born on July 31, 1962, on a farm in El Centro, California. You know what is weird about that? Somehow my grandfather, Fritz Kuhn, Sr., was born on a farm 66 years earlier on the exact same July 31st day in Switzerland. Shockingly, it gets much weirder than that: My grandfather had two children, my father Fritz Kuhn, Jr., and my Aunt Vreneli Kuhn, both born on the farm on Christmas day, two years apart – Christmas Day 1929 and 1931. I was so proud to have a father born on Christmas Day AND an aunt born on Christmas Day – and not even twins!

As if that isn't coincidental (and cool) enough, my grandfather's two oldest grandchildren (by each Christmas Day child of his) was born ON THE FARM, and back on his own birthday: My oldest cousin, Diane Kuhn Wilson was born on July 31, 1952, to my Aunt Vreneli Kuhn and I (that's me!) was born on July 31, 1962, to Fritz Kuhn, Jr. Imagine the odds that your two children would be born two years apart on Christmas Day AND your two oldest grandchildren, by each of your two children, would be born back on your very own birthday? And, all on the Kuhn family farms – outside Zurich, Switzerland and in El Centro, California! How cool is that, right??!

When I was born in El Centro, California, my Grandfather (born on the same day as me), Fritz Kuhn, said, "I cannot wait to see what this boy will do in this world. I know that it will be great!" My oldest cousin, Diane Kuhn Wilson (who was also born on the same day as both of us ten years before me) told me this. She said my Grandpa could not have been more proud and Diane remembered that clearly as a 10-year-old girl.

What you may not know from all those amazingly cool birthday coincidences is that I was born on July 31, 1962, to be a writer. God decides these things when our DNA is thrown together by our Mom and our Dad at (usually drunken) conception. God also decides what our job and/or career will be when we are born. He does! We just don't know it yet. In fact, if you read Chapter 6 of this book you will see how I know that you were chosen a job when you were born by God and that DNA thing God created for us. This is not rocket-science! If some rocket-scientist from India or Germany can figure this out, certainly little ole me, your writer here in Charleston, South Carolina, can figure this out!

The second reason that **I was born on July 31, 1962, was to be an actual Author**! It turns out that I have the exact same July 31st birthday as J.K. Rowling herself! In fact, J.K. Rowling was born on my same birthday three years after me. Thus, I must thank myself for paving the way for her to write! Lol!

Likewise, if God can figure out that I need to be born on my grandpa's birthday to make him happy, who am I to argue with that? I'm sure you, dear reader, have some family coincidences (like mine above) that your mama always tells you about. Run with it! It is part of your family. It's part of your history. It is part of your DNA! And, eventually it becomes part of your job or career! And, whatever else it is you like to do!

Something else you need to know about me, right from the onset: I am a Leo by zodiac AND I happen to be the Tiger, too, by my Chinese Year! **In other words, I double down on being a cat – both a Lion and a Tiger!**

And, because I happen to be born in 1962, I am born during the Chinese Year of the Tiger. So, look out: I am a Leo (lion) through and through (that will be evident, soon!) and, worse yet, I am a Chinese tiger, to boot! Again, it is not my fault that God made me a lion AND a tiger all at the same time. But, I will **run** (like a tiger) with it! **And, as a born writer, pun intended!!**

So, how is it that the oldest boy of one of the biggest alfalfa hay farmers in Southern California does not end up a farmer on his own family farm? Especially with a Swiss-German family that loves to give their farms to their oldest boys? By the way, we will see that primogeniture played a huge factor in my grandfather coming to America, just a couple of chapters from now!

Well, you will not have to wait long (later in this very Volume of my trilogy) to find out how the youngest boy ends up with the family farm (my deceased younger brother, farmer Jim Kuhn). But, you will have to wait until Volume 2 of this autobiography to find out how I ended up settling in the incredible port city and historic city of Charleston, South Carolina. That will come after the chapters of my founding a market for Sudan hay for our family hay farm to the dairy cows in Japan during the height of the US Agricultural Recession in the 1980s. See, dear reader, you have a lot to look forward to!

Actually, I will give you a little hint as to why I am not farming hay on one of the largest hay farms in the United

States: Unfortunately for me, I am allergic to everything! I mean, allergic to EVERYTHING! Especially our number one crop, alfalfa hay! Therefore, I loved going to law school in Chicago in the early 1990s because I quickly found (when I got there) that everything in Chicago is paved over – and better yet, it is completely frozen over for five whole months (day and night) every year. Naturally, I am way less allergic to streets than plants! Lol! Therefore, for five months in the winter in Chicago I am allergic to NOTHING! How glorious is that!?? Now you know why 9.5 million people live in and love Chicago! Why else would you love Negative 30 degrees plus 40 mph windchill on top of that? **If you are allergic to everything, Chicago is the perfect city in which to live! Lol!**

CHAPTER 2

FARMERS THAT HATE RAIN

When you are born and raised on a farm you start farming at age two. Your father does not worry about things like heat, bugs, dehydration, falling off the tractor and being run over and killed by the huge, huge wheels. If father's worried about that, there would be no farming. On the other hand, mothers DO worry about exactly these things. Therefore, you cannot be a farming mother if you worry. You just cannot. Now, my mother worried about all these things! So, she solved that problem by just not coming out to the farm to see how we boys were doing.

Speaking of boys, there were just two of us: My younger brother, James ("Jim") Kuhn, was born on April 21, 1964, on the farm, of course! Jim's birth date, April 21st, turned out to be important to my dad because he immediately pointed out that it was perfect to now be able to remember the sugar beet harvest season. April 21st just so happens to be the first day of Sugar Beet harvest, and my birthday, July 31st, just so happens to be the last day of Sugar beet harvest! So, my farmer father, Fritz Kuhn, pointed out we could all remember Sugar Beet harvest season by the boy's birthdays! A farmer's perspective! Lol!

We grew acres and acres of Sugar Beets! For sugar beet harvest, we trucked actual raw sugar beets from our fields to the Holly Sugar Beet Factory located between Brawley and El Centro, California. They were HUGE semi-trucks with sets of huge double trailers, that go from the farmer's beet fields to the sugar beet factory, or the sugar beet railroad drop off depot. At the sugar beet factory or railroad siding drop off points, there were more HUGE machines unloading the sets of doubles into the railroad cars. We owned these trucks and there was a giant Imperial Valley Union Pacific (The UP) Railroad reception point for Spreckels Sugar and Dominos Sugar, merely half a mile from our huge Kuhn Farm Shops and Kuhn Headquarters.

Imagine how fun it was for me and my brother, as little boys, to go down to the HUGE Railroad Distribution point on one of our HUGE trucks and watch our truck drivers dump these HUGE loads of our Sugar Beets into the HUGE Central Pacific Railroad bottom unloading CP and UP Freight cars! So cool! Everything in the farming world is HUGE, even as you get older, which is why all 50-year-old "little boys" in the United States want HUGE Ford F-150 pickups, or all 50-year-old "little boys" in the United States want HUGE Chevy Silverado 1500 pickups! All we little boys, no matter what age, in the world (including Switzerland) desperately want our HUGE TOYS!! We boys embrace HUGE boats, HUGE pick-up trucks, HUGE firetrucks, HUGE campers, HUGE EVERYTHING!!

The other half of our Sugar Beet trucks would go from our sugar beet fields to the nearby Holly Sugar Beet Factory HUGE holes where the sugar beets somehow disappear into the factory after being dumped in the HUGE holes. The sugar beet factory takes the raw sugar beets and processes them into table sugar FOR YOU at a restaurant in the United States, or bags of sugar at your grocery store.

The sugar beet growing season is exceptionally long for a crop - a full year. Which is one reason they grow well in

Imperial Valley, California: The Imperial Valley is a low desert. In fact, it is 30 feet BELOW sea level! To prove that point the Holly Sugar Factory, on the main highway in Imperial County, between El Centro and Brawley, painted a HUGE "Sea Level" sign on the huge, HUGE Sugar Beet Silo for everyone to see driving to work every day, indicating that all of us and EVERYTHING in the Imperial Valley is truly BELOW sea level. All our visitors to the Imperial Valley are also reminded of this because they see the dramatic "Sea Level" Line on the huge Sugar Beet Silo when they come to our town! Truthfully

Also, because our farming valley is below sea level, it is, candidly, a desert (with cactus and ocotillos and sagebrush)! Consequently, IT NEVER RAINS in El Centro, California! In fact, we are the only farmers in the world who HATE RAIN! All other farmers in the world love rain – they need God's rain to grow their crops. But, not in the Imperial Valley: We irrigate all our crops from the Colorado River. We cannot stand rain. Rain makes it impossible to harvest our impressive crops: Organic Vegetables for Whole Foods. Sugar beets for real sugar. Alfalfa hay for dairy cows all over California, to produce oodles of milk for all Californians! Bags of regular vegetables and organic vegetables, and heaps of sugar beets, and loads of all kinds of hay for beef *cattle* and dairy *cows* (they are not the same) and horses.

Now, the John Kuhn salesman (AND WRITER) part of the story: My family also grew acres of Bermuda Hay for horses in California. But, my imagination had this idea that horses in Japan should eat our hay. So, this story goes from Bermuda hay in California to Bermuda hay all over THE WORLD – yes, when you are a God-given salesman – and a God-given writer – this is no longer hyperbole.

23

Remember, God did not intend for me to be a farmer. For God's sake, I'm allergic to hay!!! I'm especially allergic to Bermuda hay! I know this because all the baseball and football fields in El Centro – especially at my grammar school AND my middle school: McCabe Elementary School and Seeley School, are all Bermuda grass! I would go out for recess every day in 3rd grade, fancy myself as Dodger Pitcher Sandy Koufax, and be sneezing so badly on the pitcher's mound by the second inning, that I had to quit the game. As the pitcher. Every school recess!

Which leads to my sneezing like crazy at every elementary school football, soccer and baseball game. Sadly, even sneezing at recess dodge ball games. Which is not fun! Sneezing, sneezing, sneezing every day at school. And every day after school at home! Which led me to think that selling all this Bermuda hay to anywhere but my family Kuhn stackyard, would be just the ticket! Since nobody told me I couldn't, that is exactly what I did.

I came home to my Kuhn family farm after college and inadvertently decided: Sell as much hay to the Japanese dairy farms (Sudan hay and alfalfa hay) and Japanese horses (Bermuda hay) and to the Japanese wagu-beef farms (also alfalfa and Sudan). Way ahead of my time with that Bermuda hay to Japan idea – frankly I was not ahead of my time at all because Ron Anderson in the PNW of the United States thought of it way before I did! I see that the first United States alfalfa hay exporter just died in February 2025, the man who started it all, again Ron Anderson. Shout out to Ron Anderson; he was my super-hero, and I would not have done what I did in my early 20s without his setting the table – pun intended!

Just for the record, when I say I was also the first to found a market in Japan for hay, I was the one to introduce Sudan hay to the Japanese Dairy farms, which is quite different than alfalfa hay. The Japanese dairy farms did not need the protein of alfalfa hay, but they did need the roughage of Sudan hay. I absolutely figured that out on my own on my first 4 trips by myself to Japan in Spring of 1986.

But, since I am the one in the Imperial Valley with the God-given salesman traits, and I HATED Bermuda hay from the moment I kicked my first football on the Bermuda grass at age 5, I decided I would sell that damn Bermuda hay to the individuals it is intended by God for: Horses. Yes, God intended Bermuda grass to be for horses, not Humans! I just followed God's lead on that one!

Between age 22 to age 28, I read every single book I could on how to do business with the Japanese. What their business culture is (for example how to bow in Japan, which is an art-form I perfected – and I will teach you in Chapters 12-18 of Volume 2 – with flavorful (like "sushi") commentary you know that you can depend on me to deliver, just as I have so far! I will also explain to you, dear reader, in Volume 2, how the Japanese ancient Samurai Culture even effects where everyone sits in today's Japanese business meeting in 2020s – the most important (highest ranked in the room) Japanese businessman always sits the furthest from the door – no matter where the door is in the room, because he is to be "protected from the enemy by his friends," straight from the Samurai Culture and history. And you need to know this if you are to do business in Japan.

Most American salesman in Japan never understand this (because they don't try to understand the Japanese culture):

A <u>Salesman</u> in the Japanese business culture is there to serve, so he ALWAYS sits the <u>closet to the door</u>. You will learn this in Volume 2 of this book, just like I learned from Mark Zimmerman's 1985 book, ***How to do Business with the Japanese***. (Again, it helps to sell stuff when your God-given traits are reading books and writing faxes to Japanese customers in simple English they can understand and read!)

Likewise, God intended my brother to be the farmer. Jim Kuhn's God-Given traits are that he is allergic to nothing (like his father and not like his brother – lol!). He can multi-task like crazy (again, like his father, Fritz, and not like his ADD brother) and full of energy (like his ADD brother on that one!). **Consequently, my younger brother, Jim Kuhn, was a farmer – and a damn good one at that!**

However, I was not intended by God to be the famer. Remember, I am allergic to hay! I am even allergic to almost all crops!! That is a clear message from God that I am not to be the farmer, even if I am born and raised on a farm. Likewise, you are not necessarily intended to be a farmer if you are born on a farm. You are also not intended to be a lawyer just because your father was, and you were not intended to be a teacher just because your mother was. No. Your God-Given traits tell you (from as early as age 5 years old) what you are meant to be. If you love to talk and be in front of people and motivate, you should be Minister. If you are quiet and like routine, you should probably be a factory worker. And, if you like to eat pizza, you should probably be a cook. You must not mind getting your hands dirty and learning all the jobs. Every career has its downside and tasks you don't always want to do.   My dad taught me that one! Start as a dishwasher, then be a server (to learn how to be nice to your fellow man or woman), and finally, a cook!

Back to the irony of the Imperial Valley being "The Carrot Capital of the World," but disliking rain: The reason that it is almost impossible to harvest our crops when it rains in Imperial Valley is because it is a desert floor with no vegetation. We then plant all our awesome crops in the desert (with cactus, ocotillo plants, and tumble weeds <u>all around our fields</u>). Then we irrigate with long rows (1/4 mile to 1/2 mile) from irrigation ditches. Then the desert animals all come to drink water in our fields: coyotes and roadrunners (yes, we have actual Wile E. Coyote, Beep-Beep Roadrunners in and all around our fields every day). Not to mention: jack rabbits, scorpions, rattlesnakes, desert spiney lizards and all manner of lizards, California quail, Gambel's quail, and brilliant, head-spinning burrowing owls. We love having all the desert animals come and drink from our irrigation ditches because it brings life and energy to the farm, especially the exceedingly cool head-spinning burrowing owls who love being high up on the ditchbanks! A lot of the animals like to be up on the ditchbanks because they are higher than the surrounding desert floor and they can see their predators better from our ditchbanks. Really

It only rains (on average) once a year in the Imperial Valley. Therefore, we constantly must irrigate our lettuce (all 7 kinds of lettuce we grow and you buy at your local grocery store and YOU EAT at home!). And we constantly have to flood irrigate our other crops for YOU to eat: Alfalfa hay (for milk YOU drink), sugar beets, cotton (for clothes YOU wear), durum wheat (specialty wheat *only grown in the Imperial Valley in the USA,* for pasta and macaroni YOU eat). And, we have now learned how to sprinkle irrigate lots of vegetables YOU love to eat all over the United States: broccoli, kale, cress, endive, Butterworth lettuce, arugula, spinach, cauliflower, cantaloupe, honey dews, and even watermelons. We have learned to use thousands of sprinkle irrigation pipes in our fields to *save water* for the rest of YOU in the USA!

And, we farmers drive around our fields on dirt "ditchbanks" in pickup trucks. Then, when it rains our **pickup trucks slide off the ditchbanks into the water-filled canals** and ditches everywhere (because there is no vegetation in sandy ditchbanks to hold the ditchbanks together). Thank goodness it only rains once a year because all of us farmers have to stay home on the rainy days in the Imperial Valley.

Moreover, we certainly cannot harvest all our wonderful crops in this slip-slidey, sandy, muddy mess. Thus, no matter what crops we grow, in the Imperial Valley we hate rain!

Back to my birthday, July 31st being the end of Sugar Beet season: Remember the Imperial Valley is a hot, hot, hot low desert with blazing 115-degree sun all summer. By the end of July, the 115-degree weather is way too hot for the Sugar Beets and they wilt and rot and practically evaporate. I have seen sugar beets and farmworkers and housewives evaporate in the Imperial Vally sun! In fact, I have evaporated in the Imperial Valley sun!! Yes I have!!

CHAPTER 3

ONCE UPON A TIME IN A BEAUTIFUL, QUAINT COUNTRY CALLED SWITZERLAND...

Once upon a time in a fairyland far, far away called Switzerland, there was a young normal farmer boy born to a dairy farming family in the countryside (way outside the big city named Zurich). His name was Fritz Kuhn, and he was good looking (which was, in fact, true – lol!) And he learned how to milk cows by hand and grow hay by hand and be a good little farmer boy. And, he wanted to marry a beautiful girl from the big city, called Zurich! (Naturally, who doesn't want that, right?)

This chapter is about my grandfather, Fritz Kuhn, Sr. He is how I got here. Not surprisingly, my grandfather was also born on a dairy farm.   But, not in this country. No, he was actually born in the most famous dairy country in the whole world: Switzerland.

You know Switzerland! Home of all those Black and White Swiss dairy cows you see on posters all over the United States! Posters with all kinds of dairy products, like: Milk and Cheese. Butter and Ice Cream. Yes, Ice Cream!

Anyway, my grandfather was born on an actual dairy farm just outside Zurich, Switzerland, on July 31, 1896, where they have had the "Kuhn Dairy" farm for over 800 years in the same little town called Dietlikon. Yes. 800 years in the same family! We cannot even imagine that in the United States.

However, to really make that happen, you really must practice "primogeniture." Which we Americans think of as a bad thing. Until you go back to Switzerland in 2025 and see that the little Kuhn family dairy farm is still right there. And still in the family, just as it has been since about 1225.

So, how does this primogeniture work in real life? You have to bequeath the family farm to the oldest son. Every generation. Every time. Or it doesn't work. In the United States, we invariably bequeath everything to our children, equally. Turns out that works fine with money. But that does not work fine with little family farms. When you do that, your children must sell the diary and the land to split up the money equally. Voila, you lose the family farm.

In Switzerland, they are "old-school." Which, if you grow up Swiss, is great! Because when your parents die, and you are the oldest son, you get the WHOLE dairy farm upon which you grew up. You keep it going and keep it in the family, generation after generation. However, if you are not the oldest son, it doesn't really seem so great!

However, my great-grandparents, the "Kuhn's" in Switzerland, at least said to my grandfather, "well, you do know how to dairy farm because you grew up on this dairy farm here in Switzerland, and you are a dairy farmer! Which is worth something." And, to make it up a little to my grandfather (the youngest boy) they decided to pay for him to go to Agricultural School in Zurich for 2 years. Which, in those days (the 1910's) was a big deal.

And, *as with all great adventure stories*, this one has an excellent ending for my grandfather, Fritz Kuhn, Sr! Because this is how it transpired: especially

When this farmer boy got older, he began to dream that he would meet a beautiful Swiss princess and get married. But, he realized he had to work especially hard to make that possible.

By the way, all of us Swiss are taught from the day we are born that "our cows never miss a day of giving milk, including Christmas day!" Thus, you must milk the dairy cows every day of the year. Every year. Likewise, we learn from our parents, if we work hard at our jobs and never miss a day of work (just like God's cows) then God will bless you with a respectable life and worthwhile things – like Vanilla ice cream, Swiss Cheese and Milk Chocolate!"

Then his parents decided to send the little farmer boy to the big city (Zurich) for agriculture college to learn where he could find his own dreamy country. Little did Fritz Kuhn know, but he was about to meet the Swiss Princess he dreamt about. In fact, in agriculture college in Zurich he met the daughter of the President of the college, Ida Glattli. She was immediately smitten with him, and vice versa. Unfortunately, the feeling of Ida Glattli's parents was not at all mutual. They were a prominent Swiss family in the City of Zurich, and it was not okay at all for this provincial, broke, young, Swiss farm boy to be dating their lovely City Princess – especially, of course, the **younger boy** with NO FARM WHATSOEVER. This was not a match made in Heaven, at least as far as the prominent, long-established, city-dwelling Schwarzenbach-Glattli family were concerned.

Naturally, the Swiss Glattli family, in short order, put the kybosh on this courtship. But, it is very difficult to stop *true love*. Oh yes, it is. Even in those olden days.

While 18-year-old dairy farmer Fritz Kuhn was in agriculture college in Zurich, in 1914, he learned about a new farming area that was being developed in the far, far away country of the United States.   In fact, in a fairyland called California – the "land of fruits and nuts" (pun intended!). It turns out that this farm development was in a fairyland called the Imperial Valley in Imperial County, California. Moreover, if the truth were to be known, it was NOT a fairyland at all! El Centro is in a hot desert, below sea level, without much water. But, humans were attempting to build a HUGE Agricultural Canal from Yuma, Arizona, 50 miles to Imperial Valley to transport water from the Colorado River to the sandy desert in California.

The idea was to bring water to the Imperial Valley with this huge canal that ran along the Mexican Border and then land-level the already flat sandy soil and irrigate it directly from a new-fangled canal system. If it worked, it would be the largest man-made Irrigation System in the whole world. More importantly, the farmers in California believed that if you watered the sandy desert soil it would be perfect to grow gorgeous vegetables in the winter (because it is hot in a desert all year). Best of all, you could ship these beautiful vegetables in train cars from Los Angeles to New York and Boston for New Yorkers and Bostonians to have incredibly delicious California vegetables all snowy winter long in their grocery stores and restaurants every day as early as 1910. And, they would be delighted to pay for that.

However, there were two perplexing problematic issues: 1. Could they really build a huge 100-foot-wide irrigation canal 50 miles through the low sandy desert, especially with 1910 excavators? 2. Could they level the soil in the Imperial Valley desert successfully enough to properly irrigate the ground?   Because the outlook was, in fact, so bleak, at least the new land in the Imperial Valley would be *free* to all farmers who moved there.

Fritz Kuhn realized this is not genuinely a gamble if you are a farmer without a farm! Ida Glattli realized, on the other hand, this was a big gamble for her, especially coming from a long-established Swiss family. Fortunately for the Schwarzenbach-Glattli family, their 16-year-old Princess was not likely to leave Zurich for this California fairytale adventure halfway around the world. **But…as we all know from fairy tales, *love* is (oh-so-often), much stronger than "not likely!"**

When Fritz Kuhn graduated from Schreckholm Agricultural College in Zurich in 1915 he immediately took a train to the Port of Le Havre, France (that is a 525-mile train trip – quite a long way in 1915). Then, he boarded a ship to Los Angeles, California, to immigrate to the United States (7,661 nautical miles, through the newly opened Panama Canal in 1903), but 30 days all lonesome in a boat as a 19-year-old Swiss dairy farmer boy, crossing the whole Atlantic Ocean and part of the Pacific Ocean! **Unimaginable to me**. As you probably know, but don't methodically digest, this is what almost all our ancestors ALL did! Unbelievable!

Moreover, his young Swiss girlfriend, Ida Glattli, announced that she is absolutely not going with him. It was over. A happy day for her parents. An unhappy day for young Fritz Kuhn. I'm sure that made the one-month long ocean voyage to a strange land very sad and lonely.

Fritz immediately came down to the Imperial Valley and claimed his free 160 acres. And prayed that the canal would function, and he could start his own little dairy farm. Low and behold, the canal did work! In fact, my grandfather helped build some of the actual original Imperial Irrigation District irrigation canals that were sections of the canal in Calexico and Seeley, California.

My family's first dairy was out in the countryside, 3 miles south of Seeley, California, and 10 miles north of the US-Mexico Border. I'm telling you, it is extremely southern California, and it is hot, hot, hot. The average temperature every afternoon every summer day is 107 degrees (in the shade!!). Then, gets all the way "down" to a "lovely" 78 degrees minimum every night. You do not want to be in El Centro, California, in the summer, unless you are farming.

Dairy farming turned out not to be ideal in these hot conditions. So, Fritz Kuhn had his hands full trying to keep Holstein Cows happy in the unbearable heat. On the other hand, the winter vegetable plan worked brilliantly! The vegetables were immediately luscious and bountiful, and you could grow almost any vegetable in the Imperial Valley all winter long. Better yet, the sandy soil drained perfectly. Thus, the vegetables were consistently perfect and constantly record-setting in quality and size.

Now, back to the Swiss Princess fairytale: It turns out that the United States always prided itself in having a terrific postal system. And, Switzerland, prides itself in having a great postal system. Moreover, young couples who are in love will use these mail systems without their parents knowing anything about it. Thus, in 1916, Ida would mail Fritz a letter in Zurich (to "Podunk" Imperial County, California) and a month later the love of her life would get the letter. Then Fritz would write Ida back 9,000 miles away in Zurich, and low and behold, a month later, Ida would get the letter from Fritz at her home in Zurich. Without Ida's parents having any knowledge of this at all.

Thus, when Ida Glattli announced 9 years after young Fritz Kuhn left Switzerland for the USA (never heard of again or coming back) that she was eloping to California and marrying Fritz Kuhn, her parents literally fainted. Then, of course, they denounced such a ridiculous plan. Next, Ida Glattli (age 26 and with the love of Fritz still in her heart) announced to her family in Zurich that next week she was taking a boat from La Havre to Los Angeles to never come back again and marry her Prince in Los Angeles and immediately move to his little dairy farm in the desert in California. And that is exactly what she did!

Five years later, in 1929, *on Christmas Day*, my father, Fritz Kuhn, Jr., was born to Swiss parents on a little dairy farm in the desert in California. Two years after that, *on Christmas Day* 1931, my aunt Vreneli Kuhn was born to Swiss parents on a little dairy farm in the desert in California.

33 years later, on my Grandfather Fritz Kuhn, Sr's exact birthday, I was born on the same farm in California. Imagine how proud my grandfather, Fritz Kuhn, Sr., was to have his first grandson born on his own birthday out on his own farm! (It may have been topped by having his oldest granddaughter, Diane Kuhn Wilson, *also born on his birthday*, 10 years before I even came along!!!)

And, that folks is how I got here on July 31, 1962, on a family hay farm in California.

Oh, and Fritz and Ida Kuhn (my grandparents) *lived happily ever after* in the little California farming town called El Centro, California!

CHAPTER 4

OXYGEN TENT

Fairly soon after I was born, I ended up in El Centro Memorial Hospital. Not for what most farm boys end up in the hospital for: being badly injured by the farm machinery like tractors, or shop welding accidents, or grinding a finger off with the heavy hand-held spinning grinder.

No, I had a much different (but also severe) problem than most farm boys: I was born with weak lungs and terrible asthma. As any proud farmer father would be, my dad had me out in the fields in his pick-up truck from about age one onward. Out on those ditchbanks. Going field to field.

In those days my father had built one of the largest alfalfa hay farms in California (and consequently, the whole United States) because, the easy part is growing the alfalfa in the famous mid-western and eastern states but because these states have so much rain. But, a farmer in those states cannot dry out the alfalfa when it is cut by cutting machines and left in the field to dry and bale. In fact, in the eastern states are so humid that you cannot possibly bale the hay dry. Therefore, the alfalfa will, literally, mold in the haystack and internally combust, and then burn the whole 5,000 ton haystack to the ground in 20 minutes. I have seen this many, many times. Even in El Centro, where it is dry as a door nail. You need a full four days in a row of sunshine – and no rain at all – or you cannot bale the hay. Again, now you know why Imperial Valley farmers hate rain!

Therefore, imagine how hard it would be to bale the alfalfa hay in the Midwest with huge rainstorms all summer long – and even worse in the East with huge rainstorms uprising at any time without warning. Likewise, horrible humidity will absolutely cause the stack to burn inside your barn and burn your barn to the ground.

My father figured out in the 1950s that the Imperial Valley desert is perfect for growing AND curing the alfalfa hay all of the year. Thus, he decided he would be exclusively an alfalfa hay farmer. Slowly but surely, he built up the hay farm one field at a time. Solely due to his work and ingenuity, we had a huge alfalfa hay farm that my father built from absolutely nothing. I asked him how he did it – because I wanted to learn – and he said: "Stick by stick, Son. Stick by stick." And, as if that wasn't enough, my mother chimed in: "Rome was not built in a day, John." Message absorbed and learned. In fact, I built three huge businesses from scratch over the next 30 years based on that advice alone.

My businesses grew like my father's, as well. Not on Wall Street with somebody else's money. Not with government money that was taken from somebody else (called taxes), either. No. I went to Japan 40 times in 72 months and built an alfalfa hay market from absolutely scratch by going – the equivalent of – door to door in Japan with nothing but my farming photographs. I promise you that I will have 10 chapters of how to do business with the Japanese at the second volume this trilogy autobiography, titled *I Tell It Like It Is!* And, you will have 10 more chapters in volume three of this autobiography on how to build a law practice right out of law school, slowly but surely from no clients to 6,000 clients doing Will packages or Probate or even Revocable Trusts. This will be one of the most informative business manuals you will ever read on Japanese culture and successful business from scratch with Japanese companies. And, on how to build a law practice from nothing, "stick by stick," as my farmer father, Fritz Kuhn, Jr., said.

Back to the hospital in Imperial County, California:

It turns out that I was born with very weak lungs and sort of sickly. Probably not a good start for a farmer's oldest son. So, we will blame my mother and her family, who from time to time, produced more sickly children like I was at the beginning! My mother is not here to defend herself, so I can get away with this now. I wouldn't dare do that if she were alive because she was from the Silent Generation and you said as little as possible about your family and any "problems" you might have. You know how this is with families, right, dear reader?

Worse yet, alfalfa hay tends to be vicious to children with health problems, especially weak lungs. Nobody in my family had any idea that all these trips out to the fields in my father's pickup truck were causing me "hay fever." So, every time my father would take me out to the fields when I was really young, he would scoop me up and take me in his arms to look at the hay and the balers and the hay rakers and the windrowers (cutting the hay is called windrowing on a hay farm of any size). Also, remember, there were no such thing as car seats in 1963. Those did not come around until about the 1980s. In fact, we didn't even have seatbelts!!! Those came around in the 1970s. So, scooped up from that pickup seat, I went to field after field in my father's arms at ages one to two.

Until I got so sick and coughing and phlegm gumming up my lungs and sneezing: And sneezing and sneezing and sneezing and sneezing. Finally, when I was about 2 years old, I had a cough attack so bad I almost broke a blood vessel in my face, and just couldn't stop sneezing, and coughing up phlegm. I even had trouble breathing. My father threw me in the pickup and drove as fast as he could down Old Highway 80 to El Centro Memorial Hospital and said to the doctors and nurses, "what is happening here?"

The doctors and the nurses rushed me to the emergency room and took about five minutes to figure out I had extremely weak lungs and asthma and hay fever. They told my father that I could die any minute from this if I continued to be exposed to hay fields and farming.

They also said that they just got this new contraption called an Oxygen Tent that would be perfect to immediately put me in and see if I did not recover. In the Oxygen Tent I went.

I will never forget the Oxygen Tent. It had two positives and one downside: First, it was fantastic for getting rid of contaminates in the air (like alfalfa dust and farm dust). So, right away I started to recover and feel better. Not to mention, it was full of pure oxygen, which my lungs loved, of course.

Second positive for me: It was in the very front of the hospital by the entrance way. Remember, I am a zoological sign "Leo" so I love the center of attention. Not my fault. I was born that way. So, I was THRILLED to be in the front of the hospital greeting everyone who came in. I was exactly 2 years old at the time. I had my 2-year-old birthday in that Oxygen Tent, so I remember that well, too. Two-year-olds love to say "hi" to anybody and everybody who comes in the door. Never mind the fact that there is a clear plastic wall between yourself and everyone. Over to the edge of the tent I would trot and greet anyone who came in the El Centro Memorial Hospital.

The downside (as with most things in life, the downside is usually the exact other side of whatever you love). In this case, the transparent plastic wall of the Oxygen Tent made sure I really couldn't greet anyone. I became painfully aware of that in a day or two. Worse, the doctors and nurses told my father and mother I would have to be in the Oxygen Tent for two full weeks WITHOUT ever coming out or meeting anyone, while my lungs healed. First, a 2-year-old does not really understand how long 2 weeks is. Fourteen days in a tent not talking to anybody is an ETERNITY to a 2 year old. Second, I could not understand why everyone else got to be out and go home and not me!

Fortunately, the Leo side of me did take over and I concluded that there was still nothing better on the planet than having everyone coming into and out of the hospital all day, every day, and greet me! And I greet them.

The other thing I will remember is that my father was busy farming every single day of his life but he was so worried about me that he came to the Hospital every single afternoon for every single day for the next two weeks and spent the whole afternoon in the lobby waving at me and saying hi and making sure I was entertained. I knew, from that moment onward, no matter how many school events my father missed (because he was farming) and how many dinners he was way to late to (because he was farming) that nothing was more important to him than me and my brother. I knew from that fortnight forward that I was unequivocally loved by my father. Even later, when he wasn't hardly ever around while he was farming and we were in elementary school.

Just for the record about our human memories: First thing I remember as a child was being a 2-year-old in the Oxygen Tent. You know we all have that "first thing that we remember from our childhood." No matter what it is. We never forget it. That was me with those 2 weeks in the Oxygen Tent greeting everyone who came into El Centro Memorial Hospital the summer of 1964. I don't remember anything else about my childhood (until about age 4 or 5). Which is normal. But I absolutely remember my time in the Oxygen Tent in El Centro Hospital like it was yesterday. It still seems like yesterday.

CHAPTER 5

SWIMMING UPSTREAM

After several more episodes of asthma attacks in the fields – and even at school with that AWEFUL BERMUDA GRASS that we play football and baseball and run around on at recess that is lethal to a child with asthma – and my missing school, my mother, Madeline Kuhn, took me to the local El Centro Doctor she knew well from church, Dr. Keith Macgaffey, to see what could be done about John.

By the way, there were to be many, many more meetings over the next few years with doctors and teachers and everyone else who could help, about "what to do about John." This was because there were lots of "issues" with John, such as: he is hyper-active, "ADD," has asthma, cannot run on a Bermuda field without wheezing and coughing – and all playgrounds and football fields were Bermuda fields back then.   And, these concepts were really not even known at the time: I did not hear "ADD" until I was about 40 years old. I did hear "hyper-active" pretty early on. But, they had no idea what asthma was until the 1970s and we certainly did not have "inhalers." Truly

Dr. Macgaffey was an exceptionally nice guy, but he had his hands full with me – for two reasons, in fact: 1. In 1967, he was to help my mother with this asthma and "hyper-active" child problem. 2. He was my Sunday School teacher every Sunday morning at Saints Peter and Saints Paul Episcopal Church in El Centro. Thus, he was tasked with teaching us little ones to read the King James Version of the

Bible. It turns out, I am very indebted to him for both! Moreover, it also turns out that it is not hard for young hyperactive children to read out loud in Sunday School when the material they are reading is interesting – and how interesting is the Bible? It doesn't get any more interesting than that! No problem focusing when we were reading something interesting. That is the same for ALL children. Get them interested in something and you will no longer have them acting up and not focusing. We can all focus when we are interested.

Back to Dr. Macgaffey's first task: To help John get over this asthma problem and get over "acting up in school." Dr. Macgaffey said to my mother, we have this new drug out called Ritalin, and it will probably help John focus in school and do better in school. My mother said, "will it help him learn more?" **(My mother was always more interested in our learning than in grades. I love her for that.)** Dr. Macgaffey said, "I doubt it, but it may help." Then my mother asked what the side effects were, and he did not know that so early on. Then, Dr. Macgaffey said we really do not know what to do about asthma yet, either. But we know his lungs are weak.

So, my mother came home that day and said to my father, Fritz Kuhn, "they think John should get on this new drug called Ritalin and that may help him focus in school." To which my dad replied, "and will he be able to go out on the farm and work in the fields? What will it do for hay fever and asthma." To which my mother replied, "I don't think it addresses those issues."

My father said: "We need him out in the fields, eventually. He is smart. And, he had no trouble paying attention out on the farm. In fact, the more difficult something gets, the better John seems to be able to deal with it. We need him out on the farm. Working."

Remember, my father's side is Swiss, so it is ALWAYS about working. And, my brother and I got a double dose of that because my mother's family were hard-working bankers in the Province of Alberta, Canada, with lots of hard-working farmer friends in Pincher Creek (farming country in Canadian plains, not too far from Montana in the USA), where my grandmother, Dorothy Embury Hall, is actually from. Consequently, "working" is the "whole ballgame" on both sides of my family.

Working, just like all of America enjoyed doing, up until Lyndon Johnson's Great Society decided to Pay Americans not to work. Lyndon Johnson's policies are, sadly, still in place in America today: US Government, take American workers money (as taxes) and pay other Americans not to work with that tax-money from the workers. That was Lyndon Johnson's primary policy, and we are living his "Great Society" in America right now with our government taking lots of working folks' money as taxes and paying other people not to work. I grew up in the desert in California where everyone works or you die. We know that paying anybody not to work is unsustainable. And, it takes away **your God-given talent that you will enjoy using** in the real world and the working communities and means you have no confidence or self-satisfaction.

The Mojave Desert that I grew up working in every day is right next to the desert in the State of Arizona. In the State of Arizona there are gorgeous wide-open free spaces where they have done great things such as build whole cities from deserts, like Phoenix, Arizona. But, in the State of Arizona, and in the State of New York, if you don't work, you die.   Ayn Rand tells us in her book, **Atlas Shrugged**, that ALL animals will work hard to eat every single day they are alive – EXCEPT human beings are the only animal who will not work to eat, until they must.   The American spirit that came from England at the founding of our country was to be the hardest workers on the planet and be rewarded for it.   That comes from all countries in the world, when you think about it.   The United States needs to leave Lydon Johnson behind and get back to work and get back to self-confidence and clarity.

Because I grew up next door to the State of Arizona, I grew up a "Goldwater Republican."   Barry Goldwater was the United States Senator from Arizona in the 1960s and ran for President of the U.S. in the 1960s on the "libertarian platform" of "do not take from me what I worked for."   That is American Freedom.   That is the thinking that the founding fathers built this country on: No more taxes than necessary for roads and schools.   Period.   And, always let me be free to choose what I want in my life – from whom I date to where I work – and let me use my God-given talents to improve my world.   I believe in that.   And so do you, actually!   You just don't know it yet.

Look up the Libertarian Party website and tell me it doesn't believe what you do – because I know it does.   It is your party, whether you are a hard-working school teacher (like my mother was), or any other manner of diligent American.   And, we are not interested in the color of your skin or your religion.   We are interested in Greatness.   Whether you are be best welder in the world, or the best New York Banker, or the hardest working Opera singer, or the kindest schoolteacher.   You are America and you are Libertarians.

Back to my mother and father's conversation about "what do to with John." My father said, "I do not trust the medication to get my child to learn in school, nor do I see how that is going to help him get over his terrible asthma. When I was at the hospital with him and he was two years old and in the Oxygen Tent, the doctors said he needs stronger lungs. Instead of putting him on Ritalin, a drug nobody even knows much about yet, why don't we build a normal-sized swimming pool, teach him to swim, and make him swim laps and strengthen those lungs? That will strengthen his lungs." And my mother added, "and that will be a pollen free environment here at our house in town where he will not have the horrible allergies to Bermuda grass on the playground." So, when I was age four, they immediately set to work building a swimming pool in our backyard and then made me swim laps every day.

My mother, always the teacher and worker, decided to sit by the pool every afternoon and make sure I swam and wore myself out. She was not interested in talking about it, she was interested in my swimming hard every single day to build my lungs up in a pollen-free environment.

Another thing that happened that was awesome, was that lap swimming really, really wears you out. So, almost immediately, I was able to focus and study every evening because I was tired out from swimming. Thus, every single night from age 5 to age 12 in Elementary School, I have no trouble studying. This "ADD," hyper-active" boy had no trouble focusing in school from then on.

Better yet, I also had no more trouble with asthma. It, literally, went away from that day forward – although I certainly could not have played baseball or football on those

Bermuda playground fields! That would have been 100 percent regressive.   Unfortunately, it happened to me every time I got on a Bermuda field. Thank goodness, I had no more trouble with alfalfa, though. To my father's delight, back out on that alfalfa farm, and permanently, I might add.

Let us not forget who the person is to be most commended in this whole process of raising John Kuhn. It was not my doctor, Dr. Macgaffey, who does deserve all the credit in the world. Nor was it my father, who deserves massive credit, too.

No, instead, it was my mother, Madeline Kuhn. Remember, she is the one who said, "We need to be in Church every Sunday, no matter how busy we are on the farm. And, John and Jim need to be in Dr. Macgaffey's Sunday School class reading the King James Version of the Bible at age 6." And, my mother who said, "what can we do to help John focus in school?"   And, more importantly, she made sure that actually happened. Not just talk about it. Happen.   (Reminds me of The Who Song "**Let's See Action**" with: "Let's see Action. Let's see people. Let's be free. And see who cares!")

Lastly, our Episcopal Churches (and Anglican Churches) need to go back to teaching the King James Version of the Bible – and I mean at every little Episcopal Church everywhere in the United States. Right now. In 2025. We are doing our children a HUGE DISSERVICE not teaching them to read the King James Version of the Bible. First, how are your children supposed to learn all the great things in the Bible if they don't read it in Sunday School? Second, the King James Version of the Bible is jam-packed with astounding, difficult, expressive, long English words. Thus, it trained me at ages 5 to 9, as I read it out loud every Sunday in Sunday school, to have confidence in reading and pronunciation for the rest of my life. Plus, I inadvertently learned almost every single long and difficult word in the English language. Right there in a little tiny rural church in the desert countryside, with Dr. Macgaffey leading the way!

People ask me how I absolutely aced the SSAT verbal section at age 12 years old in this little farming community (not originating in our famous city schools). Easy. I knew every word on that SSAT in 7th grade because myself and Jenny Macgaffey, and two years later Neil Macgaffey, with my younger brother Jim Kuhn, and ALL our friends, read it aloud for an hour every Sunday in our rural Episcopal Church.

The Roman Catholics understand this, to this day, and I commend them. The Jewish people understand this, to this day, and I commend them! Please, please get back to reading the King James Version of the Bible in every single Episcopal Church in America. And, please get back to reading ANY Bible in the Sunday schools of all the Protestant Churches in America. I pray you do that at your church.

CHAPTER 6

AS AMERICANS IT IS IN OUR GOD-GIVEN DNA TO WORK

By the way, back to the Who Song:

Let's see Action!
Let's see People!
Let's be Free!
And see who cares!

This is so true for you and me. In fact, it is true for all Americans!! You and me, we are Americans. Therefore, it is in our DNA to care!! We care about each other! We care about other people. We care about People all over the world – which is why we have helped everyone all over the world, from helping the Allies win World War I and World War II (and losing millions of American lives in those wars) to the "Marshall Plan" afterwards that our U.S. Congress passed (and we as taxpayers paid Billions of dollars for) to rebuild exactly those countries that we destroyed in the two World Wars: Namely Germany, Italy, Austria, and Japan. They do not tell you this in the American Schools anymore. They tell you we are racist. What a lie! We are not racist!! We helped Japan and its PEOPLE with billions of free dollars to rebuild their country and to rebuild their economy. That is not racist. That is the opposite of racist! That is awesome!

Back to the Who Song: It is also in our DNA as Americans to work! We love to work!! And now our government is paying over 50% of us government checks to not work. That is not us at all!! We all love to work! We love to be nurses and teachers. We love to work at construction jobs! We love to work at helping each other. And, being friends with each other in the workplace! Why are they telling you in high school and college that the "workplace is a scary place."??? That is nonsense. The workplace is where you first make new friends out of school. More new friends for life. And, it is at your workplace where you feel productive! You get a sense of self-esteem from helping other people: by teaching them, by nursing them, by building their homes and offices. What on earth are they teaching you in school? That we are racist? That we the workplace is "scary?" Hogwash on that. Hogwash on your teachers for teaching you that! You want to have self-esteem? Go to work!

In fact, God has created it so that all cultures like to work! In all countries! That is God's plan. You don't have to go to Church to learn that. I have been to Japan over 40 times. The Japanese LOVE TO WORK. I have been to Switzerland many times. The Swiss LOVE TO WORK. In fact, that is true of all peoples: God made the Italians cooks and chefs and servers. God made the French remarkable at building cathedrals. The Spanish too. God made the Germans amazing mechanics – look at the Porches and Beamers and Audi's!! He/She made the Indians amazing engineers – and terrific at phone calling and public service. And being unusually kind.

He/She made the Chinese fantastic farmers. They grow everything from rice to all kinds of vegetables, and every kind of meat you can imagine in China. God made the Russians great at making Vodka and great at farming, and great at writing! It does not get any better than Fyodor Dostoevsky's *Crime and Punishment* (everything from the jaded student –

to finally being an actual love story – that you do not see coming!) and it does not get any better than Leo Tolstoy's **War and Peace**. Brilliant! Both books are brilliant! And how about English writers like Dicken's **Tale of Two Cities** and Hardy's **Beyond the Madding Crowd**? And, don't you just love those "love stories" – Ms. Everdene finally picks the right man! Unbelievable writing and suspenseful! Can you believe we are lucky enough that God made us healthy enough to work every day? And lucky enough to watch football every weekend (in fact, pick your country and you can even pick your definition of "football!" And, God made us so we can read hundreds of years old authors in a book or on a computer, like it was yesterday: Dostoevsky, Tolstoy, Dickens and Hardy, included!! How amazing is God!

How lucky are we to be able to work hard and play hard – no matter what our nationality? And how lucky are we to be able to find our God-Given talent (which is not hard to find, either). It's usually obvious to us by age 5. Whether we want to be a nurse in a hospital or a teacher in a classroom – or even a secretary – we all get that sense of satisfaction you get from hard work.

You want to know why so many of us Americans are on Valium or Adderall, and all kinds of other extremely heavy drugs? Because our government pays us not to go to work. And our schools teach us that we are racist and that work is "scary and to be avoided."

You want to not be on drugs of any kind? Do you want to be the person God intended for you to be? Go to work. And have a job in the part of life that you love!! And stop worrying about whether it is a "respectable career." All careers are respectable. All of them!!! From dish washing to chef, from secretary to lawyer, from construction worker to

Contractor. From welder to tractor driver, to irrigator (long hours because you like it!) to harvester. God made all the different careers for each of us: from ditch digger to doctor. There are 7 billion people in the world and we are all different! We are all unique. And, we all have a God-given talent, and, therefore, <u>a God-given job.</u>

Do not forget, America was built on thousands of different jobs and careers: from Irish (Union Pacific) and Chinese (Central Pacific) transcontinental railroad builders, to teachers in every schoolhouse, to farmers and cowboys (which the Musical *Oklahoma!* says "must be friends") to nurses and factory workers. God knows we need them all!

What is your God-given talent? Use it! Now. Not next year. Now! And you will immediately feel a sense of confidence and self-esteem. You will immediately create new, awesome, friendships, and immediately get off the drugs prescribed by your doctor.

Most of us do not need self-medicating hemp and marijuana either. Your great-grandparents knew that. But they are no longer around to tell you. So, I'm telling you for them since your grandparents are long gone. That is the point of John Kuhn's book! (That is the book in your hand, you idiot! Lol!!)

Why am I authoring this book – my autobiography? Simple. Because <u>in my heart</u> – since I was about 5 years old to be precise – I've known that it is my God-given talent to write!! And, I know in my heart that I have learned how to write (at places like school) for – <u>here it comes</u>: As the Who says: "FOR PEOPLE!!!"

CHAPTER 7

AMERICAN FARMERS WILL NOT EAT THEIR OWN FOOD IN THE GROCERY STORES THEY KNOW BETTER!

115 degrees average high temperature in the Summer on my farm I grew up in El Centro, California. No, that is not a typo! That is the actual high temperature all day long when I am farming – and all of us farmworkers are farming on tractors and harvesting vegetables by hand and digging irrigation ditches on our property every time we irrigate. We irrigate every day. So our farmworkers are out there digging ditches in the brutal sunshine from 6:00 am to 6:00 pm. How brutal is the sunshine every day? Remember, the Imperial Valley is a desert that is completely below sea level. All of it is low desert and the whole farming valley averages **45 feet below sea level**. Therefore, there are no trees anywhere. NO TREES. NO SHADE. Only cactus and desert animals trying to find shade under desert mesquite trees. It is miserable to work in every day for 6 months of the year. Can you imagine all of us working every day in that grueling heat to put vegetables on your table and milk in your glass? We must me crazy. Well, we are crazy!

But hard-working Americans, of course. And we know now that we Americans like to work. All of us!

The other side of the coin is that in the Imperial Valley it never, ever snows in the winter! So it is perfect for

Canadians and Chicagoans to come stay the winter. In fact, Palm Springs is just North of the Imperial Valley and that is exactly the same desert I grew up in and where Chicagoans and Canadians do come to spend the winter. In the old days, before airplanes, folks from the Sierra Nevada mountains in California, also flocked to Palm Springs to get out of the snow, too!

I cannot make this up! My brother and I were also out there in our family fields from age 5 onward to completing high school. Why that early age of 5 years old on the farm? Because that is when boys have the most energy and that is a perfect time for them to be out on their parents' farms. Unfortunately, for Jim Kuhn and myself, we just happened to live in the only farming county in the US where it is by far the hottest farming valley in the whole world! That is because our Imperial Valley is actually a reclaimed desert. What reclaimed desert means is that our forefathers, like my grandpa, Fritz Kuhn Sr, went out into the low desert when there were no fields and ditches in the 1910s and staked out 40-acre fields and 80-acre fields in the desert.

Then had the audacity to bring in huge Caterpillar tractors and huge excavators and land levelers and D-8 Caterpillars (from Peoria, Illinois where those awesome factory workers – who loved their jobs – made those awesome machines, because those men and women liked doing that with their lives) and we farmers ran over the sand dunes and flattened them out and made fields!

Sound like fun? Of course it is fun!! Oh, and naturally, I have more Kuhn Family in El Centro, California, doing that for the past 80 years, as well: I am proud to report that my Swiss cousins, also from Dietlikon, decided to move to El Centro, California shortly after my Grandparents, in the 1930s, and it just turns out that their God-Given talents are with heavy machinery: Huge Caterpillar Excavators and digging actual 80-Acre fields out of that God-Given desert that we reclaimed. Not surprisingly, Walter Kuhn (cousin to my grandpa Fritz Kuhn, Sr) and his boys and girls are the best on the planet at digging 80-Acre fields (and cutting and filling dirt exactly with huge Caterpillar Tractors with little wooden signs every 100 yards), *painstakingly precise work with HUGE tractors*! And, my 2nd cousins are the best in the Imperial Valley at it: Walter Kuhn, Bruce Kuhn, Freddi Kuhn, Jeanine Kuhn, Merry Kuhn and Trudi Kuhn.

Then they got Caterpillar graders and trenched irrigation ditches about 5 feet deep on the end of every 40- and 80-acre field. Then they cemented the ditch with real cement, mostly by Ryerson Company, who did most of the cement ditches in the south end of the Imperial Valley in the 1920s to the 1980s. And, my father, Fritz Kuhn, Jr., is a master at this!

This is actually amazing ingenuity and amazing grit and amazing fortitude, all in that miserable blazing sun heat!! Ouch! But, remember, that is what made America great! All these men and women coming over from countries all over the world to "make a new start!" Often with their loved ones in toe! That would be your forefathers, too. From Africa to farm in the rice and cotton fields of the Deep South. From Poland to work in the garment factories and restaurants in Chicago. From Israel to be bankers and farmers in the new world. Where anything was possible. And where you could use your God-given talents, without your parents telling you what career you had to be in.

In fact, my uncle, Walter Kuhn, specialized in this big heavy equipment and was one of the best ever at what we call "land-leveling." Again, it was Walter Kuhn's God-Given talent to love BIG machinery, so naturally, that became his job. Again, this is not rocket-science. This is doing what God gave you the gifts to be good at. And he was one of the best in the Imperial Valley because he had an eye for seeing exactly which sandy dunes needed to be leveled and where to move the good soil for better crops and where to move the bad soil that would not grow plants – for example, put the bad soil where you were going to dig your cement ditch and put the good soil in the middle of the field. This is clearly a gift from God. And Walter Kuhn loved it.

Mind you that Walter Kuhn also escaped Switzerland to America to farm because he was also a youngest son in farming family. Again, can you imagine leaving your home and your Swiss family (of over 800 years in Switzerland) and getting on a miserable boat over 100 years ago and coming to the hottest county on the planet earth to farm? Realize that Switzerland is the exact opposite! The whole country is high mountains (So high that Hitler couldn't even get in the country during World War II and that was his neighbor country). And, El Centro, California: Below Sea level desert with actual hot sand and cactus and lizards. Switzerland: Snow covered alps, actual Swiss glaciers, and frozen lakes with God-given milk cows wandering all over making milk for Swiss families and families all over Europe. Then getting on a horrible boat ride to a country you know absolutely nothing about so you can do what you love and were brought up to do.

This is not today, where we can fly anywhere we want, including Zurich from New York City in 8 hours. And, we can get a brochure for anything, or better yet, look up any Swiss valley and ski area on our cell phone. No. In 1910, you knew nothing at all because El Centro is not going to be in the Zurich newspaper in 1910. Worse yet, your family in Switzerland, says "what, are you crazy??!!!" Yes, you are crazy. However, your girlfriend in Switzerland is also young, foolish, and crazy too! So, she is 19 and just out of high school, and to her parents' chagrin, says "ah what the heck, I'll go with you Walter!"

And there you are, that is pretty much how America was founded: By Irish potato famine young girls and boys doing the same as my grandparents. And by Russian families coming over to the US to work in garment factories and as Russian cobblers in NYC and LA, oh, and one named Peter & Son in Charleston, South Carolina, of course! And by German girls and boys leaving their little towns in Germany and coming over to the Midwest to farm, or Germans in the United States building airplanes in our factories in WWII to defeat German Hitler and Mussolini and Japan's Emperor. And, Dutch families (best dairy farmers and flower farmers in Europe), leaving their beautiful windmills (now that's the sign of a farm: a windmill!) and getting on the horrible boats that make you seasick for 2 weeks straight, and coming over to Wisconsin to dairy farm because America needs milk. Dutch dairy farmer families all over the USA – including thousands of Dutch dairy farmers in just Los Angeles itself, buying my father's alfalfa hay and producing milk for EVERY Los Angeles family and every Los Angeles schoolchild. That is a lot of alfalfa hay we are producing in El Centro every year to feed thousands of dairy cows in Los Angeles for all of you to have fresh milk at home and fresh milk in your school lunches.

Again, every child in this USA of yours has been drinking milk from the day they were born through high school in every town and city in the USA for the past 200 years, every single day. Do not tell me they were stupid. The great workers that built this country, every day for the past 200 years, are all the proof you need that you need to go back to drinking milk. But you must demand of your US government and its multinational corporations that are shafting you with Pasteurized milk, so stop Pasteurizing your milk – and ruining God's gift to you: That fresh glass of milk: "Raw Milk" is by far better for EVERYONE than heated, pasteurized milk – all the way from your baby bottle days, up to old age, like me!

It's not rocket-science. It is common sense. It is thinking for yourself. Something we were also awesome at in America until we lazily let our cell phones do our thinking for us: We Americans were the best on the plant at thinking for ourselves for the past 300 years. That is why our founding fathers left England. They wanted to think for themselves and not have England and the English government doing the thinking for them. How do you think we Americans invented the: 1. Airplane, 2. Telephone, 3. Rockets to jet engine ourselves to the moon. **Unbelievably great, your country is (as Yoda would say in "*Star Wars*").** Oh, and how about our movies being the best in the world? You have to love being American. And you have to love your great-grandparents for all getting here from their various countries. When you get to Heaven, be sure to thank them!

Nothing like it – this USA. It's awesome! And we Americans are awesome, whether we come from India or China or Italy or Switzerland. We are all doing our best and have been for over 300 years. But our media tells you different, doesn't it? And your teachers (who never learned what their great-grandparents taught them) are telling you differently, aren't they? Now you know why so many of us older people are frustrated. **We know exactly how great Americans are. All of us**. And we are frustrated with your media and teachers lying to you. And they are lying to you.

My father's cousin, Walter Kuhn, loved this land-leveling so much that he ended up land-leveling all my father's fields when he finally made enough money baling hay for other farmers that he could buy his own ground. And my dad, Fritz Kuhn Jr, still could not afford expensive ground over on the East End of the Imperial Valley (where most of the Swiss lived and the Imperial Valley Swiss Club is to this day). So my dad took a huge gamble and bought desert sand dunes on the West End of the Imperial Valley and he and Walter Kuhn land-leveled about 700 acres and prayed like hell that it would work! And did it ever work. But, only because they made it work with the American discipline and hard work.

By the time he purchased his own ground, my dad had been custom farming alfalfa for other wealthy farmers and was already a terrific farmer. Again, my dad's God-given talent was to manage me (Swiss manager, right) and an engineering mind, and the Swiss farmer discipline to stay up all night in the other farmers fields he custom farmed all year and wait until "the moisture came into the Valley – at about 3:00 am – and bale hay like crazy for 4 hours – from 3:00 am to 7:00 am – when the alfalfa leaves had just enough moisture to stay on the stem – which made for the perfect amount of protein in the alfalfa hay for the dairy cows to make the maximum milk.

That would be in Los Angeles – and eventually Chino (LA area) – where we would deliver our alfalfa hay bales where the LA diaries made all the milk for Los Angeles grocery stores and school children. That is a lot of families at grocery stores and a lot of children drinking milk in schools in the whole of Los Angeles, that my California family farm has been producing "milk-cow hay" for in the Imperial Valley for over 70 years. Real, genuine, cow's milk that comes in milk cartons.

You need to know something: They are lying to you on your cell phones and in our current media that Almond Milk is good for you. That is a lie. **Human Beings have been drinking cow's milk for at least 4,000 full years BEFORE Christ and another 2025 years straight since the Birth of Christ.** Not Almond Milk. Almond milk is fake milk.   Cow's milk and goat's milk are real milk, and have been since God invented it. Again, milk that is hand milked directly from a female cow – or machine milked since the 1980s – but still all the milk in the world comes straight from a Cow's udder.

Raw Milk is God's perfect and complete food. Why have you been lied to by your media when 7 billion people have been drinking Raw cow's milk on this planet for every single day for the last 1,000 straight years? Do you really think your grandparents were stupid? Do you really think the Chinese for the last 3,000 straight years are stupid? Do you really think the Russians for the past 3,000 years are stupid? Ruining our milk with Pasteurization just started in 1927. For 10,000 years on this planet earth, there was no Pasteurized Milk. None. All milk in all countries for the last 10,000 years has been non-pasteurized raw milk. Everywhere.

Do you think the Germans and the Swiss (and their Swiss cows for children's milk for the last 3,000 years and their cow's milk and cheese and yogurt and butter and ice cream and milk chocolate) are stupid? That is exactly what you are saying every day to me! I am 62 years old and I know that you are being lied to by your cell phone and by the multi-national food corporations. The US Food plants and distribution companies are only interested in the dollar and are not interested in your health. The muti-national food corporations are not interested in your health; they are only interested in their financial health.

In fact, you are nothing but a number to these multi-national corporations. You need to listen to those of us who actually care about you: Your parents and your grandparents. With our 3,000 STRAIGHT YEARS of dairy cows and non-pasteurized raw milk.

And, for thousands of years (until about 1927) your families were eating unprocessed food. Your parents care about you. Not your cell phones. And not your media who are all sold out to the big, huge corporations, like Coca-Cola, because they want to sell you sodas that will kill you with their preservatives, simply because they want the shelf life of preservatives and pasteurization. Coca-Cola Company hates real raw milk. But, your body does not hate real raw milk. Your body loves real raw milk.

What we do need to stop is the pasteurized milk that the US corporations invented less than 100 years ago. It is not healthy. We farmers hate it. We know it is not God-given milk from a cow. Pasteurized milk is processed and horrible for you and your stomach. For 3,000 straight years the 7 billion men, women and children in every single country in this world have been drinking milk straight from a cow. Cow. Hand milk the cow. Fresh Raw Milk. Put it in a bottle. Not a plastic container. A glass bottle. Serve it fresh to you in your home and your school lunches. Now the stupid USA has Pasteurized milk and they say it is safer for you. Another lie. It is heated and processed milk. It is making you sick.

And it is making you need big pharma drugs (more multi-national corporations making money on you every day because you are drinking their horrible, pasteurized milk). These are people who only care about money and do not care about you or me and our children. And they love to sell you lactic acid free milk – to compensate for what is not God's milk: Pasteurized milk. **Process the milk and ruin it. Process your food and ruin it. That is what you eat every day now.** In every grocery store in America!

Your farmer wants you to eat fresh vegetables and fresh meat and fresh raw milk. And, your farmer wants you to make the choices you want to make for your own body. Your multi-national corporations do not want you to make these choices. They only want you to pay them more and more money. **How about we pay the farmer instead of the multi-national corporation?!! Now your talking!!**

Thank you, my dear reader, for reading my book. **I am just telling you what your great-grandparents would tell you if they were here**. And, I promise, your great-grandparents would love you way more than anyone else. And they would have your best interest at heart. I will keep on eating cheese and butter and drinking milk because I do know that it is the most complete food God ever made for mankind and womankind.

But, it has to be Non-Pasteurized Milk. In other words, not processed milk. In other words, NATURAL MILK. And the cheese and the butter must be made from Non-Pasteurized

Milk (Natural Milk), or the cheese and butter makes us sick. I know this because the last 20 years even I am sick from too much Pasteurized Milk. **This is because I also take the easy way out and eat the bad Pasteurized milk. Note to self: John Kuhn, you need to stop it, too.**

This is my plea to the farmers in the USA to go back to Natural Milk and make us all healthy again. Please, pretty please, Mr. and Mrs. Farmer, please go back to Non-Pasteurized Milk and make every single school child healthy again.

There is a place in my hometown where they do care about you and where they do get it. It is called "Earth Fare." They are awesome! They refuse to sell you GMO (Genetically Modified) food from GMO cows and chickens. Earth Fare also refuses to sell you vegetables AND fruits from Mexico and South America that ALL been sprayed with the chemical DDT (that we US farmers are not allowed to spray on ANY of our fruits and vegetables because it is illegal and unsafe to eat), but the US Government immediately allows All Mexico and all South American fruits and vegetables and grapes, all sprayed with illegal and unsafe DDT and imported right into the United States and put on ALL of our grocery store shelves – something we US Farmers are totally banned from doing the our same US government. **How sick is that, that the multi-national corporations will allow you to eat fruits in vegetables right in your grocery store from all over Mexico and Chile and Argentina and Brazil that have the exact same DDT sprayed on all the fruits and vegetables that has long been banned DDT in the US by our government?** That is called money-hungry. And eating that food everyday from your grocery store WILL KILL YOU. It will kill you. Your great-grandparents would tell you that if they were here. **Again, thank you very much, Earth Fare, for counteracting that. We US Farmers and your US food consumers both appreciate that more than you know!**

If it is Genetically Modified food, do you think it is good for you? Do you think Genetically modified animals' food is good for you? They even Genetically Modify your corn and wheat. The GMO corn and the GMO wheat – which goes into your daily loaves of bread and sandwiches – so your bread is bad for you too. And, your bread is full of preservatives from your food manufacturers so that it can ship from their one plant in the whole United States, in whatever state the manufacturing plant is in, then the **"fresh bread" in a truck and on a grocery store shelf for two weeks is healthy?** to your grocery store and the chemical preservatives in your bread make it seem fresh after two weeks in a warehouse and a truck. **Your bread and your breakfast cereals and potato chips with all their chemical preservatives are killing you very single day. Every day**.

Your body cannot take those chemical preservatives every day. It is very slowly killing you every day you eat our food. And you eat it every day, don't you?

Then, when you eat your processed restaurant food and your processed grocery store food, every day, it slowly becomes Cancer in your body and it kills you. And when you eat cheese and butter and ice cream made from Pasteurized milk – and its ALL PASTEURIZED MILK – it is slowly creating Cancer in you. And it is slowly killing you. I'm telling you that your Cancer is coming from Pasteurized Milk, because it is. Cancer does not come from real, raw natural milk. It has not for 10,000 years in every country in the world. Please demand that your milk (and cheese and butter and ice cream) no longer be heated and ruined and no longer ruin your stomach and no longer give you Cancer. It's that easy.

Your farmer knows better and he and she will not eat these chemical-laden foods that we are sometimes forced to buy by big corporations (who won't buy our corn if it is not Genetically Modified – so we farmers have no choice but to sell our crop to these big corporations). But we won't eat our own crops and meats! **That should tell you something: If your farmer will not eat the GMO food he is producing, and the food manufacturer is lacing with chemicals, do you think you should eat it?**

And big pharma loves the horrible Cancer they caused in you, with their highly processed food, and their preservative laced food, and their Pasteurized Milk, because they can then sell you their astronomically high priced and astronomically powerful side-effect drugs, every day after you get Cancer from our food in our daily restaurants and daily grocery stores and our daily school lunches, and in our ice cream and cheese and butter.

When you eat all this grocery store and restaurant food day after day, you will then have to get on their big pharma drugs that they say will help you to get well.   The side effects on those drugs they are giving you (because of the chemical filled food they are selling you) are so unbelievably strong that those big pharma drugs will also kill you – if your grocery store and restaurant processed (all of it is ***processed food***) doesn't kill you first!! Your restaurant food is all processed. And most of it is full of preservatives. How do you think it stays in the factory warehouses (without refrigeration) for a week and in the distribution trucks (without refrigeration) the second week to get to any restaurant in the US? Those preservatives are banned in Japan because they will kill you!! Why do you think the Japanese outlive the Americans? Because they don't eat preservatives in their food, and most of their food is fresh from the farmers' fields, just like ours used to be in the US until 60 years ago.

The Japanese government protects its citizens' heath by banning all preservatives in the Japan internal food manufacturing and in their food imports from any country. This is awesome!   I know this because I had a shipment of U.S. potato chips shipped back to me in the US from the port of Tokyo for having preservatives that my manufacturer in the US said it did not have in the potato chips. And, my US food manufacturer said to me honestly, "I did not know that we had that much preservatives in our food. I just did not know." My Gourmet food producer did not know and he was being honest. However, all the big US food manufacturers know the amount of preservatives in their own food, don't you think they will sell it to you all day long on your grocery store shelves and do not care. In fact, their food lobbyists all lobby our US congress to forget about the people it represents (and that voted them in office) and support the big corporations and their donations?

So, all hail to Earth Fare Stores for actually caring about you and refusing to sell you preservative laced and artificial food! Here is Earth Fare's Advertisements in big headlines all over all of their stores:

OUR FOOD PHILOSOPHY
WE PLEDGE OUR FOOD IS FREE OF:

Added Hormones
Antibiotics

Artificial Fats and Trans-Fats
High Fructose Corn Syrup
Artificial Sweeteners
Artificial Preservatives
Bleached or Bromated Flour
Artificial Colors or Flavors

By the way, having been in the food business myself for years in the Untied States, and knowing that Earth Fare (and myself) care so much about the health and longevity (without Cancer) of our clients, I know that Earth Fare would unquestionably have on their list of their food being free of: GMO. Genetically Modified animals and chickens and eggs. (First, Genetically Modified, how bad does that even sound?!)

American food is so rampant with GMO in practically every cow, pig, and chicken; and, in all kinds of food such as **basic corn on the cob**, that Earth Fare just cannot even find Non-GMO foods to sell you in the USA. How bad is the food in the USA from your huge corporations (From Coca-Cola to Nestle, to Kellogg's to Mars Candy to General Mills to Ben & Jerrys to Starbucks) that we cannot even find Non-GMO beef and pork and wheat and corn and chicken? What a nightmare for you and me. And sad that our food is laced with chemicals and artificial Sweeteners and Artificial Preservatives and Artificial Colors and Artificial Flavors!

If you think about it, **you will realize that if it is natural and it came from God, then it is good for you**, **including milk**. You also realize that if it is "Artificial," then it is made with Chemicals by Man, and the Chemicals will eventually kill you – because God did not intend for you to keep feeding your body chemicals. God intends for you to put in your body Natural Foods and chemical free food.

No matter what God you believe in – and I believe in all of them, from Buddha to Jesus Christ – and I believe in both because, remember I have been to Japan on food business over 40 times and I believe in both Gods; I even believe in any God you believe in, including No God, if you believe in no God so do I. Therefore, no matter what God we believe in, we must understand that: **If it is Natural food it is intended for your body and healthy for you,** *including Natural milk, straight from a cow*. If it is Artificial food, or heat-treated, or freeze dried, it will wreck your body and wreck your health!

In fact, I am walking over to my Earth Fare right now for lunch because I will not let multi-national US corporations kill me with their lies and their processed, preservative laced, food, that I know will kill me. And, I know that if I eat the healthy organic vegetables and the non-GMO meats and non-GMO milk and non- pasteurized milk, I will stay healthy and strong, right up into my 90s. I know this because everyone in my family has eaten healthily for years in both Switzerland and the USA, on both sides of my family, we all live into our 80s. This is not luck. This is simply not eating something that God did not make.

And because the Swiss will always do their own thinking and will not eat bad food daily. Oooookkkkaaaayyyy: Just a little Swiss milk chocolate from raw milk, every once in a while. Or….. Swiss Cheese from raw milk every single day of their lives – and still all the Kuhn's and Schwarzenbach's live into their 90s! Remember, we Swiss do not lie! (Dear reader, you are supposed to laugh at that!)

You, dear reader, would also do your own thinking but the media hides the facts from you. It's extremely difficult to know what to do if you don't have the facts. It's even more difficult to do your own thinking if you are lied to by your media every day. Otherwise, you would not eat this Cancer-producing, processed, chemical ridden, horrible food in the USA if you just knew about it. Therefore, I am telling you about it and you can get healthy for the first time in your life. And you can know that your cellphone is lying to you about Almond milk!

Truly think about it: Almonds do not make milk. Human beings make that "milk" from almonds with their **processed food manufacturing plants**. GOD makes MILK. In fact, God makes Milk from lots of animals (none of it Pasteurized): Goat milk, Cow milk, Sheep milk, Camel milk, Buffalo milk, Human milk – certainly your mother's milk is not pasteurized, is it?

If it is not milk from a female mammal (sheep, goat, cow, or female human); but, rather it is made from a plant, such as an Almond plant or an Oat plant, it is not actually milk, is it? Thus, almond milk is a big fat lie. Oat milk is also a big fat lie. Let's go back to natural milk, from any of the female mammals above!

Moreover, Let's go back to looking at every food as a farmer would: The first question every farmer (male or female) asks is: Is it natural?

CHAPTER 8

THE HAND THAT ROCKS THE CRADLE RULES THE WORLD

Well, I guess it is time to introduce her. Who? *Who do you think?* As J.K. Rowling says in the Harry Potter Series about Malevolent Lord Voldemort (so you know from the beginning, as the reader, how powerful he is): "You-Know-Who." or "He-Who-Must-Not-Be-Named." Well, in my case, that would be my mother: Madeline Louise (Hall) Kuhn. **She-Who-Must-Not-Be-Named**. Ah, look at that, I did name her!! Lol! Unambiguously!

First of all, if I am honest, I must readily admit that my mother was unambiguously fantastic in every possible way, and I was incredibly lucky to be raised by her. Even though I will jokingly refer to her throughout this book as "She-Who-Must-Not-Be Named," the truth is that Shea and I named our first-born daughter for her! You certainly cannot get better than that.   My wife and I named our oldest child for my mother!

She-Who-Must-Not-Be-Named (my mother) was born in the "Silent Generation" and these folks really had it difficult. Worse yet, in my mother's case, she happened to be exactly age 2 to age 20 during the Great Depression. **And that Great Depression left very, very lasting marks on all of them. ALL OF THEM. We cannot possibly understand what that must have been like.** My mother (like ALL HER PEERS) never believed she had enough money. Her whole life she thought she was going to go broke. They grew up with their parents going broke overnight. And their friends' parents going broke overnight.   When you grow up your whole childhood broke – as that whole generation did – you are so emotionally scarred that you believe in your heart that you are just one day away from going broke again. It was Horrible. Absolutely horrible.

My mother also believed in hard work. Again, that whole generation did. They had to work. They had to work hard. They had to work days-on-end for almost no money. Their parents had to work days and days and days for almost no money. Just to eat. **Just to EAT!**

And, they also believe that they had it rough. And, they did. In fact, imagine growing up that way for the first 20 years of your life. From age 1 to age 20. Broke and going broke and scared. And, eventually, scarred.

Then, you just finish high school (age 18) and you now must immediately, by law, register for the draft to go fight a war on a different Continent against some unknown juggernaut called Nazi Germany. When you are 18 years old! And you already grew up broke, and scared of going broke and watching everyone you know go broke.

Then, register for the draft, be scared you will get called (because, of course you will get called, because Murphy's Law says so!). Then, at age 18 you are uprooted from your family and your home. At age 18! Then, put in the Army, taught to march with a gun you will be married to for 2 years (not a wife to be married to – a gun!). Then, you and your new Army brothers, 3 months later get put on a Military transport plane, to a completely unknown place. At 18 you get sent to a country you cannot even find on a map to fight, AND die.

You, literally, wake up the next day in The Philippines fighting the Japanese!! Some people you never even heard of. Fighting Kamikaze Pilots. Fighting overnight at Guadalcanal, age 18, hardly know how to tie your combat boots. Overnight, you are in Iwo Jima!! Age 18. *In one day*, US landing forces suffered 6,821 killed and 19,217 wounded. You are only 18 and are now dead. In one battle in one day, you are one of the 6,821 dead. **6,821 dead on the first day of the Battle of Guadalcanal and 6,821 18-year-old boys in caskets on a transport plane home for your 17-year-old girlfriend to drape an American flag over your grave in your hometown.**

Worse, you are sent to Okinawa. Bloodiest battle of World War II. You are fighting Japanese. These kamikaze guys who are busy killing you. And your whole platoon. And, your whole Company. Killing all of you instantly!

How would you like to be born in 1927 like my mother? How would you like to be born in 1927 like my wife's Grandfather, Charles R. Hipp, Sr., in North Carolina. At age 18 drafted. Gone from his hometown. Immediately sent to the Pacific Ocean, at age 18 with a bunch of new friends in the Army. Then, have 66% of all your friends in your Regiment killed in 180 days. Literally. Not good. Decidedly not fun.

Or be born in 1927 like my wife's stepfather, John Gantt, in South Carolina. From a nice family but absolutely broke. Remember, it is the Depression. Age 1 to 20 totally broke. Everyone. Then, age 18, drafted and off to war, overnight. In his case, again, against the Japanese in the Pacific. A long, long way from South Carolina. **Then, same thing. He lost**

over 50% of his friends overnight. In Okinawa. John Gantt, Sr., was so scarred by that, he never, ever could talk about it. Ask him anything. Ask him anything and he will answer. Except that. Never, ever talked about it. That is scarred. That is sad. Oh, and that is the whole generation. Big Chaley Hipp would never, ever talk about it, either. And he was a salesman. Both of them, Charles Hipp Sr and John Gantt Sr, were actually salesman extraordinaire, and would talk about anything – because they loved to talk, because they were God-Given salesmen. But, not about the War. Neither of them would ever talk about the war. They were unbelievably scarred by WWII. Their years in the war having all their friends killed fighting every day right next to them. Dead instantly! Unbelievable, really.

By the way, because God decided they both would live, and come back to South Carolina alive from the war, I was extremely lucky to end up spending so much time with them. Being as they are amazing God-Given salesmen, just like I claim to be – as you will see in later chapters of this autobiography, in my 40 trips selling alfalfa hay in Japan (how is that for full-circle)! I had (and still have) the utmost respect for them.

My mother, Madeline Kuhn, was also born in 1927 in this Great Depression thing. This is the "Silent Generation." Now you know why they are silent. There is not much to talk about when that is the initial 20 years of your lives. **Everyone of you reading this book**, born during the 1910s to 1930s, with the same awful first 25 years of your lives, that I just described, at least flat broke, if nothing else.

My mother had it hard. She said she did not want any child to be named for her because she did not want that child to have as rough a "road to hoe" (another farming expression) as she had. Also, that whole silent generation was completely adverse to adoption. That was a thing. To this day, I am not sure why. But they don't care for adoption. Probably another little surprise that you don't know what your are getting. And, we see how surprises worked for them, right? Going broke every day from age 2 to 20. Then, drafted and uprooted from your home at age 18 and sent to fight overnight (and die overnight) in places like D-Day and Iwo Jima and Okinawa. Surprises just did not work out for the silent generation, in the end.

So, Shea came up with this absolutely brilliant Southern solution: We will name our newly adopted baby for her grandmother. Because you cannot possibly dislike a child with your own name! And, that is what we did!

And, it was brilliant!! Literally brilliant! And of course, it was magic: My mother instantly loved the newly adopted little girl, because she was named for my mother! My wife, Shea, is so smart.

My mother was also really great at proclamations. (Sadly, something I have also inherited. I, too, love proclamations! Again, I cannot help it. I was born that way!!!) (lol!)

Now for the really great stuff: All you young ladies (age 14 to age 30) reading this: My mother was absolutely correct about one thing. She graduated from Stanford University in 1948 – one of the earliest women to do so – **and a full year before** the first female U.S. Supreme Court Justice, Sandra Day O'Connor, graduated from Stanford. (Thus, I will have a Justice Sandra Day O'Connor story for you (in the next volume of this trilogy because my mother knew U.S. Supreme Court Justice Sandra Day O'Connor before she even went to law school).

This story will also be incredibly encouraging to <u>all of you young ladies (all over the world, not just USA)</u>: After graduating from Stanford University, my mother, Madeline Kuhn, then eventually got married to my farmer father, and then quit teaching high school so she could stay home and raise children (myself and my younger brother, Jim Kuhn). And, I said to her, "Why aren't you out of the house with a job or career like so many other trailblazing women in America in your generation?"

This is where it gets unbelievably encouraging for all of you young ladies **(in all 195 countries today)** that are reading my book: My mother said to me, "John, do you think it is more important to have a career, or do you think it is more important for me to stay at home and raise my children – and teach my children my values and my work ethic and my honesty and my optimism?"

Then, my mother brought up an expression that she learned in History Class at Stanford University (and she was a History Major): She said to me: "The hand that rocks the cradle rules the world."

Wow. **<u>As a young woman, you want to be powerful</u>? Think of that one: "The Hand That Rocks The Cradle Rules The World."**

First, you now understand, that means that men do not rule the world. Lol! We men may think we rule the world, don't we? **But, we men do not "rock the cradle," do we?** Second, all of you young ladies, ALL OVER THE WORLD, every one of you ladies are actually raising ALL THE CHILDREN all over the world, aren't you?

That means you women are raising all the children and teaching your values and ethics and your moral standards to

76

the WHOLE next generation. That is incredibly powerful! That is one option for you now that you may not have thought of! That means you may "honor your body clock" and your desire to raise your own children. I promise that God will bless you if you do – no matter what or who your God is. God blessed my mother and her children.

I say we commence having far more respect for Stay-at-Home-Mothers than the media allows. I am tired of the media putting down Stay-At-Home-Mothers. As a woman, you want to rule the world? Then rock the cradle. Be a stay-at-home mother, if you want to. **It is your God-Given right to be a stay-at-home mother.** And from this day forward, respect yourself for it, no matter what the media says.

Of course, as human beings all women have choices, that were not as prevalent in the olden days. In fact, one of your choices is to be a C-Suiter as a woman! My mother would tell you to be the best C-Suiter ever!! As a woman, just be your best and always be honest. And, remember the Henry David Thoreau I quoted from *Walden* that quoted as my biggest influencer: "Rather than love, than money, than fame, give me truth." Why is truth more important for all human beings than anything else: Because if you are always truthful, three things happen: First, you will climb any ladder and always be respected and relied upon if you are always truthful. (Even if you are a stay-at-home-mother, your children will know they can believe you and rely on you to tell the truth). Second, when you always tell the truth, you can always remember what you said. Third, you will always sleep well at night!

An outshoot of being a woman C-Suiter, is that you can aspire to be just like my beloved Dagny Taggart from Ayn

Rand's novel, *Atlas Shrugged.*   Dagney Taggart is probably the first woman in a novel to not be married, not have children, and be the greatest businesswoman of all time, by being first and foremost, honest with what she said to everyone, from the Track welder to the President of the United States, and true to herself.

Also, remember, Dear Reader, my all-time favorite William Shakespeare quote from the **first page of this book**, that is from the Shakespeare tragedy *Hamlet*, Act 1, Scene 3: **This above all: To thine own self be true.** Isn't that your goal as a woman and a mother and as a human being? It was Dagney Taggart's goal, and she achieved it in spades! Same with U.S. Supreme Court Justice Sandra Day O'Connor. She could not change her personality (because she was true to herself) at a Washington, DC, dinner with famous NFL HOF Running Back John Riggins, when he said to her "Losen up, Sandy, baby." U.S. Supreme Court Justice Sandra O'Connor kept her composure with the "drunk boys" and never changed who she was as a person – even laughed at it later that week in a Speech at Pepperdine Law School! Lol! But, great for both of them, Dagney Taggart and Sandra Day O'Connor! And, great for you, dear women, too!

Back to another choice as a woman is to be a stay-at-home-mother, like my mother. The goal is still to be honest and hard-working and have your own self-worth, since society is no longer very supportive of this incredible option! Remember, as a stay-at-home-mother, that is your choice, and you are just as valuable as a C-suiter!

And, that is what my mother did every day at my house with me and my brother, Jim Kuhn. Brought us up as two fine boys from age zero to age 28, when we both got married to our College Sweethearts! On my mother's behalf, the proof is in the pudding: She could not possibly raise two better men than my mother did: My brother being an amazing farmer, both before high school and after college. In between, my brother, James Kuhn, was an amazing student at St. Paul's boarding high school in New Hampshire and at Stanford University as a Russian Language Major. As for little old me, at age 62, I am finally emerging into my own as a writer. Something my female English Professor at Vanderbilt 40 years ago saw coming when she taught me Freshman English, and said, "you can really write creatively and with energy – you need to do that for the world!" Even further back in time, my high school English teachers at Culver Military Academy in Indiana taught me to do every day for four years: They taught me how to write.

The more I think about it, I am surprised that the expression, "The hand that rocks the cradle rules the world" is not more well known! This statement by my mother should give very young women daily self-confidence as a mom! In fact, this statement should give all young ladies immense self-satisfaction and self-respect as a mom!   You oversee your destiny and you can teach the whole next generation everything there is to know. And give the men and women of the next generation YOUR morals and values. Pretty powerful.

CHAPTER 9

RESPECT FOR THE VERY YOUNG MEN (OF ALL RACES) WHO DIED

Not only did I learn how to write in English classes in Military High School in Indiana, but my high school classmates also taught me how to march with a gun – a gun we were all married to in Military Boarding high school. Just like my father in Korea, and Shea's grandparents in World War II, many of us in the United States have been taught how to march. And, how to march with a gun, and how to shoot that gun so you can kill someone before they kill you.

I also learned military history at Culver Military Academy every year from 9th to 12th grades. And, to this day I am sad for **all the young men <u>who died or were injured</u>**, overnight on battlefields: 1776, Revolutionary War against England. War of 1812, again against England. Civil War in 1861, against each other. World War I in 1914 in Germany and Europe. World War II in Japan and Italy and Germany in 1939 onwards. Korean "Conflict" in 1948. Vietnam War in 1961 through 1973 – where we started to have women die on the battlefield. Finally, Persian Gulf Wars in 1991, and War in Afghanistan starting 2002, and War in Iraq in 2003 for almost a decade.

Lots and lots and lots of United States 18-year-olds died (and wounded) on battlefields for this country to free itself from England, and to end slavery, and to free Europe from fascist tyranny in 2 World Wars, and to free Korea and

Vietnam from Communism, and to free Afghanistan and Iraq from Muslim tyrants who kill us. We have done a lot of good. We have lost a lot of extremely young men, too. The price is high.

Let's not forget that price: The half million young (very young) men, who died. And, over 1 Million young Americans who were severely, severely injured. Let's stand up for the National Anthem again, as we did for 240 years as Americans, in honor of over Half-a-Million very young men (of all colors) who died for that National Anthem in the past 250 years. And, let's salute our flag, again. How about that for another Madeline Kuhn (my mother) proclamation!

Again, it is what your great-grandparents would tell you if they were here, let's stand and for the National Anthem since so many Americans died for your Freedom and for that flag, from men and women in the Revolutionary War all the way to the Afghanistan War. So, I will say for your great-grandparents to you now, with the historical explanation that is needed to understand where they are coming from.

CHAPTER 10

THE CAT OUT OF THE BAG

Back to the amazing birthday thing: Full Circle: Guess who also has the same birthday as me? Besides both my grandfather AND my First Cousin – have you already forgotten the very first paragraph of this book? Tsk, tsk, tsk, Dear Reader!

Okay, I am going to let the Cat Out Of The Bag: The Other person who has the exact same birthday as me is Harry Potter! Yes! Harry Potter!! Oh, and a little factoid you will (not surprisingly) learn from me now is that Harry Potter's Creator, J.K. Rowling, also shares the same birthday as myself and Harry Potter!

And now you are saying, "Ahhhhh. That makes sense. Of course, J.K. Rowling would give her greatest creation the same birthday as herself! Makes perfect sense, Mr. Kuhn!" How auspicious am I to have the same birthday as J.K. Rowling AND Harry Potter? I am very fortunate, indeed!

CHAPTER 11

I AM THE CAT

Okay, dear reader, are you really that bad at remembering??? That was the First Chapter, as well!!! Remember, where I point out that I was born a Zodiac Leo (end of July, so I am a Lion – which is a Cat). And, I am born in the Year 1962, which is the Chinese Year of the Tiger (which is also a Cat.). So, I double-down as a Cat, right? Again, it's not my fault. God made me that way.

Oh, and just to remind you a little bit more about cats: Then, as a cat, I love to sleep! I am happiest when I am sleeping. Of course, I am happiest sleeping! That is all Cats' favorite thing to do on the planet! Our favorite thing to do is sleep! And, I am no exception! My wife, Shea, wants to come back as a cat so she can sleep anywhere, anytime, without a care in the world!

The other thing that makes us cats the least happy, is to be woken up! We do not like to be bothered while we are sleeping. We do not. From lions sleeping in Kenya to Tigers sleeping in China, to Tabby Cats sleeping on your porch or Siamese Cats sleeping in Japan, we do not like to be woken.

But, what happens if you pester a Cat enough while it is sleeping? If you poke them enough, with blinding speed, they will wake up, swipe you with their paws, and cut you with their claws. Literally all in one instant motion! And, it will hurt you. And, you will bleed. And it will be sharp pain for you (or for their prey).

So, why would you wake a Cat (of any kind, including me) when it is sleeping? If you poke me enough and poke me enough, *and eventually wake me, oh no*…. I will whirl around and kill you and eat you so fast that you will not know what hit you. But, you asked to be my dinner by poking me enough times. My warning, dear reader, leave me alone when I am sleeping.

And leave me alone when I am watching hockey on TV! Lol!!

So, again, it makes sense that I was born the same day as Harry Potter, July 31st. And, the same day as another quite good writer, Harry Potter's Creator: J.K. Rowling. Again, we are all three born on July 31st.

Therefore, we are all three Zodiac Leo's with the exact same July 31st birthdays (J.K. Rowling, Harry Potter, and me!). Being as all three of us are creative, and as cats we like to nap, read and write, and create, and… EVEN pull mysterious magic from, a, well, a Quidditch!! Or yes, pull magic from a Wand!! Or, even pull magic from a real well, such as an Ink Well! Again, like J.K. Rowling, pun intended!!!

Oh, and not to leave out my favorite cat from the WHOLE 1980s, off we go to English Composer Andrew Lloyd-Webber and his Broadway Musical **CATS** – which he based on "terrible anglophile" and terrific American poet T.S. Eliot and his Cat from **Old Possum's Book of Practical Cats**: Mr. Mistoffelees. Now, why is Mr. Mistoffelees my all-time favorite cat? That is easy! According to T.S. Eliot's poem (and Andrew Lloyd Webber's showtune) "The greatest magicians have something to learn from Mr. Mistoffelees' conjuring turn….and we all say Oh! Well I never was there ever a cat so clever as magical Mr. Mistoffelees!"

And why do I say "terrible anglophile" about our American poet T.S. Eliot? Two reasons: First, I am also a "terrible anglophile," from loving the rock band "The Who" to loving British history and British Authors (such as Jane Austen and J.K. Rowling) way too much, to loving British tea even more than that – just truly terrible, terrible on my part. Second, on the other hand, at least I am not as bad as T.S. Eliot (in my opinion, greatest American poet of all time, bar none!), who up and expatriated to England. I promise you, dear reader, I will not do that – even though I have straight out stolen "dear reader" from amazing British novelist Charles Dickens. Yes, guilty as charged, I am, from The Who to the Dickens to the Rowling, to sadly, the tea, to which I am addicted! Lol!!

Anyway, I am now singing as loudly as I can: "And not long ago this phenomenal cat produced seven kittens right out of a hat!" Join me all of America and all of England – not to mention the rest of the world!

CHAPTER 12

FROM BOLTS IN THE FARMYARD TO BALING HAY

Writing about the farm again, I am. (Again, thank you, Yoda!)

My farmer father believed that a farming son should do every single job every farmworker did on the farm so that we (my younger brother Jim and myself) could relate to all the farmworkers, and so that we knew every single job implicitly. This would mean we could make good decisions as Foremen, when we got older, and owners, eventually.

Fortunately, all farmers' sons in this country start extremely early in life on the farm, so we never complain about our jobs. But, because we work so hard our whole lives, all farmers do love to complain about the markets when we sell, especially when they don't pay us enough for our crop that we toiled daily for months to produce. And we toil daily, including Saturdays and Sundays.

I will never forget my dad said early on, when I was complaining about going out to our farm at 5:00 am to work on a Sunday: "John, do you think the female cows don't give milk on Sunday? The cows need to be milked on Sunday – and on my birthday (Christmas Day) – so you have to milk the cows on Sundays and even on your birthday and on Christmas, or the cows will get sick. So, Johnny and Jimmy, we work on Sundays. Get out there boys, the cows need you." My father had a booming voice. I inherited that, too.

With that comment about female cows, my father was also making sure that Jim and I knew, <u>utterly</u>, that female cows make milk, not male cows, who are not called cows, they are called bulls, and male steers make beef and female cows make milk. And don't forget, female cows all over the world, make Non-Homogenized Milk. Our United States farm factories ruin our milk with factory treating called Pasteurization. (I am not letting you forget that, dear Reader! I Tell It Like It Is.)

So there we were, Jim Kuhn and John Kuhn, in the Farmyard by our huge mechanics shop, age five, barely able to stand, picking up bolts (to recycle the good metal bolts that got lost in the yard) and picking up the discarded metal iron shards form welding (so the metal iron shards in the farmyard don't pierce the next big tractor tire that comes in the yard). In the 105-degree heat. Remember, this is El Centro, California and it is summer and it is hot all day long!

I also remember my mother saying to my dad: "Why are they, at such a young age, picking up bolts in the yard, in the blazing heat?" My father said when they are exceedingly young like that, they are still exceptionally short, so it is much easier for them to pick up the metal shards and discarded bolts in the yard than for a grown man. Right, he was!!

Next job I had, at age 7, was to go behind the Sugar Beet irrigation pipe layer all day (that is 12 hours every single day, with just Sunday off), and put the small plastic irrigation pipe on the hydraulic machine every single pipe for a whole field, 12 hours every day, for 1,600 acres of sugar beets. In other words, for three months out there behind that machine:

That would be an ingenious hydraulic machine that some practical farmer invested, behind a real International Harvester Tractor (**IH Tractor, for short for the rest of this book**, and with the sad huge IH Tractor multinational company going completely bankrupt because of the huge US Agriculture Recession in the 1980s – I promise to cover that red, white and BLUE (i.e. sad) USA story, too!).

Back to my farm job every day at age 7: Piece by piece by piece, methodically, I would place a plastic irrigation pipe on that hydraulic arm, all day long. The hydraulic machine would then jam every single piece of short plastic irrigation pipe into the soil (it would take about one minute to do that part) so the irrigation water could go from the cement irrigation ditch (on my right) to the one-fourth mile irrigation bed (on my left, where the sugar beets would be planted **by another farmworker** on a tractor). Moreover, we would have to redo every field again, every single time you watered a sugar beet field. Again, my dad said, "You are seven years old, short, young and have no back pain, so you can feed every one of these pipes all day long onto the hydraulic arm of the pipe inserter. Someone must do it, John." (Booming voice, again!)

Believe it or not, I sincerely loved that job! Being hyper-active and Attention-Deficit Disorder (ADD for the rest of my book), nothing will get your attention like a big hydraulic machine that you just repetitively, precisely place plastic pipe on, without fail, quickly, over and over again for a whole day. *Thus, no time for ADD and no mind wandering there*! And never *mind* the fact that the hydraulic machine could cut your finger off instantly. Farmers take this all for granted. But next time you buy vegetables in the store, or sugar in the store, remember this and thank the farmers, who start at age

4, doing all of this for you! Remember me at age 4, picking up all the metal bolts and the metal welding scraps in the shop yard so the farm pickups and farm tractor tires don't blow out repetitively.

The other reason I loved that job is because I got a **huge pay increase** for this job!! At age 5 and 6, I was only paid 50¢ an hour for picking up iron shards and bolts in the yard. That would be 12 hours x 50¢ = $6.00 per day. And all summer the farmyard was hot as "he - double toothpicks" But, at age 7, my father paid me "a penny a pipe"!!   And that was a lot of pipes!! I would average 800 pipes a day, every day, all summer long! Now, 800 pipes at 1¢ a pipe comes to $8.00 a day! **And, we all know $8.00 per day is way, way, way better than $6.00 per day! Lol!** (My dad was not stupid, was he?)

By the way, little did I know, that this precise motion I practiced every day age 7, did come in handy when I was age 15 and a sophomore in Military High School, in the Artillery, where it was my job to load the 105mm howitzer shells (ammunition) in Four Gun Drill cannons for 21-Gun salutes in high school – and it was imperative that you not get your hand caught in the cannon's loading block or it would instantly cut your finger off. I loved that job, too! Imagine how cool it is to load real cannon shells by hand into the back of a 105mm Howitzer, especially when your friends back home don't even know what you are talking about. It surely makes you "cool" overnight! (*More on all the fun times I had in military boarding high school as a real farmer, later in this 1ˢᵗ volume of my autobiography, I promise!*)

Remember that mechanic's shop I mentioned in the paragraph about myself and Jim picking up bolts and metal spikes and shard at age 5? Well, that huge, metal, outdoor, mechanic's shop is where they repair all the tractors when they break. And the tractors break ALL THE TIME. But, if your father makes you do every single farm job on the ranch, you learn not to break the tractors and not to break the equipment you are pulling behind the tractor, at least not quite as often! It is extremely expensive to break a tractor. Then the tractor comes back into the mechanic's shop for repair, with its big tractor tires waiting to get punctured by the metal welding shard in the machine yard. Oh, good news, Jim and I just picked those up, so that is one win for the Kuhn Farm Team!

It also is terribly time consuming and costly to break a disc, or a landplane, or a hydraulic sugar beet pipe injector, or an alfalfa seed planter, or a hay rake, or a hay baler, or even a subsoiler. By the way, I also spent a whole year on our HUGE Caterpillar Tractor D8, with massive metal tracks, when I got kicked out of Vanderbilt University for bad grades after my Freshman year of college. You have that whole story coming in Volume 2 of this Autobiography, *I Tell It Like It Is!* (which comes out next year), and I promise you will laugh wholeheartedly at me in that chapter because it is certainly funny!

If you drive a tactor into a sugar beet field and you are "topping beats" with a hydraulic "plant-top haircut" machine, or drive a tractor in an alfalfa field spraying with an unbelievably long-armed spray rig, you need to know how to maneuver that spray rig carefully while spraying for aphids (and oh do we hate those pesky, awful aphids that kill lovely alfalfa plants and kill lots of great vegetables that you eat every day at your restaurant and your grocery store). That is why we spray the aphids!!

By my father sending Jim and myself out to all the fields on tractors at age 12, we eventually learned how to not have that tractor break by going up a steep ditchbank too fast; or, actually have the tractor tip over because you climb a ditchbank that is too elevated.

Oh yes, I have tipped over a whole tactor. A whole red IH Farmall 806 tractor, with a hay rake on the back, that I flipped over backwards at about age 16 in one of our fields near my Tractor Foreman's house.   Not fun listening to my dad's booming voice on that one! That is also when I learned the Spanish phrase from my Tactor Foreman, "pinche puto cabron." Looking back on it, yes, Juan Leal was right on that one! Foreman Leal was quite a bit older than I and he did get to laugh constantly watching "little Juanito" (that would be me) slowly learn how to be a tractor driver. He certainly had **lots of laughs at me – and with me, too**, out there in those fields!

Or, you learn how to not have the long metal spray arms break (on the aphid sprayer), by sloooooooowly, hydraulically bringing them in at the end of every alfalfa land BEFORE turning to the next land. And turn sloooooooly to the next lane. And not go over the alfalfa bed too fast. **Yes, I managed to break the huge alfalfa field spray rig. Twice, in fact**. Jual Leal was kind and explained to me that I would need to slooooooowly go from alfalfa land to alfalfa land with the metal spray arms out. *But, I kind of forgot about that three hours later*, and in one fell swoop, I had a whole spray arm broken off in the field. Juan Leal was able to weld that problem back on in the field, so that was improvement.

The second time with the same spray rig? Ahhh. Not so good. My father, himself, came out to one field and kindly said, "You need for diesel fuel for that tractor. The Farm Shop is just down the road a couple of miles, so go there and fuel up. And, remember, John the diesel fuel tank in the yard is covered by a big wooden shed.   As you know, that wooden fuel shed has been there for countless years. Don't go running the long spray rig arms into the shed and knocking the whole shed over. That has never happened since I started the farm and that would be just like you, John, to break the whole shed (stern face of my father)."

Well, I just did not realize how long the spray rig arms were, even when they are folded in hydraulically. So, well, I just did not see the wooden shed as being that big and sticking out that much. Middle of a sweltering day in August at the El Centro Farm Shop. I bring the IH 1066 tractor into the yard. Apparently, I already did not remember what my father said. I drive the tractor around the back side of the wooden shed to fuel up and: WHACK!!!! CRACK!! BANG!!! OMG, I knocked the whole flipping wooden fuel shed over! Plus, every farm worker in the yard is watching this and laughing immediately at stupid John. And saying, "OMG, look what son Juanito just did!!??!!"

My father? Not impressed. In fact, the booming voice went exactly like this: "How can I trust you kids with ANYTHING around here???!!! I tell you how to do it. I tell you to look out for the shed and look at that! In one ear and out the other. Stupid Boy."

My punishment? Spending a whole week fixing the old wooden shed over the diesel tank, of course! My father: "That will help a boy to remember to be careful with machinery and equipment."

My only redeeming situation was the next week I asked Juan Leal, "Is it REALLY true that true that NOBODY has ever knocked over that wooden diesel shed? I cannot believe that!" To which Juan Leal pulled me aside and said, "Your father is correct when he states that it hasn't been knocked over in a long time. However, the reason your father knows this so well is that he, himself, at about age 16, with a new Farmall H Tractor and a hay rake, knocked the whole wooden diesel shed over, all by himself. So, I suppose your dad knows what to tell you when you are learning, right?" **Like father, like son. It's not that bad when you take after the old man, now is it?**

Who was Juan Leal? Like I said, my father's Tractor Foreman. I loved him because he helped me all the time with the tractors and was nice to me. He was "simpatico." (A Spanish word that I love and does not truthfully translate well to English. Everyone loves that Spanish word!). I thought he was meaningfully younger than my dad. Just about that time, I moved elementary schools from McCabe Elementary School (near my house in El Centro), to Seeley Elementary School (near our Farm Shop on the West end of the Imperial Valley). This was because "She-Who-Must-Not-Be-Named" (my Mother – lol!) decided that Jim and I were not learning nearly enough at McCabe School (near my home) and we were bound to learn a lot more at the farming area school, Seeley School, 8 miles farther out and conveniently next to our Kuhn Shop Headquarters on Drew Road in Seeley.

Low and behold, I arrive at Seeley school for the first time for sixth grade, and in my diminutive class, there in my class is my Tractor Foreman's son, Juan Leal, Jr. Also in my class is my Irrigator Foreman's son, Jesse Rodriguez. AND, there is my Shop Mechanic Foreman's son, Frank Gutierrez. I'm thinking, how is it that Juan's son, Macho's son, and Leo's son, are all in my tiny sixth grade class in Elementary school? That shows you how small a farm community is!

There is the son of an amazing welder and manager of men, Juan Leal. There is the son of an amazing genius with water and irrigation, Macho Rodriguez. There is the son of a true mechanical genius, and whose shop I desperately wanted to work in, Leo Gutierrez. It also showed me perspicaciously, that we are all the same, and made in God's image. Whether we are farm workers, or farm foreman, or we are farm owners, we all have our own God-Given talents and our own God-Given brains that we are to use to make God's world a better place. Even little ole me from that **same small sixth grade Seeley Elementary school class**, now writing my book, my autobiography for the big bad world out there!

Back to me as a tractor driver: To be honest, that wasn't even my worst move with a tractor. Want to know why I brought up the tractor driver job of "topping beets" with a hydraulic "plant-top haircut" machine? Well, that was another summer job I had.

After you plant the sugar beets and water them for 8 months in the dirt in our fields, the sugar beets grow large enough to harvest them. The last job before the huge beet digger comes though the field to harvest the sugar beets for sugar, is to drive a piece of equipment that cuts the green leaf tops off the sugar beets, through every single row of sugar beets on the whole ranch. And that is with an IH tractor that goes fairly fast and with the "beet topper" behind you cutting the greens off the top of every sugar beet plant. I was given that job one summer when I was 15.

Now I loved that job too! It was fun driving the beet topper all summer, and it was fun having lunch in the sugar beet fields with our Mexican workers, who loved having the son of the *Patron* around to feed the best Mexican food on the plant (from their wives). And, the son of the *Patron* around to tease, of course.

I also loved the fact that the tractor went way faster than most, because beet topping is comparatively simple. Or... at least in theory, it is simple. Lol!

But, being a novice, I did not realize that you should **slow down the beet topper** if there is a section of sugar beets with lots of greens. That is going to take a slower pace. Or you will clog the beet topper and have *Jefe* Juan Leal back over to fix what I broke, again! Of course, my dad warned me about that too. So, you learn quickly where to slow down in the field, and where to speed up, by the sound the topper makes, and even the sound the tractor engine makes, as well. If the engine is straining, slow down. It's too much vegetation for the beet topper. I got superb at that. And, I learned a lot about farm machinery and listening to the machinery noises while I worked.

By the end of the summer, I got bored though. And I got a little cocky. So, I did not think I needed to listen to the whirring beet topping mechanism anymore. I also contracted this great idea in my head that I should buy one of those new great big boom boxes with a cassette tape in it. Plus, a set of those new Koss Headphones – that were my generation's version of noise-cancelling headphones! And, I love the rock band "The Who," remember? So, this was the best idea I ever had! I would listen to my Who albums on cassette tapes in my new boom box with my new Koss

Headphones. Nobody would even see the Boom Box and Headphones way up there on the tractor with me! I was right, of course! And, I LOVED listening to The Who – The album **Who's Next** to be precise, with "Teenage Wasteland," the greatest song ever – on that contraption!!

Until, of course, I messed up again! Because I am joyfully listening to The Who on my boom box all morning, topping sugar beets, I did not really notice that I had gotten into a part of the field where the green leaf sugar beet tops were much bigger, and I needed to slow down. And, I could not hear the engine straining, either, because I was blissfully listening to my headphones! What do you think happened next?

Well, of course, the beet topper gets completely full of vegetation and gets fully gummed up and the gear box breaks entirely. The metal blades flat out break, too. My obligatory walk all the way to the end of the field to my pickup and drive over to *Jefe* Juan to explain that I broke the beet topper. To which he said: "Now, that is a first! Nobody has actually broken the beat topper. Well… truthfully, that is the second time in two years because your brother, Jim, last year also broke the sugar beet topper. He completely forgot to turn it off when he left the field. Then, he got on the paved road and the whirling blade broke instantly when it sucked up a piece of concrete. So, you are in good company on this one."

Just for the record, that is NOT what you want to do with a beet topper. That is worst case scenario. Imagine the BANNNGGGG sound of the whole metal farm implement being torn up by a piece of concrete halting a 6-foot steel metal rotary blade in a millisecond. Not. Good. Two days in the shop on that one. However, if I am being honest, my scenario is substantially worse because my dad told me not to listen to music while operating farm machinery. Things that make you go: Hummmmmmmm.

My father; not so forgiving as Juan Leal. I thought I hid the Boom Box with the cassette tapes (like Styx's **Grand Illusion** Album) and the Koss Headphones. But, oh no. Dad saw them right away when he came over. "John, didn't I tell you to listen to the engine noise of the tractor? Didn't I tell you to listen to the beet topper all the time to know if the vegetation is too condensed? How do you think you are going to listen with that G__ D___ music contraption you have there?!!!! I am throwing that whole thing out at the shop, immediately." In one fell swoop, that was the end of my Who tapes and my Boom Box and my Koss Headphones. However, I am proud to report that I did not break the beet topper again all summer, nor did I break the IH tractor either, after that! Progress is made in baby steps! Or, as my father used to say: "Piece by piece, John. Piece by piece."

Baby steps is right. Although I did not break the beet topper nor the tractor the rest of the summer... I may have hit the diesel shed again! Of course, this time I collided with the diesel shed with the sugar beet topper itself. Fortunately for me, this time the tactor nor the equipment broke. But, I think I broke my father's patience with this one: After I broke the wooden diesel shed the prior summer, I re-forgot by next summer that the farm equipment is wider than the tractors. In the case of the beet topper, it is just a little wider than the tactor. But, a little is a lot when you are talking about inches and metal equipment.

I just felt **I had to prove my father correct the prior summer** when he said (remember): "I tell you how to do it. I tell you to look out for the shed and look at that! In one ear and out the other. Stupid Boy!" Well, Stupid Boy just had to go and do it again this summer. I analyzed the beet topper, and I knew it was not any wider than the tractor, so I knew I was good to go! I brought the beet topper and tactor into the Shop yard and drove around back to get diesel at the pump under the new wooden shed I had to build the prior year (so I wasn't going to hit that again!!) Until: WHACK!!!! CRACK!! BANG! The whole damn NEW wooden shed, over the diesel pump, crashed to the ground, again. This is because when you are out learning to farm, it is baby steps.

Hey, at least I did not break the actual metal farm equipment on the wooden diesel shed, like I did last year, right? Right?? My dad admitted that was true. Later, my dad also told me it was exceptional for all the Hispanic farmworkers to see that you really cannot mess up as bad as the two sons!

He said that did have its advantages. The farm workers knew three things after that: 1. They could not possibly blunder as badly as John. 2. Fritz Kuhn's sons were not privileged. 3. The Kuhn boys worked every job they worked and learned everything from the ground up (pun intended).

This was also when I leaned the most important thing as a businessman in my whole life, from my own father, when he said to me and Jim: **"Show me someone who never makes mistakes and I will show you someone who does not work."**

And, *let me repeat that*, because it is one of the most important statements you will read in my whole book: **Show me someone who never makes mistakes and I will show you someone who does not work.**

That has helped me my whole life. Why? Because it is incredibly encouraging to anyone in the working world. It means, if you mess up, you are working and trying and doing your best. That is to be commended. And if you do not mess up, then you are simply not working at all. Working is to be commended every single time. And, that beats not working every single time.

Remember, that Kuhn family Swiss work ethic? There it is in a nutshell.

CHAPTER 13

MY MOST IMPORTANT FARM JOB – IRRIGATOR – AND CADDYSHACK REVISITED!

Remember my 7-year-old job at "a Penny a Pipe" putting in vital plastic Irrigation pipes on the head ditches of the sugar beet fields? I got really good at putting in pipe my whole farming career – all kinds of pipe: from little plastic sugar beet irrigation pipe, to cement feeder pipes from the cement irrigation ditches (that we paid Ryerson Cement to build in our fields), to big cement pipes at the ends of Drain ditches, I have put in every kind of pipe by hand.

When I say by hand, I mean by getting a standard work foot shovel out of the back of my Ford F-150 pickup and realigning a sugar beet plastic irrigation pipe – like I put in at age seven – when I am the Irrigator for that field. Yes, we have lots and lots of Irrigators. We could not irrigate the fields without Hispanic Irrigators. And, remember my dad's rule: We Kuhn boys were to do every single job on the farm. Especially being an Irrigator.

In fact, my farmer father, because he did all the jobs on the farm when he was growing up, as well, had another rule that truly made all our Hispanic workers always want to work for Farmer Fritz Kuhn at Kuhn Farms, no matter what else happened on the farms around us. The farm employee management rules he came up with were truly ingenious. First, all of our employees knew that if you worked for Kuhn

Farms you were full-time and NEVER seasonal. My father said there is always some work to be done on a farm, no matter what the season. As you know from this book, you can, at least, pick up all the discarded metal bolts in the yard, especially in the winter when farming is slow and it is not so insufferably hot!

Second, my father said that we would always pay one dollar more per hour than all of the farms around us. This served two purposes: 1. We rarely lost good employees to other farms around us. 2. We would not have to train all new farm workers every year because our employees stayed with us because we paid the most.

Third, my father said that if a farmworker comes to work, that means we called them in to work and they must show up. If, for whatever reason, there turned out to be no work, we would always pay every employee that showed up for work a minimum of 4 hours pay. My father said that they are called in to work, they must dress in their work clothes, spend gasoline money to drive from their homes, and must wait until we no longer need them. Basically, messing up their day. Consequently, we paid every employee who showed up for work a full 4 hours of pay, even if they only stayed one hour. Naturally, we had a whole lot of very happy employees at Fritz Kuhn Farms and they LOVED working for my father.

Irrigation water runs through our fields for twelve hours to twenty-four hours a day, every single day of the 365 days in the year. The irrigation water comes from the Colorado River (which borders California fifty miles from our Imperial Valley) because we perfected our water rights in 1903 in the Imperial Valley – the first farm valley in the United States to do that!   Then, our water comes to our Imperial Irrigation District from Yuma, Arizona, just as it has every day since 1903, to our Imperial Irrigation District (IID). Lastly, the IID delivers the water in their HUGE canals to our little cement irrigation ditches we built and own on each of our fields.

Our reclaimed desert sandy soil is the best on the planet to grow vegetables. This is because sandy soil drains so well that the vegetables grow to their God-Given size and grow healthy and beautiful and delicious. So, Irrigator is another assuredly important job! And Jim and I have irrigated hundreds of fields hundreds of times. When you have no rain (because it is a desert) it is vital to irrigate the soil all the time to keep the vegetables (and sugar beets, which grow deep in the soil, too) growing healthily every day! This is not wasting water. Hispanic irrigators, Irrigator Foremen, and Farmer Owners do not care to waste water. We pay a high price to the IID for every acre-foot of water we order every day at our farms. Because we pay a high price for the water every day of the year, we don't want to waste it. What we do want to do with that water we pay for is grow your awesome vegetables and awesome alfalfa hay (for your milk) that we sell all over the USA every day at the least cost. Wasting water makes you go broke.

My father, my brother and I trained our Hispanic Irrigators to use as little water as possible, every time you water. A farmer will survive if you do that. You will go broke if you don't do that. Moreover, all the farmers in the Imperial Valley do not waste water when we grow your crops that you eat. One hundred percent of us farmers want to grow all our crops as inexpensively as possible. Of course.

So, when I am driving around a field that I am irrigating, and I see a cement pipe from the **Irrigation Ditch** to the field, not working properly from my pickup, even if I am not the actual Irrigator, I MUST hop out of my pickup, grab my shovel, climb over the big cement irrigation ditch (full of water) and go fix the broken cement pipe. Or, temporarily fix the flooding water by rapidly shoveling the dirt next to the hole in the pipe, to over the pipe hole, until the leak stops. In other words, cover up the water hole with dirt as quickly as humanly possible. Then tell my Irrigator Foreman, Macho Rodriguez, to remember to have our ditch repair crew go over to IID Fern Canal Gate 89 and fix the problem with real cement when the water is gone and the ditchbanks are dry.

Or, if I see a Huge **Drain Ditch** with a Huge Cement Drainpipe that is now leaking, I jump out of my pickup, grab my little shovel, and go down deep in the Drain Ditch (12 feet down or more) to see what is going on down there in the dirt drain ditch. Probably be compelled to rapidly figure out where that water is going and shovel like crazy to get that runaway water stopped before it ends up all the way down at Salton Sea.

Who is that "Macho Rodriguez?" Well, just like Juan Leal, he is another Foreman on the farm. Macho is our Irrigator Foreman. And he is talented at figuring out water flow and figuring out irrigation. Plus, he is terrific at teaching Irrigators how to irrigate. He is also great at directing men and hauling men and women in his pick-up truck to the precise IID gate number at the correct fields all over the 10,000 acre ranch every day to irrigate with that day's twelve hour and twenty-four hour huge water orders that are coming in from the Imperial Irrigation District. So, he was vital to the farm, as well.

Do you know what the Number One problem for farmers in the Imperial Valley when it comes to dirt ditch banks, or dirt drain ditches? Gophers! We hate Gophers! We actually treat all Gophers just like Bill Murray does in the movie *"Caddyshack."* (BTW, shout out to Bill Murray, because he is a friend of mine – just met him along the way through life here in Charleston, South Carolina!)

Why do we Imperial Valley, California, Farmers treat all gophers just like the movie *"Caddyshack?"* Because the gopher digs a gopher hole all the way from our actual field, under the great big dirt ditchbank that we created years ago. We drive our pickups AND our tractors on our huge ditchbank roads to get to and from our farm fields.

The gophers love to dig their holes from our fields, under the dirt ditchbank road, to the huge dirt drain ditch on the other side. Usually about 15 feet. Then, guess what happens next? We don't know where Mr. Gopher burrowed, but we will certainly find out the next time we irrigate that field! HOW? Oh, within *minutes* of the irrigation water reaching that part of the field with the gopher hole, the water will find the lowest point – now the Gopher hole)! The water will instantaneously change directions (from our beautiful flat field) and will now entirely flow hundreds of gallons of water *under our awesome farm roads* we drive on, washing our farm road out instantly!! And, voila, we have an instant disaster. From the gopher hole. The whole farm road is gone in seconds. And, we pray that it does not happen just when a pickup is driving over the dirt road or the pickup will directly disappear in the huge washout. Which, of course, has happened to almost every farmer and irrigator in El Centro, at some point. Not good to lose a Ford F-150 pickup truck to a gopher. That is one for the gopher and none for the farmer.

Then, we must desperately radio in to our Farm Shop and call our emergency Caterpillar Grader M14 to come repair the whole ditchbank immediately, before the whole dirt ditchbank rushes down the drain ditch – which does happen from time to time, to every farmer. Did I mention that WE HATE GOPHERS??!!

My grandpa, Fritz Kuhn, Sr., hated those gophers more than anyone in the family? Why? Because when he was younger, there were no "Caterpillar Graders" which were designed in the 1950s by Caterpillar Company precisely for repairing ditch banks and irrigation ditches. So, when Fritz Kuhn, Sr., was younger, every time a Gopher destroyed a ditchbank or destroyed a road, he and his farmer friends would all have to spend A WHOLE DAY with just hand-held shovels, fixing the whole ditchbank and bringing the dirt road back to shape. Horrible work in the old days. Made milking cows by hand look easy.

Anyway, from my age 3, I kid you not, my Grandfather, Fritz Kuhn, Sr., would come by our house early in the morning and pick me up in his old chevy car, and take me out "Gopher hunting." And, I loved Gopher hunting. Because, it did NOT involve a shot gun. No, we would take Gopher Traps with us on all the ditch banks every day and find those pesky Gopher holes, and we would put a trap in each Gopher Hole and catch the Gopher before he "Got Us!" **As you can imagine, a 3-year-old boy would think Gopher Hunting was the most fun thing on the planet!** And it WAS the most fun thing on the planet! I miss my Grandpa, Fritz Kuhn. actually

CHAPTER 14

GRADUATED TO THE MECHANIC'S SHOP, FINALLY!

Back to the massive metal mechanic's shop in the middle of the Kuhn Farms headquarters at 1625 Drew Road, south of the little town of Seeley, California (where a lot of our farm workers lived, and where I was now in sixth grade with my three Foremen's sons!)

Just for you to be shocked: We are the southernmost point in the whole State of California and **all our fields are all within ten miles of the Nation of Mexico!** Five miles south of our shop and headquarters, for the past 80 years, is the Mexican Border. Just across the border in Mexico, is the City of Mexicali, an actual Mexican city of over 1 Million people! Compare that with 80,000 in the whole Imperial Valley! Now you know why we get so many farmworkers from Mexicali, Mexico.

By sixth grade it was my desire to work as a mechanic on our tractors in our tractor shop, which is run by our Mechanic Foreman, Leo Gutierrez. I thought working on the tractors would be way more fun than driving them. So, my dad put me in Leo Gutierrez's shop for the year (1974) to learn under Mr. Gutierrez how to work on tractor engines and work on all the broken farm equipment.

You think driving a tractor is hard? You think Irrigating is hard? Try working as a mechanic in a farm shop with 150 pieces of equipment coming in and out, broken, all summer.

My first rude awakening is that every single problem that comes in will be "something we have never seen before, so we will have to figure out how to fix that." Oh, and not later. We must figure out how to fix it NOW!!! Why now? Because the machinery is now not in the field doing its job. That means the plants could wither and die because we are not tending to them with what they need that day.

That means that if today's broken machine in the shop is for subsoiling, then the plowing will be delayed. Next, the discing will be delayed. Then, the landplaning will be delayed. And the forming of crop beds will be delayed. And, then the planting will be delayed. And, then the irrigation will be delayed. And then your crop will come up too late in the season and will die prematurely from heat or cold. **There is nothing untrue about this. This is farming in a nutshell.** Farming is the biggest domino effect you have ever seen!

Imagine this truth: On every farm in America, every day, hundreds of thousands of dollars are gambled. On this exact wager and this exact precision timing AND on the markets for our products being high enough to survive when we sell our crop six months later.

Being not old enough, or mature enough, at age 11, to understand all these dollars gambled and domino effect, my biggest concern every day when I went into the Kuhn Farms Mechanic shop was my stomach! More precisely, every day that summer I went to work at 6:00 am looking forward to the Mexican food the workers bring from their wives to work for lunch.

By the way, there you go women, another great woman's job created by your particular God-Given talent: COOK! There are millions of ladies cooking lunch for their husbands all over this great big world. That is a lot of women all over this great big world cooking lunch for their husbands (or vice versa, even, men cooking lunch for their wives)! Add onto that all the cooks at McDonald's, plus hundreds of cooks at military outposts, all over the world, plus hundreds of cooks in the food and beverage industry in Charleson alone. For centuries we have revered great French cooks and Chinese cooks. We even celebrate our Mess Hall Cooks, such as General Washington's cook in the Revolutionary War. Everyday in this world there are lots of cooks who are doing an amazing job!

Anyway, I knew that the Mexican wives always cooked the BEST Mexican lunches for their husbands every single day, all over our Kuhn Farms (irrigators, tractor drivers, alfalfa hay balers, even shopworkers – like me!). Thus, if I were in the Mechanic's shop with all the Mexican Men (and not out solo on a tractor in the field), I would have a better chance to trade my sandwich for their meal. Daily, at work, my goal was to trade my Madeline Kuhn (my mother) prepared, BEEF-TONGUE sandwich in exchange for their great Mexicali style, burrito colorado, or their carne asada burritos with homemade flour tortillas, or their shredded beef tacos with homemade corn tortillas. Now, dear Reader, you may salivate!

Yes, there is such a thing as a beef-tongue sandwich. And, when you grow up on a farm, you eat beef-tongue! What is that? Exactly what it sounds like. Beef-tongue is the beef part of the cow's tongue that is below the skin of the cow's tongue. I have eaten thousands of them. That is not an exaggeration! Why have I eaten thousands of beef-tongue sandwiches? Because that is some of the tenderest of all the beef on a steer. We farmers know that! And they are delicious! So, Jim Kuhn (my brother) and I had one for lunch almost every day at school prepared by Ms. Norma Cancio, our live-in housekeeper!

Just for the record, my wife, Shea, does not think they LOOK delicious! But, they are delicious. More importantly, Mexican farmworkers think they are delicious. And, they will trade their awesome home-cooked Mexican food for incredibly delicious home-cooked beef-tongue sandwiches. That is a fair trade for both of us, and I knew it!

Also, remember, these beef-tongue sandwiches were cooked daily by my mother, Madeline Kuhn, or my housekeeper, Norma Cancio, so shout out to them both as fantastic women cooks! Another one of their many jobs!

CHAPTER 15

BEEF TONGUE FOR MY NEW BRIDE IN CHARLESTON!

Back to my wife, Augusta P. Kuhn (Shea Kuhn). Another wonderful woman cook! But, remember, she certainly did not like the look of the beef tongue sandwich! So, here is the story:

Of course, it never occurred to me that my wife would never have seen a beef tongue sandwich when we got married! We farm boys think everyone has seen a beef tongue sandwich. And, because I love them so much, within two weeks of our coming home to Charleston from our honeymoon, and Shea was already back to work at her paralegal job in the city, I decided to make my 22-year-old bride a wonderful BEEF-TONGUE Sandwich from scratch for lunch when she came home. So, being an exceedingly nice new husband, I went down to the local Harris Teeter grocery store for a nice fresh beef tongue from the butcher shop – like we get at the Safeway in El Centro. Well, they told me they did not have beef tongue. In fact, they never *heard* of beef tongue! I thought, that is strange! Everyone loves beef tongue!

Not to be a man denied when trying to please my new bride, I then went to the best wild game cook in the family, 65-year-old John Gantt, Sr. (he is the one I told you above fought in WWII and would never, ever talk about it). So, I knew that John Gantt has a Christmas tree farm on the Edisto River in South Carolina, and is the best game, venison and all types of meat, cook in the family. I knew this because I dated Shea for 4 years, with many visits to Charleston and out to the "Edisto Tree Farm" and many "Sunday Dinners at exactly 2:00 pm" at John and Lisa Gantt's house.

I arrive "on the Boouuleevard," as John Gantt called it for years, to see my father-in-law. "John, where can I get a fresh beef tongue?" He immediately laughed so hard that he literally spit out his morning coffee. And, he said, "Son, what on earth would you want a fresh beef tongue for?" I said, "Why, to surprise my new bride (your daughter) with a super beef tongue sandwich for lunch when she gets home from work." He laughed even louder. "I am not sure Sheeeaaa is going to like that, but alright." John Gantt continued, "Now John, the only folks in the South who eat beef tongue are the black folks. But, they do love their beef tongue. So, I know just where you can get one right away. You go up to The Meeting Street Pig and you go to the butcher shop, and they will certainly have one."

Fantastic!! Off I go to the Meeting Street Piggly Wiggly in my soft-top Jeep Wrangler that I drove out all the way out from the farm (by my little lonesome), when I got married in Charleston.   First surprising observation on this jaunt to the Pig: I realize that in 1990 almost no Charlestonians go North of Broad Street. And, this is waaaayyyy North of Broad Street. And, I park my jeep in the parking lot across from the Newspaper and go into the Meeting Street Pig by myself. Only to find that I am the only white person in the Meeting Street Piggly Wiggly. Again, I grew up on a farm with all races of farmworkers, so that is no problem for me. Except, I cannot understand one word from anybody in the grocery store from the minute I walked through the door. Not a single word. I must be in a foreign country. Oh, I am in a foreign country!

I have spoken with many African American workers on my farm. But, they speak normal English. What on earth is this they are speaking at the Meeting Street Pig? Ahhh, I find out later, from none other than John Gantt (who also loves the Meeting Street Pig) that they speak a completely different dialect in Chhaaaarlessston. It is called Geechie. And, it is impossible for a farm boy to understand (unless, of course, you are a farm boy from South Carolina, like John Gantt!)

John Kuhn has entered the Meeting Street Pig to purchase a beef tongue. Talks to the ladies at the register who ask, *"what is it you waaannntt?"*

> *"A beef tongue."*

> *"We don't have that here."*

> *"Mr. Gantt said you do."*

> *"We don't"*

Then, from the meat department, an older gentleman hollers over, *"OHHH I like Mr. Gantt. What he send you in here for?"*

I said, *"a beef tongue."*

"Never heard of it, son." But then the gentleman asks me, *"What piece of the steer is it from?"*

So, I point to my tongue.

"OH," He says! *"Yes, we carry beef tongue! My favorite part, in fact!"*

Sure enough, the old black butcher fumbles around in the cold meat case for something at the bottom. Low and behold, he pulls out a full-sized beef tongue from under the rest of the meat! I, of course, am delighted!!

I ask him, *"How much is it?"*

"Oh," he says, *"the white folk don't like beef tongue, so it ain't spensive. It only cost you 99 cents!"*

That is even more awesome! Beef tongue in California is a delicacy and it cost 10.99 a tongue back in 1990. But, not in Charleston! 99 cents! Are you kidding! Yippee!!

Back into my Jeep to drive home to cook my beef tongue from the Pig for my new wife. I arrive home, and of course, realize, I have no idea how to cook beef tongue! But, I have an "ace in the hole."

I have Norma Cancio, my Mexican housekeeper. In other words, our live-in lady who raised me from about age 6. Cooked for our whole family and made most of our beef tongue sandwiches growing up (after my mother taught her how). In 1990, there are no Cell phones. There are not even computers! Nothing like that at all. Heck , we just got fax machines in 1985.

So, now I must call Norma to get her to tell me how to cook beef tongue for my new bride. I do know that we farmers (and everyone on the farm) get up between 5:00 am and 6:00 am. Even though I am calling Norma at 10:00 am Charleston time, the three-hour time difference will not be a problem. And, I know that Norma will answer. Because that is how we operate on farms!

"Norma, soy Juanito," I say.

"Ah, que bueno! Que paso?"

"Oh, yo quedo cocinado un beef tongue por Shea."

"Ah, que bueno!"

Yes, I am fluent in Spanish! When you grow up with a Spanish-speaking housekeeper from age 6 onward – essentially, in my case – our surrogate mother: Norma! Then you know Spanish as well as you can, or you cannot find your "calcetinas" to go to school in!

So, of course, Norma is delighted to hear from me only 1 month after I am married in Charleston, on the real telephone!! Not a letter. The Bell telephone!

But, she asks me in Spanish: "Do you really think that Ch$\overline{a}$ (no Spanish speaking folks can say Shea – it is not in their language – it is ALWAYS: Ch$\overline{a}$ – with a long a!) will really like beef tongue, Juanito? (Norma laughs out loud, because she knows where this is going!) I, of course, have no idea where this is going. I am moderately new to the opposite sex, and I am not very smart, to boot.

But, Norma explains to me, just put 2 bay leaves in the boiling water and boil the beef tongue for 2 hours, and it will be perfect. Not a minute shorter.

Got it! Now, being Swiss, I am very good at following directions. It is in our DNA as Swiss people to be exacting and precise! From Swiss watches, to making Swiss cheese. We follow complicated directions well.

So, I boil the beef tongue for 2 hours in a big pot on our stove at our old new apartment in Charleston. Sure enough, the beef tongue is perfect!

Also, Shea gets home right when the beef tongue is done, and she sees that I am cooking.

She says, *"Wow, that is great that you are already cooking so soon in our marriage! I did not see that coming! What is for lunch?"*

I am so proud! *"Well, just take the lid off the pot and you can see what is boiling in the water!"*

Shea pulls the lid off the pot and, and, and almost throws up!

I'm like, *"What is the problem?"*

Reply, *"What on God's earth is that ugly thing?"*

"Oh, that is beef tongue. My favorite, you know!"

"Oh my GOD! IT IS DISGUSTING! Get it out of here. NOW!"

"I have spent all morning finding that for you. Cooking that for you. Calling Norma for you. How can you not like it?"

"John! Look at it! It is disgusting! I would no more eat that then fly to the moon!"

For my children's age readers: Things that make you go, "Hummmmmmm."

"Well, honey, looks like we will be going out for lunch," I said.

"John, that is the best idea you have had all day!"

Dear Reader: Just a side note. Look at this: You have my whole marriage and children thing not even coming until Volume 3 of this Autobiography!   You think this beef-tongue chapter is funny? Think of the laughs I have in store for you in Volume 3, two years from now!

CHAPTER 16

HAND-HELD HEAVY METAL GRINDER IS NOT EVEN THE MOST DANGEROUS JOB

Back to my favorite place on the farm at age eleven in 1974: The Kuhn Tractor Repair Shop. The Repair shop is a HUGE metal framed shop out on Drew Road and has been there since my father built it in the 1950s as the repair shop. It has always been across the dirt driving expanse from the Fritz Kuhn Farms Office. Daily, that summer I worked in the repair shop. Across the yard in the Kuhn Office were my father Fritz Kuhn Jr., the Irrigator Foreman, Macho Rodriguez, and the Head Foreman Arnold Wilson. Arnold, incidentally, was my Aunt Vreneli Kuhn Wilson's husband (my father's sister's husband) for whom we all liked to work!

Remember, I am now working under the Head Shop Tractor and Farm Implement Repair Foreman, Frank Gutierrez, whose son, also named "Frank Gutierrez," and my good friend now that my mother moved me out to Seeley School for sixth grade.

I am 11-years-old and my job that summer is difficult. For twelve hours a day, every day, I am in charge of the hand-held 20-pound, heavy, gyrating, metal grinder. It is hand-held and it is WHIRLING at high speed all day long and I must take it anywhere in the shop that metal needs grinding off for twelve hours every day. This means where the farm implement I need to work on is, I must climb up with the 20-pound spinning grinder (usually 10 feet up on a tractor, or 10 feet up on a huge metal farm disk or hay rake or any farm implement that is broken), plug it in, and for an hour slowly grind off the metal protrusions, or cut a piece of metal off, before it can go back in the field.

First, I did not realize there could possibly be soooooo many metal welding bumps to grind off!! Every time the metal shopworker who is the actual welder in the shop (David Gomez was our best Welder!) welds together two pieces of metal, to make one piece of metal, our shop welder has to spend 10 minutes, with BLINDING LIGHT and a huge dark glass helmet needed to see the welding spot in the BLINGING LIGHT, This happens about six times a day in every farm implement repair shop in the United States. This is how, for example, you get the arm of the farm implement to permanently stay on the body of the implement. Or, get the HUGE landplane bucket, back on the huge landplane. Or, get the actual rake that John Kuhn broke off by going up the ditchbank too fast on his tractor, welded back on the metal hydraulic rake frame. You see why we must weld every day in the farm shop in the whole United States. And, we must grind off the metal protrusions left by the welding or the tractor driver will cut his hand badly on the welding surface, if it is not ground smooth by John Kuhn in the shop.

Second, this is exhausting for an 11-year-old boy every single day for twelve hours. Plus, it is precise work. You must tightly grip the 20-Pound hand-held grinder because the big metal grinding disc is spinning at high-speed; otherwise, every piece of metal you grind off will jar you immediately on the cement floor of the shop. The big whiling metal grinder blade will cut you so badly you will be in the ambulance to the hospital. This happens to every single one of us in the shop sometime during our career. My turn was that summer. Half the time that happens you immediately lose a finger, or a leg by gashing your rectus femoris (very front upper leg muscle) so badly that you lose your leg in the hospital. I am not exaggerating here. It happens instantaneously with the huge spinning metal grinder that is hand-held by each of us on every tractor or implement that comes into the shop. I was extremely fortunate that summer because I only gashed the front of my lower leg shin with the whirling metal grinder and though my Levi jeans, so that was not too bad and I did not bleed enough to go to the hospital. The shop first aid kit tourniquet and the big bandages, plus the shop 100% alcohol cleansing liquid (we use at the end of the day to get the actual grease off our hands) did the job and saved me from the hospital. Again, I was fortunate.

The reason that my job at 11-years-old, the summer of 1974, in the Kuhn Shop, was to be in charge of the Hand-Held 20-Pound Heavy Metal Grinder and work on that twelve hours a day, six days a week, is because that is not even the most dangerous job in the shop! The most dangerous job is the Welder Job, at which David Gomez was the best in our shop for 20 years. The welding machine is so dangerous that I was not allowed to do it!! Imagine how dangerous that is! I already told you that it is, literally, blinding light. It is from an arc welder machine.   And it is important that everyone in the shop clear away from the welding site when the Welder is doing his job (with the ultra-dark mask) or you will be blinded in 30 seconds by the arc light.

My father told me, Welding is the most dangerous job in the shop and it takes years to learn how to do it properly and you will not be doing that job. Grinding with the 20-Pound

Heavy Metal Grinder is much safer, my father said! And, he was telling the truth, actually.

I also learned that you must line up the two pieces of metal to be welded, to exactly the correct spot, with up to six metal clamps at a time, or the weld will fail. Consequently, I ended up helping with clamping metal in exactly the correct spots, to weld, every day at the Kuhn shop.

Yes, I worked from 6:00 am to 6:00 pm every single day, Monday through Saturday, just grinding down metal welding bumps on every piece of machinery and implement they brought in broken from the field. Every single farm worker, including me and my father, worked 72 hours a week on that farm! In fact, on every farm in the Imperial Valley. That is a whole lot of farm workers and Foremen and owners. Of course, my Dad also worked every Sunday, as did Macho, the Irrigator Foreman, because you have to water alfalfa when the alfalfa needs watering. Not when you feel like it. When the soil is dry, you irrigate. And, my Dad was the best at anticipating when the farm ground (in the 100 degree El Centro sun) would be parched and the crop would need irrigating. Especially on Sunday. Remember what my father said earlier: "Cows need to be milked every day, including Christmas Day – which was his birthday, recollect, dear reader?

In fact, I worked one summer on the farm when I failed out of Vanderbilt University with bad grades – another Chapter in this first Volume of three, for you to laugh with me – on our HUGE D8 Caterpillar tractor (with huge metal tracks). That summer I worked from 6:00 pm to 6:00 am every single night, **7 <u>nights</u> a week**, because my father was so mad at me for not keeping my head in the books and getting kicked out of Vanderbilt.

So, he put me on the D8 as the driver, to "learn how to really work and remember to learn at school instead of goof off " That was the whole year of June 1981 to June 1982 when I had the night shift 7 nights a week under Tractor Foreman Juan Leal. Also, my poor brother, Jim Kuhn, got stuck on the day shift on the same caterpillar Tractor, **7 <u>days</u> a week**, so, as my father said, "Jim, you might as well learn John's lesson ahead of time, because we don't need to go through this again while you are at college." Again, poor Jim. Punished for my failures! Sort of like the coach of a football team, or hockey team, where the coach makes the whole team run sprints for one team member costing them the game!

You realize, that means I worked 365 straight days (without a day off) that year on the D8 Caterpillar tractor. The second reason for this is that the **D8 Caterpillar costs so much money to buy and so much money to run**, that my father figured out if the two boys keep it running 24/7 for a whole year it will expense out less for the farm. In other words, the cost of the machinery and maintenance is much less than if you run it full time than if you run it half the time. So, full time, 24/7, with the Kuhn boys on the day AND night shift, it was! (Not lol! A lot of work, for both of us, that was!)

CHAPTER 17

THE BIC, THE BID, AND THE BURRO!

I am under Shop Foreman Leo Gutierrez in the Kuhn Shop working every day. At lunch, I am figuring out how to trade my beef tongue sandwich with the Mexican Farmworkers. We spend one hour every day (from 12:00 to 1:00 pm, of course) having lunch in the very small, hot, dusty, shop office, with the shop workers. Now, the three farmworkers who are there all the time with me are our best welders: Victor, David, and Alvero. And, they think I am funny. Why? Because I have such a hard time sitting still. And, I always want to trade my beef tongue sandwich for their great Mexican food – which they also think is hilarious.

And, because I can talk, and talk, and talk, and talk. I take after my mother. In fact, I take after my mother's father (my maternal Grandfather, Jack Hall), who could sell anything to anyone and could talk and talk and talk and talk. And, whom I am named for: My grandfather's name was John Hall. So, I am named John Kuhn, for him. But, they called him "Jack' and they just called me "John," to avoid confusion.

Anyway, it is lunch in the shop. And there is a very heavy metal table (that Victor welded) in the corner of the shop office, upon which we all ate lunch. So, here is this 11-year-old kid going to eat lunch and I decided to have a fake horse race with my hands on the metal table. And, my fake horses were to be named: Victor, David, and Alvero. So, they think this is genuinely funny.

Subsequently, I start "Announcing the Horse Race," just like my favorite announcer I have heard on TV! And, to make it super easy in this fake horse race, I decided to shorten their names to:

The Bic.   The Bid.   And, the Burro.

Here we go, "The gun sounds and tthhheeeeyyy are offffff!"

"Wow, the Bic takes the early lead and takes the inside rail. Oh my, he is just not got enough steam, so it looks like the Bid is catching him! This is going to be a long race for the Burro. Now the Bic has hit the first pole first. Perfect position to win the race. Oh my, now it looks like the Bid has way more energy than the trainers thought!   Looking better for the Bid as he catches the Bic! Still looks like it is just not the Burro's race. They are tearing down the backstretch at Churchill Downs! There are still a lot of race left, but the leaders are tied!"

"Wow, looking down the backstretch it looks like the Burro is coming out of nowhere to make this a three-horse race!! Where is this energy and drive from the Burro coming from? Some trainer played this close to the vest! The Bic is now tiring. Yes he is! The Bid has taken a five farthing lead over the Bic! And, the Burro seems to be making some noise, but probably just too late.

"Not too late!! In fact, the Burro has closed the gap on the middle horse and is tied the Bic! But it is so close to the finish! Too little room left. Oh my, not too little room left as the Burro has now found a new gear! The Burro is passing the Bid! For first place in the Kentucky Derby! No, the Bid has got him in his eye and gaining back. It is going to be a photo finish!! It is a photo finish!! But, the Burro wins at Churchill Downs, with the Bid second and the Bic a distant third!!!

Naturally, after this John Kuhn fun at the farm lunch table, David, Victor, and Alvero are laughing hysterically at me! And, David, who had the best English of the three, said, "How on earth can you announce like that? That fast and that funny!" I said, "Well, my grandfather, Jack Hall, is just like that, so I am sure it comes naturally." David said, "Certainly not your farmer dad. He would not be talking that fast." I said, "No, he wouldn't."

But, I also knew that I was a huge, huge LA Dodger fan, because the only baseball games we could get on the transistor radio on the farm in El Centro in the 1970s, were Vin Scully and Dodger baseball! I loved Vin Scully! And, I loved Dodger baseball. I could say the whole starting line up! AND their batting averages! Everyone in the Imperial Valley were huge Dodger fans. San Diego Padres Baseball radio did not come over the mountains to our transistor radios.

I would watch World Series games at home on TV and my mother commented, "I think you will grow up to be a sports announcer, like those men on TV do!" She was probably right. **But, I also knew I could do something most people could not do: That is, I could write.**

Consequently, you, dear Reader, are going to find a few chapters from now in this first volume, how I, as a freshman in high school, took over the Vedette Newspaper and wrote thousands of words in every section of the newspaper. Not to mention, that in the Vedette Sports Section, I would write about my beloved Dodgers and Walter O'Malley, owner of LA Dodgers, and coincidentally from my very same high school in Indiana, would see what I wrote! How coincidental is that? That the actual owner of the Los Angeles Dodgers, Walter O'Malley, graduated from my very same high school in Indiana, Culver Military Academy, in 1922?? Ohhhh, and later in this very Volume 1 you will find out TWO more owners of actual Major League Baseball teams who graduated from my same boarding high school in Indiana – one in 1922 and the other major league baseball owner in 1945. All coming a few chapters from now!

In four years in high school, I wrote so much for the student newspaper, The Vedette, that the English Teachers at Culver would help me with my writing and proof reading. Eventually, my senior year, I became Editor-In-Chief of The Vedette Newspaper and my senior year, my Vedette staff and I took our high school newspaper to Number One high school newspaper in the United States. We were voted the top high school newspaper in the USA (as voted by the National Scholastic Press Association in 1979), and my senior year. All of this is coming a few chapters from now!

Meanwhile, Victor and David and Alvero knew I would not be the boy staying on the farm (like my brother, Jim Kuhn did) after watching and listening to my made-up horse race!

CHAPTER 18

THE YEAR WE MADE A KILLING

Many people have asked me: "Why was your dad so successful at farming?" This is why: He was a genius at machinery. Specifically, farm machinery. And, he was a genius at gently moving everything and everyone along in the same direction every single day, no matter what the cost. Moreover, he was enthusiastic. And he never took no for an answer.

I'll never forget: Our Chino, California, Hay Salesman: "We cannot sell the hay at that price this year?" Dad: "Why?" Salesman: "Because the trucking is backed up and we cannot get the hay to Los Angeles Daries. Dad: "Fine. We will buy our own trucks and sell our own hay." And next year, we were doing exactly that.

My other favorite: He loved machinery. So, one year he read about this new electronic sugar beet thinning machine just developed in Idaho by engineers (Engineer, another great God-Given talent and profession!). He said bring one down here to the farm and let's see it work. It did not work well at all. But my dad spent every waking hour for three full weeks out in the sugar beet field until he made it work correctly. Then, he planted double the sugar beets that he had the prior year, which would quadruple your costs with the field crew thinning that many acres of sugar beets. Some farmers in the Imperial Valley said, "Fritz, that will never work." (Which means he will go bankrupt if they are right).

But, oh no, dad spends every day in the sugar beet fields for the whole month making the new electronic beet thinner work properly. He was the first farmer in the Imperial Valley to thin all his beets without a crew. Wouldn't you know, God is good. My father had no idea this would happen; yet, this is what happens when you try hard and do the right thing every day: Low and behold, the US government decided that very year to quit regulating the sugar price. And 1974 was the year the sugar price tripled in seven months (April 1, 1974, was 22 cents a pound and November 4, 1974, was 55 cents a pound) and we had twice as much sugar as we ever had because my dad made that beet thinner work. My dad sold his double the amount of sugar in November 1974 for triple the price. In fact, if you are old enough to remember, 1974 was the year the sugar price in the US tripled in six months and that was the year your candy bars went from 5 cents to 25 cents from Summer to Christmas 1974. Remember, everyone in the United States was shocked that candy bars could go up from 5 cents to 25 cents in one year!

My father had gambled on his own ability to make that new sugar beet thinner work, and he did make it work – eliminating a whole beat thinning crew in all his sugar beet fields all summer. Because he believed in himself and believed he could spend hours in the field and make that pesky newfangled electronic beet thinner work, he decided to double the acres of sugar beets he planted in 1974. What an excellent move. His hard work and ingenuity resulted in our having double the sugar production from the prior year. And this was the very year the price of sugar tripled. Thus, he made 10 times the revenue in 1974 that he did on sugar beets in 1973.

Remember, though, this is not luck. You must be out there in the fields, do the work, and gamble on yourself. It is not luck. It is work. And, I learned how much work it was that year, too, because I learned how to dig the sugar beets out of the ground with a shovel when the beet digger missed one – because each sugar beet was worth a lot of money that year. Like father, like son.

Another thing I learned from my dad that year: My dad's friends in the coffee shop said to me: "Fritz made a killing." I came home and told my dad that and he immediately retorted something I will never forget: "Nobody makes a killing in business. Show me a man who makes a killing, and I will show you a man who killed somebody to make that killing (figuratively speaking)." My dad said, "**There is no such thing as a killing in business**. There is HARD WORK and ingenuity."

And, did I mention, hard work? You work hard every day and do the best you can, every single day, and you will be rewarded by God's natural law and you will help people.

I am telling you, dear reader, all of this, because these are life's lessons. You don't learn these things in the newspapers. You don't learn these things in the coffee shop. You don't even learn them in school. You do learn these things at work. At your own work. Which is fun, actually!

And, maybe, if you're lucky, you will learn them in my book. Lol!

CHAPTER 19

LOVE IS THE ANTIDOTE TO ANXIETY

I am writing this Chapter specifically for my children who are ages 27 and 25 and 23 and of the generation that believe that you need to take either an over-the-counter medication or a prescription drug to solve any problems God may throw your way, such as ANXIETY.

For over 10,000 years (that is not a typo) on the planet earth there were no Doctors anywhere on the planet earth prescribing drugs or mediations to anyone. That changed in just one decade, the 1960s. In the 1960s we went from hardly any drugs for anybody anywhere, to everyone in every big city needing over the counter drugs or prescription medications.

I am pretty sure that is why Mick Jagger and Keith Richards of the Rolling Stones wrote the Song "Mother's Little Helper" in December 1965! They knew that they grew up in England before prescription drugs were anywhere.

But, virtually overnight, in the 1960s, in England and the United States, drugs started to be prescribed by Doctors for everything you could think of. The most popular thing in the 1960s was to get Valium from your Doctor for anxiety. Wow, how sad is that? From 8,000 BC to 1960 AD (10,000 years) we do not need prescription drugs in the world for anything. Suddenly, we now need prescription drugs for every little thing that is bothering us?

This is because God did not intend for you to take prescription medication. If you get a headache, He intended for you to go over and see your friends and listen to music and forget about your headache. If you got anxiety, He intended for you to go to your friend's house and talk about the football game and escape the worry. Humans were intended by God to be social animals and for 10,000 years were.

How about we stop taking any prescription drugs or medications, just like our forefathers did not do for over 10,000 straight years in this God Given world of ours? How about we trust in our bodies and our friends and loved ones and go back to just talking things over with our friends and partners? That will go a lot further than drugs or medications. Just like it did for first 10,000 years on this Planet Earth.

I tell you: **A mind filled with love will heal a lot faster than a mind filled with anxiety.**

The best antidote to anxiety is love. Good, old fashioned, love. As the Beatles sang in another song in the 1960s: All You Need Is Love. Well, that is correct! Love is a much better answer than drugs and medication. In fact, Love is the perfect answer to outclass and outlast anxiety.

If you give LOVE a chance, it will win every time over ANXIETY. The Beatles and the Stones and The Who all knew that! Nothing better than The Who song, "Love Reign Over Me" on the Who Album **Quadrophenia**! Listen to the original **Quadrophenia** recording and I promise you that your anxiety will disappear immediately! I know. Because I do just that when I feel anxious. I have never taken a drug in my whole life. **And my antidote is ALWAYS The Who or the**

Stones or the Beatles songs – to everything. Try it. You'll like it!!

Or, try something new! Try **Tchaikovsky's 1st Piano Concerto**! That will conquer all worry and anxiety and stress. So will **Beethoven's 6th Symphony ("Pastoral")**, or **Mozart's 41st Symphony ("Jupiter")**. You will transcend to another world you cannot even imagine. Anxiety will take a back seat to the beautiful and the magical and the gorgeous! Trust me on this one!

CHAPTER 20

CHOCOLATE IS THE ANTIDOTE TO EVERYTHING!

For 10,000 years on this Planet Earth, Chocolate was every Girl's antidote to Anxiety. Oh yes it was! From Egyptian times right up until now. **Every little girl wants Chocolate.** Yes, CHOCOLATE! You probably do not know why. But I know why! Because it is delicious! And, as soon as you eat it your anxiety and cares go away! They vanish in happiness!

So, you do not need prescription drugs for anxiety! You need to turn to every "Mother's Little Helper" for 10,000 years before the 1960s and Valium: **Chocolate. For over 10,000 years, all women know that it makes all anxiety go away.**

Now, what country do you think perfected Chocolate? Why, Switzerland, of course!! Remember the country with all those Black and White MILK Cows? Switzerland. Naturally, the Swiss Invented Milk Chocolate!! And, of course, it is even better than God's original dark chocolate. Why? Because is a mixture of God's Cow Milk AND God's Dark Chocolate.

Because Switzerland has the most milk Cows (per person) in the world, of course they invented milk chocolate! In fact, in 1875, in the French part of Switzerland, Daniel Peter invented Milk Chocolate. Why? To impress a young woman, of course!!

Dear reader, let me set the record straight. This idea that men think they need to impress women has been going on long before Anthony and Cleopatra in Egypt! In fact, we do know that it goes all the way back to Adam and Eve, the first man and first women. Too bad they did not try harder to impress God (and less effort impressing each other!) and we would not have snakes! And, we would have endless Milk Chocolate!! Sounds just like Heaven to me!!!

Oh, is that a Cure Song? Yes, it is! Top 10 love songs of all time, that "Just Like Heaven!" Full circle, I am sure that Robert Smith of the Cure wrote that song to impress a girl. I just looked it up! Of course he wrote it to impress a girl. AND, the girl was so impressed that she married him! How is that for an antidote to anxiety? In fact, listen to "Just Like Heaven" and that will ALSO get rid of your headache and your anxiety. **Could even lead to better things…** Just saying!

All I have to say is: Nice job Mark Anthony, nice job Daniel Peter, nice job Robert Smith!

And, if you want to know more about Anthony and Cleopatra, don't worry, they were so famous that Shakespeare wrote a play about them as lovers! You can watch that play in the United States – or probably in ANY country in any language in the whole world, now that I think about it (especially since Mark Anthony is Roman and Cleopatra is Egyptian!)

CHAPTER 21

MY VINYL RECORDS TO JUVENILE HALL!

What did the Rolling Stones say: It's Only Rock n Roll if You Like It! Or, The Who: "Long Live Rock – Be It Dead or Alive!" Why are these songs important to Rock n Roll? Because most of my mother and father's Silent Generation, who grew up listening to Frank Sinatra, could not possibly believe that Rock n Roll, "and all that damn noise and racket" could survive after one decade of the 1960s. The Rolling Stones and The Who began to realize our parents were wrong and wrote those two rock anthems (which sold over 1 Million 45's each) as an "in your face, parents," response to the whole prior generation. It sure turns out they were correct. It's 2025 and Rock n Roll is still gong strong!!

"She-Who-Must-Not-Be-Named" (my mother) certainly did not buy into that one! Ironically, little did my mother know; but, my father had the best 45 Records Rock N Roll Singles collection ever – starting with 1955's Iconic Bill Haley and the Comets: *"Rock Around the Clock"*

Yes! My father, Fritz Kuhn, had a first printing of *"Rock Around the Clock"* in his 45 RPM Collection of rock and roll singles. He had Elvis Presley's *"Heartbreak Hotel,"* as well! At my age 16, when I stumbled upon this forty or so 45 records, I was just stunned! My mother certainly was not telling me, nor was she telling my brother, Jim, either!

My mother probably knew that my dad had those 45's shortly after she started dating him when she met him at a Bowling Alley in El Centro. When I found the 45's, they were in a nice burgundy plastic box, neatly ordered with paper dividers, numbers, and a handwritten (by my father) index card to all forty of those vinyl records. That was well thought out. And, some girlfriend or boyfriend had handwritten at the top of the index card: "Fritz, Show-Off Kuhn!" So, I knew that my mother knew about that. My mother knew everything. She did not have to fake anything. She did know everything. Lol!

By the way, my younger brother, Jim Kuhn, was into the records several years before I was. Why? First, my younger brother was always trying to be cool. And, I was always trying to please my parents. Why? Because, isn't that normally always how it is in families? The oldest child is completely dialed into pleasing their parents, because that is the first person you need to please before anyone else is around. In fact, it is exceptionally difficult for the oldest child to break that parental bond. Some of us never get there. I never did. Even when we think we have!

And, the youngest child is always trying to be cool. Why is that? Several reasons: First, they internally think their older sister or brother is cool, so they do everything they can to copy them. Second, it is a lot more fun to be cool than it is to suck up to parents. Third, wouldn't you rather be cool than not? Older children always realize this last. Consequently, my record collection was already way behind my younger brother's!

My brother, Jim, was no different. Quite frankly, he was always way cooler than I was. Even I knew that. Even my mother knew that! There I was going to McCabe Elementary School, with my "high-water jeans." What are high-water jeans? They are jeans that were from the prior school year, and you have grown three inches, and your mother still puts you in the same JC Penny's blue jeans as last year, and they are now three inches too short and "high-water jeans." And, you get laughed at unmercifully by your classmates when you go to school with "high water jeans."

Does this also happen to the youngest boy? Oh no. This only happens to the oldest boy! The youngest boy is way too cool for that. All hell will break lose when Jim Kuhn is asked to wear his same blue jeans the next school year. Frankly, I was too stupid to know better! Half the time I did not even know I was being laughed at until my good friend Benny Furrer told me, "You know, John, you probably ought to get new blue jeans next year before school," and explained to me while we were playing cowboys and Indians in his back yard on the farm. Benny then elucidated me on the whole situation of my being laughed at behind my back at McCabe School.

The other reason the youngest child is usually much cooler than the oldest child is that they pay attention to all their friends in school. That is human nature, really. My brother watched everyone at school, made friends much faster than I did, and would bring his friends over to our house to play all the time. Plus, my younger brother was much better looking than I was. How do I know? All the girls our whole life would be, "Wow, I sure would like to go out with your brother, he is soooooo good looking." They were not even remotely saying that about me. I can hold my own. And, like my mother, I got better looking every ten years. But, not in the early days were any girls remotely interested in me. We all know where we stand in this department, from a young age, don't we?

So, my bother has been buying rock n roll albums for a full two years before I was. All **The Kiss** albums were his first albums. That was two years before I even knew what an album was. The first album he bought that I listened to was Elton John's <u>**Rock of the Westies**</u> in late 1975, and I thought that "*Island Girl*" was the best song ever! And, "*Grow Some Funk of Your Own*" was even better.

Then, I started listening to the AM radio, on my transistor radio, of course, about that same time. And, the first song I ever heard on the radio one early morning in El Centro, was "*Here Comes the Sun*." I thought, Wow, that is AMAZING! Immediately afterwards I knew I was pretty dumb again, because I thought, "I will wait and see who sang that song because I am sure the DJ will tell us afterwards. And, the El Centro DJ said, "That is 'Here Comes the Sun,' and we all know who that is by." And, I thought, "how stupid is the DJ? Of course, I have no idea who that is!" I believe it took me 4 months to find out that song was by The Beatles.

I did manage to listen to a whole lot of Rock n Roll on the transistor radio in the next few months. And, managed to make up for lost time, by going to the JC Penny at the El Centro Mall and buying my first two 45 singles for exactly $1 per record. Little did I know that I could buy records at the same JC Penny department store where my mother bought my blue jeans. But, I did!

What were my first two singles? In September 1975 I bought Helen Reddy's "*Ain't No Way to Treat a Lady*," and I bought Sweet's "*Fox on the Run!*" Not much longer thereafter I bought Sweet's "*Ballroom Blitz*," and screamed the lyrics and danced around my living room like a maniac! To this day, I know every single note to both of those (Band)

Sweet songs (pun not intended!) and if I hear even one second of either song, I will still dance around the room and sing as loudly as possible!

And, like everyone my age, when my parents were not home, I listened to them on my parents' record player; that, heretofore, had been relegated to my mother's favorite album, **Swing and Sway with Sammy Kaye**! Moving up in the world, Jim and I were! (There you go again, Yoda!)

By the Summer of 1976 I knew my Rock n Roll well enough to have bought the Beatles **Sgt. Pepper's Lonely Hearts Club Band** album. That was my pride and joy. And, my brother had graduated to Elton John's **Goodbye Yellow Brick Road** album. We were pretty proud of ourselves.

On the other hand, "She-Who-Must-Not-Be-Named" (my mother), was not so impressed. Not at all, in fact. Remember, our parents' generation grew up during World War II, so they followed all the rules and they did not like loud noise, either.

My mother was much more proactive than most mothers though! She found Jim and me listening to these albums named above, and a few others, like Styx's album, **Grand Illusion**, and she screamed at us, "that is nothing but a bunch of noise! That is going to give everyone a headache and I am not going to put up with it anymore."

To which she then said to me and Jim one fine day in the Summer of 1976: "That is it! I am done with all your loud Rock n Roll music. You boys grab all your records and bring them to the front of the house here." Which, being the oldest child, I did as my mother demanded. And, I was all proud of myself bringing all my records and all my brother's records to the front of the house. About 10 albums and 10

45s for Jim, including his **Rock of the Westies**; and, about 5 albums for me and 5 singles for me, including my beloved **Sgt. Pepper's**!

Then my mother said, "Put all those records in my car and we are going on a field trip with them. You boys get in the car, too! We're all going." I couldn't imagine where we were going, but we did as we were told and got in mom's car with all our record albums.

Once we were all in the car she started up the engine and said, "We are now going to Juvenile Hall and we are going to give ALL THESE ALBUMS AWAY to the kids in that drug infested place where they belong! My children will not be listening to this druggie music and I am no longer listening to this loud Rock n Roll anymore!"

My mother literally said, "The kids at Juvenile Hall are just the kids who should be listening to this God-awful music and just the kinds of kids that should be having their minds ruined by this trash."

It took about five minutes to get to Juvenile Hall, and when my mother got there, she grabbed all our record albums from the back seat and said, "Come in here you two with me and help me give these horrible, noisy, things away to someone who will appreciate them."

And, that is exactly what we did. And, I will never forget the smirk on the face of the manager of the Juvy Hall, because he thought it was hilarious that we were bringing these "drug infested records" into the Juvy Hall as a gift to the kids!

Just for the record (pun intended!), my bother and I did not even know what drugs were. I am not even sure we had heard of such stuff until I went to Boarding School for High School in the Fall of 1976, when I enrolled at Culver Military Academy for Freshman year of high school and the Commandant of the Military high school said, "there will be no drugs at Culver and if you are caught with them or taking them, you will be immediately dismissed." And they meant it. Remember, I am the oldest child, so it is my job to follow the rules and not be cool, so I never went near drugs for any time in my four years in high school. I knew that if I were dismissed from Culver for drugs, I would be enrolled by my father at that same Juvenile Hall. Not doing that.

Now, I was none too happy that my beloved, awesome, non-drug-infected, **Sgt. Pepper's Lonely Hearts Club Band** album, with its unbelievably cool album cover, and its really cool grave on the cover (because Paul McCartney was dead, remember?) was gone from my house. Jim was also none too happy that his hard work on the farm for the past two years had just been given away at a place we had never heard of called Juvenile Hall! Both of us thought, "you know, at least we are not listening to Pink Floyd! How bad can Kiss and the Beatles and Elton John be, anyway?!!"

Now, once you tell adolescents in the United States of America (or kids in any other country, I am sure!) that they are "never going to listen to that noise again," what do you think the adolescents are going to do next? Buy as many Rock n Roll records as humanly possible, right? Only, we get much smarter after that. So, we then buy all the same records again, only incognito. And, we keep these "drug infested records" out of sight from our parents! Naturally, Jim and I proceeded to buy all the exact same albums over the next six months and keep them hidden away.

And, you know what we Kuhn boys did? First, every day, we would figure out exactly when our mother was coming home after school every day. Then we would play the albums as loudly as possible on our new "drug infested turntables and amplifiers and speakers" way back in Jim's room in the back of the house, until the moment my mother's car drove up into the driveway. Then, EVERYTHING would disappear immediately, as though the lady on **Bewitched** twitched her nose, and my mother would walk in the house, nothing left in sight! Gone with the wind! (Pun intended!)

Like we love to say in America: What goes around comes around. This was not intentional on my part. It just happened. **Inadvertently,** I got back at my mother. Without much thought, I would buy every single record I loved. And, it turned out that I loved Rock n Roll music, as you will see from this point forward in many coming chapters of this book!

Boarding high school: Bought records every week. My first actual album was Don McLean's **American Pie**. **Not bad for a first record, right**? Summer working on the farm in the middle of nowhere. Got to have music! So, every summer, lots of records without my mother noticing.

By the time I was a junior in high school, I had every Beach Boys album. (Of course! Remember, I am from California, and we LOVE our Beach Boys!)

Before I even got to college, I had one of the biggest vinyl record collections in the United States, especially if you include my 33s (albums) and my 45s (singles). One of my favorite 45s, to this day, is still Elvis Presley's *"Jail House Rock."* You need to watch the world renown TV episode with that Jail House Rock "music video" and you will be blown away how timeless that is. And, you will see it is truly a forerunner to Micheal Jackson's *"Billie Jean"* music video.

It's not my fault that I have one of the best record collections in the United States. When your mother takes your whole record collection at age 14 to Juvenile Hall, what do you think will happen?

The good news: Even my mother, in the early 2000s, had me play all my favorite Beatles records for her, and said, "Wow, they are really good, and I can see now why you like them."

CHAPTER 22

MARGARITAVILLE

My most vivid memory in my whole life on the farm, was in the Summer of 1977, when my brother, Jim Kuhn and I, were put in charge of my grandfather, Fritz Kuhn's house, which, was right there on the same property as our Kuhn Farms office and shop, as it had been for 50 years and counting. By my father, we were put in charge of making the grass grow and the magnolia trees grow, in the despondent dry desert soil. It was not the job I remember so much as the heat. And, it was not the difficulty of the job, either, that I remember. As with all junior and senior high school (pun intended) aged children in all of America, what we ALWAYS remembered the most was **"The Song."** The song of the Summer. And, that summer it was the Jimmy Buffet's song, *"Margaritaville."* Out of our Transistor Radio, *Margaritaville* was the song that played incessantly, all that summer by my grandpa's house in the heat, as we impossibly tried to get the St. Augustine grass to grow in the sandy scorched soil.

Transistor Radio? Yes. Never heard of it? Oh, in the 1970s, almost every person in America lived with their transistor radio on all the time. What is it? It is a milk-carton-sized radio, mostly made in Japan, that has one 3-inch speaker, and you can put your ear up to the speaker and listen to ANY radio station you could ever want to listen to in your area. Mainly, in our case, that would be KLOS FM 99.5 "Rock N Stereo" Radio in Los Angeles, where you could hear all the hits, all over Southern California, all the time.

As if that were not great enough, on our little Transistor Radio, we could get Vin Scully and Dodger Baseball on KLAC, AM Radio 590. No matter where you were in Southern California (that was 30 million people!), including in the little, hot, desert town of El Centro, you could get Rock N Roll on KLOS and Dodger Baseball on KLAC, on your little Transistor Radio. I would stay up every night after my parents put me to bed, stay wide awake, and listen to "Dodger Baseball" on the pillow on my bed with my ear flattened up against my orange Transistor Radio speaker on low, so my parents would not hear me or catch me. My brother, Jim Kuhn, would do the same with his green Transistor Radio! And, we would live and die with our team and compare notes on how our pitchers did the next morning at breakfast at home before school, because Dodger pitchers were always better than Dodger hitters! We BOTH had the whole Dodger starting lineup completely memorized every single day from 1970 to 1980.

By the summer of 1977 the AM/FM radio business had the transistor radios so perfected that you could listen to it softly in bed at night, without your parents hearing it, to having it sit on the plywood table we made in the farm shop for myself and Jim to put our transistor radio on the big wood table while we worked in grandpa's yard, and listen to Jimmy Buffet's "*Margaritaville*" as loudly as possible every day on KLOS!

Another reason I remember that summer so well is that it was the first summer that Jim and I got to work together. All the prior years, I was always in the farm shop, without a radio, because, as my father said, "You cannot hear what is going on and will get hurt by the machinery with that damn

144

radio," and Jim was always out irrigating or tractor driving most summers before that one.

Not only that, when you are high school age, your favorite thing to do is complain. Now, you were not going to complain to my father, or you would be jettisoned to a much worse job WITHOUT a transistor radio. And, you certainly were not going to complain to "She-Who-Must-Not-Be-Named," namely my mother, because she, being a former teacher, would make us write 100 times in a row at home with a pen by hand: "I will not complain about...."

Instead, we would **complain to each other** about everything, and in this exact order: "That damn Jimmy Buffet song is driving me crazy; I'm sooooo tired of that song." "This damn heat is driving me crazy." "That damn St. Augustine grass is driving me crazy." And, "Why is Steve Garvey the only Dodger player who can hit the damn baseball?"

My brother, Jim Kuhn, and I were out there in my grandpa's yard by the shop all Summer, from 6:00 am to 6:00 pm everyday (except Sunday) as we lethargically listened to Jimmy Buffet's incessant *"Margaritaville"* being played on our Transistor Radio on the wooden table we made that June in the farm shop. The reason I say incessantly played because ALL Number One songs in America were worn out by the DJ's every year on the radio. *"Margaritaville"* was no different. It spent the whole Summer of 1977 firmly entrenched as number one on the charts in the United States for the whole damn summer. I call it damn summer because Summer in El Centro, California, is damn hot. It was 106 degrees all day, every day, that summer. I now live in Charleston, South Carolina, for the past 35 years, which is the second hottest place in the United States, in my book – this book! (pun intended!)

The reason I tell you this is because there is an enormous difference between the hottest place in America, El Centro, and the second hottest place in America, Charleston. How do I know? Because I am dumb enough to have spent my whole life living in the two hottest places in America! I was born and raised in El Centro and lived there until I was 27, when I went to Charleston and married my wife, and lived here for the last 35 years of my life. If you are good at math, or, if you are imaginative like me, and you can remember my Harry Potter birthday, July 31, 1962, then you know that makes me 62 years old. **See, I will make all this easy for you, dear Reader, and you won't even have to think! Lol!**

So, the difference is the Western United States is **completely arid**, versus, the Eastern United States which is **completely humid**. And, 106 degrees Fahrenheit dry heat (like an oven), is way nicer than 96 degrees and 99 percent humidity (like a sauna). "Way nicer" being the operative words! I will take oven (El Centro) over the sauna (Charleston) every time.

Dear Reader, do you remember your Summer after freshman year in high school? The reason I ask is because I know the answer: Of course you remember your high school freshman year summer because **EVERYONE remembers their freshman year summer just like it was yesterday**. Why is that? Because you remember everything as a high school freshman. From your first class, to your first kiss, to your first dance, to your first drink, to, even, your first headache! And, you finally know how to talk. So, you love to talk. And, you love to talk to all your friends, about anything and everything.

Finally, you EVEN like talking to your siblings, because everything is so new. And, you think everyone is so smart, your freshman year. Even your siblings are smart. In fact, as you know, the only people who are not smart when you are a freshman in high school are your own parents. I mean, come on, they take your record albums to Juvenile Hall with no notice whatsoever! Obviously, they are stupid!

Finally, you remember the song that was Number One on the charts your whole Summer freshman year because it is iconic. Mine is *"Margaritaville."* I don't even like the damn song! But, I sure can sing every word, and make the slightest change from, "It's nobody's fault," to "It could be my fault," to "It's my own damn fault." Dear reader, I know that you know that same *"Margaritaville"* lyric shift, just like I do, because it is that self-depreciating humor that, in the end, wins us over. And, if that does not make us laugh, certainly the "Mexican Cutie" tattoo that he probably should not have gotten, will make you laugh! Lol!

CHAPTER 23

DALLAS COWBOY STADIUM
WHERE USA WEST
MEETS USA EAST

Trivia question for you (that I came to on my own) when I just turned 18 and drove across the three quarters of the USA from El Centro, California to Nashville, Tennessee, in my Jeep CJ5, 2,500 miles in 3 days, with a CJ5 soft-top, to start Freshman year at Vanderbilt, in August 1980. As farmers always do, I paid attention to my surroundings, when I drove across the United States on Interstate 8 to 10 to 20, to 30 to 40, a drive 4 days straight on one road **without even getting off the same road** – another thing you really can only do in the USA.

That is AMAZING when you think about what you can do in a car **for over 100 years in the USA, to this very day**: I got in my Jeep CJ5 and drove, without stopping, except to sleep at night for three full 12-hour days: 1. Day one for 12 hours, from El Centro California, on Interstate 8 and Interstate 10 to El Paso, Texas. 2. Day two for 12 hours from El Paso, Texas to Dallas, on Interstate 10 and Interstate 20 to Dallas, Texas. 3. Day three for 12 hours from Dallas, Texas, on Interstate 20 and Interstate 30 and Interstate 40 to Nashville, Tennessee. That is incredible. I need a Harry Potter broom next time! That would speed up the trip!!

Now that I think about it, not much has changed! It still takes four full days to drive across the USA, **but you spend**

over two days in the State of Texas!!! To be precise, 16 of the 48 hours to drive from the Pacific Ocean to the Atlantic Ocean are spent in TEXAS!! Just the State of Texas. No wonder they have their own star on their state flag!

And, I saw it!! What? I saw what? I saw the most amazing thing you can imagine. And, do you know where it was? It was between the 2 towns of Ft. Worth, Texas, and Dallas, Texas. A forty mile stretch of the United States, that everyone calls the same town: **Dallas/Ft. Worth, is exactly where the 3,500 miles across United States changes from ARID to HUMID**.

How do I know? Just look at it: West Texas. Famous for deserts, oil wells, scorpions, and cactus. 2,000 miles of CACTUS, from El Centro to Ft. Worth! And cattle. Cattle are even in Marty Robbins, "***West Texas Town of El Paso***" You can sing the song very loudly in your automobile when you drive though El Paso: "Out in the west Texas town of El Paso, I fell in love with a Mexican Girl!" I know, because I have done it driving to Nashville!

The other thing about the long desert from El Centro to Ft. Worth is that there are endless oil wells in picture postcard deserts, with stunning stars all night, that you can still drive by today!

Where does it end? **At exactly Cowboy's Stadium**, which is smack between West Texas and East Texas! How do I know? Because I drove it in my Jeep CJ5 at age 18 to college in Tennessee, which is humid and endless trees. You also cannot stay more humid than all the Great Lakes' states in the summer; on the other hand, you cannot be drier than Utah, Arizona, or Montana!

I just tested my theory 4 years ago when my youngest daughter enrolled as a freshman at Texas Christian University, in Ft. Worth, Texas, in 2020. I told my wife and daughter that I was going to rent a car, drive over to the famous record store in Dallas, which, as you know, is perfectly reasonable. But, really, I was testing my Western Untied States ends at Cowboy's Stadium theory. It is still correct to this day! Ft. Worth and its famous cowboys, cowboy boots, rodeos (like I grew up with in Brawley, California) and then you have the George W. Bush Presidential Museum in Dallas, with all these trees around it – in Dallas, not a cactus in site, like they have just 40 miles away in Ft. Worth! Today, drive from Ft. Worth to Dallas and you will begin seeing all the pine trees that are in East Texas. You will not see them in Ft. Worth, a western cow town. But, you will see endless trees from Dallas onward to Texarkana, East Texas. No desert. Gone is the desert. Gone are the cactus and the oil wells. **And, here comes the damn humidity**. And the pine trees and the rain and the farming and the corn and soybean crops! And one state to the East, you have so much rain in Arkansas that you can successfully grow rice!

So, Charleston, South Carolina, being the second hottest city in America, versus El Centro, California, being the hottest city in America.

As for the humidity in the East versus the aridness of the West, when I was flying back and forth, dry Los Angeles to humid Tokyo, I began to notice that the **whole world follows the same pattern**, of East of the continent being humid and the West of the continent being invariably dry, which is even more amazing, that the whole world follows the same pattern!

Just for a preview of what is coming in the second volume of this autobiography, in June 1984, at merely age 21, I started flying back and forth from Los Angeles LAX Airport to Tokyo, Narita Airport, in Japan to develop an alfalfa hay market to the Japanese dairy farms. No USA company shipping any agriculture product to Japan in 1984, to my building Kuhn Hay to becoming the largest USA exporter of hay to Japan, in less than five years. I flew 10,976 miles round trip (LAX to NRT), 40 round trips in exactly 60 months from 1984 to 1989. Just for you numbers people, that means **in less than 5 years, I flew 439,040 miles, just Los Angeles to Tokyo, and back**.

At my age 21 to 26, that was forty 10-day business trips in Japan, strictly to meet with Japanese trading companies (sōgō shōsha), and the wholesalers (tonya) all over the country who move the alfalfa hay to the end users (endo yūzā mei). In my case, the dairy farmers (Nomin nyūseihin) that I would also visit all over Japan every trip. I spent 400 nights in Japan (from the big cities to the tiny dairy farms), on a much different time zone than mine, during those five years. Thus, the second volume should be even more fascinating than the first for you to read!

Back to the East/Humid, West/Dry World theory I came up with: Just look at all the countries coming from East to West: In Asia, Japan, South Korea, China, India, are extraordinarily humid. Just like Charleston. In fact, Tokyo has the same weather as Charleston, South Carolina, and it is so humid, they grow amazing rice, just like South Carolina did for 150 years before Arkansas surpassed it in 1875!

Yet, the western Asian Continent is dry as a bone: Turkey, Israel, Greece. Then, Western Europe follows the same pattern: Poland, Germany, humid and great farming. Then, 500 miles to the West: Italy, Spain, England, dry as a bone. Surprisingly, England, like San Francisco, is the biggest anomaly known to mankind. Both are the West end of their continents, so they should be dry. But, in England and in San Francisco it rains ALL THE TIME, yet both places stay shockingly dry. Neither are like South Carolina and Tokyo, that is for sure!

Africa and South America, just the same. Sudan, Ethiopia, Uganda, Rwanda, most East African countries and humid. Over to the West Coast and dry as a bone: Morrocco, Sahara, Namibia, and Algeria, so dry! Just below us in South America, Brazil is the whole East Coast, and you cannot get any wetter than huge Amazon rain forests, Amazon river and most of Eastern Brazil. Then, western South American countries, so very dry: Puru, Argentina, and Chile, with Atacama Desert in Chile being the dryest place in the whole Mundo! It is just the way that God made Planet Earth!

Dear Reader: **Do you want to know about my 40 trips to the WHOLE country of Japan in five years, starting June 1984, developing an Alfalfa and Sudan Hay market for my family farm from scratch?** And, saving the whole Imperial Valley, and its 400,000 farmable acres, from economic oblivion, at the height of the second worst agricultural depression in US history (whole 1980s)? And, the sad American story of when almost every small dairy farm in America went bankrupt, and **immense Dow Jones International Harvester Tractor Company went completely bankrupt never to return as a company at all?**

Do you want to hear the story of agricultural Indiana Rock Singer John Mellencamp released his album, **Scarecrow,** that went straight to number one in the United States, lamenting

152

the loss of the small town American agriculture entirely, and he and country music star Willie Nelson did 3 full years of free concerts to save the family farms, called "Farm Aid Concerts?"

Then, stay tuned for Volume 2 of this 3 Volume Autobiography, *I Tell It Like It Is!* which will come out next year and will, mostly, cover my founding a market for Sudan Hay (great low-protein, dry-feed for a Cow's stomach). Sudan Hay will prevent cows from dying in dairy farms all over Japan from too much corn, which cows cannot resist because they are cow's version of "protein shakes." From 1984 to 1989 I went to Japanese dairy farms all over Japan – yes, I visited 50 of them in 5 years! I will tell you ALL ABOUT how great the Japanese businessman is, how great the Japanese dairy farmer is, and how many great Japanese rice farmers is. And, I will tell you all about the Japanese culture, which is incredibly strong and binding after 1,600 years, and is wonderful to follow and understand. Lots of chapters on my many trips to Japan, throughout all of my second volume out next year!

CHAPTER 24

BREAKFAST AT BESSIE'S CAFÉ AND LUNCH AT COUNTRY BOY DINER

You are either a Ford F-150 pickup lover or a Chevy Silverado 1500 pickup lover. But, you are never both! In America you grow up one or the other. I grew up in the Imperial Valley in California and the Ford Dealership was THE dealership, so my whole farming county is Ford. Did I mention Ford? Did I say, Ford? Did YOU say Chevy? Never heard of Chevy. Period. End of story!

So, my greatest memories as a small boy with my father, Fritz Kuhn, were in his Ford F-150 pickup, riding around in the only seat, the one looonnnggg seat, with no seatbelts. In the 1960s there were no seatbelts in pickup trucks. If I remember correctly, there were no seat belts in any vehicles. And, there certainly were no seatbelts on tractors! You were lucky to have an actual seat on the tractor at all. My father's generation had a seat on the tactor alright. It was a metal seat! **Can you imagine raking hay all year, 6 days a week, with a metal seat?** I can imagine it! Because the first tractor I drove had a metal seat. Because my father made sure that my first 3 years driving a tractor and a hay rake were with the old metal seat on the Farmall H tractor, with the narrow front wheels (to go up and down sandy ditchbanks with a hay rake). Why? "Toughen you up, kid." Of course, I did not mind because I knew that it was the EXACT same tractor my father drove 30 years earlier raking hay!

But, I also LOVED riding in my father's Ford pickup for the first six years of my life! The first thing I remember was that I would ride around as a 3-year-old in that ginormous pickup truck seat with him, and we would first stop at first gas station and get me a stick of Juicyfruit gum. His favorite flavor was also Wrigley's Juicyfruit gum. Consequently, my favorite flavor was Juicyfruit gum. I thought I had died and gone to heaven when we both put our Juicyfruit gum in our mouths! I wanted to be just like my dad. I'm sure I was!

My home, from almost the day I was born, was out on the West end of El Centro, the nearest part of El Centro to the farm, which was exactly eight miles to the West of El Centro, near a tiny farming town called Seeley. Back in the 1960s, you could drive the eight miles in eight minutes in your Ford Pickup. Why? Because there were no stop lights in America in farm communities. If fact, there were no stop signs, either. So, we could drive Ross Road from my home in El Centro to the farm eight miles west with no stops at all. I sure miss those days! (lol!)

Also, in the United States before the 1970s you did not move houses or apartments much, either. A lot of us lived in our houses long enough for the street name to change. I was that way too. I grew up in the exact same house at 2901 West Main Street for the first ten years of my life, which was technically one quarter mile down a dirt road from Main Street. My mom and brother and I would walk all the way down the quarter mile dirt road every day to our mailbox to collect the days mail. For the first ten years of my life.

When the city decided to pave the quarter mile dirt road, they named it Glenwood Road, and we got a new address, without moving at all. Our new address was 1853 Glenwood

Road. And, now the mail came right to our house in our shiny new mailbox on the street.   Several trucks ran into our shiny new mailbox over the next few years. My father, being a farmer, had a new metal mailbox made in our Kuhn Repair shop, and it was Welded (of course) to a long metal pole and then our farmworkers put the mailbox, cemented way deep down in the ground on the street. When one of my high school friends decided to prank us and pull the mailbox out at night with his Ford F-150 pickup and a chain he had, the mailbox did not budge and the Ford pickup lost an axle!!! My father and I thought it was terribly funny. The One-Who-Must-Not-Be-Named (my Mother) did not think it was funny! Lol!

My home phone number was 352-5344. Every single girl and boy in America knew their home phone number by heart. There were no other phone numbers. Imagine that. No other phone numbers. So, all of us knew our home phone number. Ask anyone over the age of 50 in this country and they will immediately recite their home phone number. Even without having said it in 30 years. I just did! Our phone numbers stay with us for life! And, without the area code. There were no area codes in the 1960s and 1970s. We were lucky to have phones in the 1960s. There was just one big United States Phone Company, too! No matter where we lived in the United States, from San Francisco to Charleston, we all called the telephone company: "Ma Bell!" But, they have been listed on the New York Stock Exchange for over 100 years as: American Telephone and Telegraph Company (AT&T – but the Ticker Symbol is still just: "T").

AT&T has gone though all kinds of reincarnations since 1965, including being sued by the US Government for being too big and then being broken up into regional companies.

The US Government should not have done that. Every time the government does something like that, God changes the whole ballgame and they should have left it alone. AT&T is a great example! The US government broke it up to regional companies just before the cell phone came in and destroyed all of the AT&T smaller companies in one decade. Please, Mr. Government, let the free market solve all these problems. Breaking up Standard Oil did not work. Breaking up AT&T did not work. Stop suing big companies. And, stop FEEDING big companies taxpayer money!

Just let companies and people live free as a bird. (Sounds like a Lynard Skynyrd Song to me! "Freebird!") Companies will continue to survive as God intended for them to. If they get so they are no longer useful, they will go out of business, in a natural way. Just like Chrysler should have done 20 years ago instead of the United States taxpayer bailing them out – that is you and me, you know. Great companies survive. If you let the free market weed them out and not bail them out. Let bad companies go bankrupt. All companies should be subject to the free market and go bankrupt if they no longer produce something that someone wants to pay for – or if they are improperly run. Taxpayers should not bail them out. Ever.

And new companies, such as Tesla and Apple, have come along to replace them. Just like G.E. went bankrupt when it cheated the people with bad accounting. Just let the free market take its course. This is Milton Friedman school of economics at its best! In other words, the Chicago (America) School of Economics. Let it be. And let all of us Americans be. Just let us be. And, let our companies be. By the way, that is the Basis of the Libertarian Party, right there. I told you, Dear Reader, that you are a Libertarian!

And I am going back to my childhood on the farm in El Centro, California, with my farmer father Fritz Kuhn every morning until I was age five, when I stated Kindergarten at McCabe School. We would go straight out to Bessie's Café for breakfast in that giant, one long seat, in my Dad's pickup truck. Bessie's Café wass in Seeley, in the middle of all of our fields. Fields in El Centro are not like in the Midwest South of the United States, where you own as **many acres around your house** as you can accumulate out in the rural areas of the whole country.

No, California is quite different. In the 1890s lots of thought went into farming in California because you needed to get water over to the farming areas, with 50 Mile long well-built canals, from all of our rivers to irrigate the fields. If you managed to get water to your farming valley, the first thing you did in California is PLAN AHEAD. That meant every farming Valley in California, when you could see you were going to get water from a long canal being built to your valley, you would then take HUGE Caterpillar Landmovers and bulldozers and scrapers and take every 80-acre parcel of land and make it perfectly flat. You not only had to pay lots of moneey for that, you then had to pay lots of money to build your own dirt (or later, cement) irrigation ditch on your 80-acre field, and then you could farm.

Why? Because now that you paid exorbitant amounts of money to level your fields and you spent even more exorbitant amounts of money for your excellent irrigation ditch, you could now irrigate the field because it was so flat the water would slowly move across the 80-acre field with gravity flow over a 24-hour period – and we have to pay 2 irrigators full wages every time we irrigate an 80-acre field. We have done this for 100s of years in the Imperial Valley for you to get your vegetables at your grocery stores all over ethe United States.

We are not done with our exorbitant costs now that we have the infrastructure in our fields, either. Now we must pay the Imperial Irrigation District every single month for the rest of our lives (and our children's lives) for the little bit of water we need at our fields every time we need to water our crop, water a field (for the rest of your life you have to pay the IID for the water every time you use it), whether for germination, mid-waterings, or watering for harvest. We have to do this for vegetables every year, and for alfalfa for dairy cows, and for wheat for your past and sugar beets for your sugar. Even for Bermuda hay for your horses all over the Untied States.

Now, Dear Reader, you know why we need to plan for over 100 years on all farms in the United States. It takes one full year to grow two crops for you: Usually, half a year to grow cotton for your shirts, or wheat, for your bread.

Then, the other half of the year for your organic vegetables: ***Seven different types of lettuce, including kale***; or, broccoli, asparagus, green beans, or carrots. Whatever you want to eat, we grow it. But, really, God grows it and all farmers would rather you eat natural foods produced by us and God. Each of those vegetables takes half a year in the field, and lots of 24-hour irrigations, to grow.

So, I am driving out to Bessie's Café in Seeley with my father at age 3 and 4 and we are now in the geographic middle of our fields for breakfast, every single day. You now learned that because we have to PLAN AHEAD in the Imperial Valley (and in California) and buy 80 acres of land that are desert with cactus on them, and then, build them into fields, by land-leveling them and putting in expensive irrigation ditches, and expensive sandy ditch banks with dirt roads around every field, from, literally, desert. Most farmers in Califorina start by renting 80-acre fields from older field owners, who no longer want to farm because they are tired of it or too old. Farmers rent one field at first. Then start fareming it and seeing what they like to farm and see how it goes. And go borke for a while because you do not get the timing right: Irrigation timing - you irriaate too early or too late. Crop timing - you plant broccoli in the fall and by Christmas harvest everyone wants cauliflower so you cannot sell your crop. Or, bank timing – you always have to borrow money (**every** farmer in the United States does) to pay for the seed, the water, the irrigators, the tracktors, the tracktor drivers, the havest crews, and the harvest equitpment. Every farmer in the United States has all 3 of these bad timings working against him (or her) every sigle year. All of us.

And, if you cannot sell your crop after the six months, besuwe there is too msuhc alfalfa or bermuda hay in the United States that year, you go broke and the bank takes yroui farm. All of farmers. Every year. I am not kidding. Why would I kid aobu this? I don't need to kid about it. It's true.

Then, why do we farm? Because we farmers all LOVE the genius it takes to outsmart the three timings I told you about above. ! We are all smart and we love the game. And, if we are not smart, we go broke the first year. Unfortunately, half of us go broke even if we are smart. It is called bad luck. How would you like to farm during the Obama recession? 62 percent of the farmers in the United States went broke (no matter how smart they were) with the Obama Recession in the one decade of the 2010s. I will repeat that. 62

percent of all the farmers in the United States, including some of my friends, went broke in the 10-year Obama recession. It is not bad luck. It is bad government from our United States Government. Usually does not matter which president is in office, we have bad economic results for American workers. President Trump, hallelujah, is the exception and he cares about American workers and American fae3mrs and put all of us first. And now he has an Democrat Secretary of Health and Human Services, Robert Kennedy, who cares about your body and your food and you getting natural foods, that EVERY FARMER in the United States would rather grow for you every day, for you to start buying again in your grocery stores, like we used to in this country under Republican President Dwight Eisenhower – who grew up in a faming community in Kansas before he beat Hitler and Nazi Germany by being one of the greatest General in United States History.

Remember, Dear Reader, I Tell It Like It Is!

Second reason is that we farmers love to farm. Remember, I told you, you have at least one God-Given Talent. A lot of us love to be out in the countryside on farms, growing actual olives, fruit, rice, wheat, vegetables, watermelons, cantaloupe, even red beets, for you to eat. We just love all the work of preparing the land for a crop, all the work of planting a crop, all the work of irrigating a crop, and all the work of harvesting a crop. Can you imagine how cool it is to go out on your farm in El Centro every day in the Spring and see all those lines and lines and lines of little plants growing from nothing at all the prior week, to full grown alfalfa hay or cotton or wheat plants, from nothing at all. So cool. So rewarding! Let's help Robert F. Kennedy, Jr, save the family farmer and lets start getting raw (unpasteurized) milk every day at your back door from your milkman, like every single house in New York City had in the 1950s. And lets get non-GMO chicken and non-GMO wheat back on our grocery store shelves so our bread chicken does not make us sick and our bread does not kill us with it's preservatives, like every single house in every state had in the United States right up until 1960.

Back to Bessie's Café in Seeley, a California town of less than 1,200 people – remember, it is a farming community of farmworkers. My friends in sixth grade in Seeley School, mostly our tractor driver's sons and daughters, right there at Seeley school with me, first to eighth grade. God's Plan to have three of my father's Farm Foreman's sons in my tiny class alone, in sixth to eighth grade, Frank Gutierrez, Juan Leal and Jessie Rodriguez. Right? Nothing is coincidental in this world. You are given the Gift of Life from God and you are given your very own personality and personal gifts from God, and you go forth as use them. Just like your ancestors, all the way back to the Stone Age. And, you tell the truth and move forward. You tell lies and you move backwards. I know this because I have told the truth and always ended up forward, **and many times I have told lies and have always ended up going backwards, every time**.

But, I am going forth with my honest, truthful book and hopefully you are reading it. And, you are thereby, getting more confidence, from every chapter of my book.

So, when I say that my father and I went out every day to Bessie's Café in Seeley, when I was ages 3 and 4, I am pointing out that in Imperial Valley farm area, you first start as a new farmer with one field. Whether you dig it out from the bare-naked desert and put a cement ditch in it, or if you start by renting your first field from a landowner, you will then have one field somewhere in the Valley. After that, it helps to stay in that area of the Imperial Valley, or you will be too spread out to farm. So, after 10 years of farming for other farmers on the West End of the Imperial Valley (his ages 16-26) he finally rented his first field from Mrs. Voorting, about half mile past Bessie's Café on Old El Centro Highway 80 (the first road from El Centro to San Diego, built in the 1910s and 120 miles long). So, half mile further West of Seeley, Ms. Voorting loved my father and said, "Fritz, if you ever want to farm on your own, you are so honest, that I would be happy to lease you my 80-acre field."   So, in 1955, my father, at age 26 years old, did just that. Thus, his first field he farmed on his own was Mrs. Voorting's field a mile past the town of Seeley, on the far West end of the Imperial Valley farming fields.

Next year, after a decent farming start on Mrs. Voorting's field, my father then called up his cousin, Walter Kuhn, whom I told you all about earlier, as being the best desert cactus land reclaimer in the Imperial Valley with all his HUGE Caterpillar ground-moving equipment and HUGE land levelers and D8 Bulldozers. He said, "Walter, we been talking at Bessie's Café for years about trying to reclaim that section of the desert around the **Silsbee Wash** just West of Derrick Road and try to turn that section of the desert into good fields by land leveling and putting cement ditches in that about 600 acres there. Want to go into a partnership there – you do the land leveling and I will do the farming – and we can be 50/50 on that ground?" To which Walter Kuhn said, "Sure, Fritz, that would be great."

1955 was a full year of desert reclamation out there in the heat of the Imperial Valley, with lots of dirt cuts and pours, and lots of Ryerson cement trucks building all new ditches, all on Fritz and Walter Kuhn's money, and HUGE bank loans, with tremendous amount of sweat equity and perseverance, for them to have 8 new fields by end of Summer 1956.

After lots of planning and work creating 8 new fields, all on the IID Fig Canal, the Kuhns finally had 8 fields of their own. They did not even know if the ground was good farm ground and it cost them an exorbitant amount of money. But, they owned it. And, my father was an outstanding farmer, already at age 28, so he got a bank loan at Wells Fargo Bank, and started farming, with both men owing the Bank a huge farm loan right from the start. And, an even bigger Revolving Line of Credit, necessary to put out the money for six months of tilling, planning, irrigating, tractor driving, harvesting, and praying that your crop would sell! My father found his real talent was growing alfalfa hay for dairy cows – probably because he and his sister, (both born on Christmas day two years apart), Fritz and Vreneli Kuhn, grew up on their father's small dairy farm, also on the West End of the Imperial Valley, when Fritz Kuhn Sr, came over from Switzerland in 1913, just to dairy farm. My father always told me he liked growing the alfalfa hay for the cows way more than he liked milking the cows, so he ended up building a farming operation, slowly but surely, from nothing at all.

You will see, Dear Reader, in Volume 2 of 3 of this Autobiography, that you will see, "Like Father, Like Son," when I built the Kuhn Hay Export Operation from absolutely nothing in 1984 to a giant hay export business of Sudan Hay to 50% of the Dairy Cows in Japan, when I was age 24 to age 30 and back on my fathers same farm, fresh out of College. This was because, by then, the 1982 decade long Agricultural

Recession had hit the United States so badly that I needed to find another market for our hay, or lose our whole 10,000-acre operation to the Bank, with mortgages on all our property, which was just about to happen – and I staved off with one long bank meeting with my asking all kinds of questions that they could not answer.   All that excitement is coming in my next Volume, just next year. I promise you will LOVE READING THAT, too!

Finally, back to Bessie's Café at Seeley for the last time. So, it took 30 years of my father renting one field; then, renting another field, and then reclaiming 8 fields out of the desert during the whole year of 1956, and, finally, in the 1960s, buying some of his own fields, for us to get to the point where we had about 80 fields all around that there Bessie's Café when I was 3 and 4 years old, sitting there at those little linoleum tables with little aluminum posts, eating categorically great fresh eggs the chickens had laid **way up there** in Brawley, California – twelve miles north of Seeley – lol! Just for the record, my father and brother liked their eggs sunny-side-up, so, naturally, so did I! (Another lol!). More importantly, every morning at 6:00 am sharp, my father would wake me up, and my mother would dress me in Levi's blue jeans, and we would be at Bessie's Café every single day at 6:30 am for breakfast. After that, out to one of those 80 fields it took my father 30 years of hard work farming (commencing with no money or anything whatsoever), to be able to take me and Jim around lots of fields every day to learn.

Once I started school in first grade at McCabe School, the whole scene shifted from Bessie's Café for breakfast eggs and hash browns (real potatoes, from Idaho, of course!), to County Boy for a great big hamburger lunch. I also loved the hamburgers at Country Boy Diner because they were just what you would expect from a farming valley lunch joint: One-half pound of juicy hamburger, lettuce, onions, pickles on a sesame seed bun – oh, forgot, that is a McDonald's ad from the whole 1980s!

My father and I ate thousands of hamburgers at Country Boy Diner in El Centro. The Country Boy is where we would see lots of other El Centro farmers at lunch, from our Kuhn cousins, to Matt and Tim LaBrucherie of LaBrucherie Farms and El Toro Cattle. Their Feedyard was exactly one mile South of Country Boy Diner, on LaBrucherie Road, so we would see them all the time. And, we would see their farmworkers all the time, too. We would even see my fourth-grade teacher from McCabe there, Ed LaBrucherie, quite often, as well. All of us eating Country Boy hamburgers and French fries.

Speaking of Hamburger, this is where I part with my cheese-obsessed Swiss cousins: I do not like Cheese on my hamburger. I like straight one-half pound of juicy ground-round beef, preferably from Brandt Beef in Brawley. I grew up with all the Brandts in Brawley and they are all still my friends. Bill Brandt revolutionized the beef industry in the United States, in one decade, with their outstanding beef! Why ruin a great tasting juicy fresh hamburger with cheese on top? Takes away from the hamburger taste, it does!

On my hamburger, I am not picky. In fact, I love fresh tomatoes and pickles and ketchup and fresh lettuce and fresh onions (the onions are often from our own farm!). You can put anything – except mayonnaise and cheese – on it! Mustard. Fine. No mayo. No cheese. No Cheese, please!

I personally know that I am on the other side of the Ledger from Bill Murray and John Belushi in the famous 1978 Saturday Night Live Skit: Cheeseburger, Cheeseburger, Cheeseburger. But, dear reader, do you remember way back in Chapter 1, where I admit that I love Chicago because I lived there all through Law School, well, that makes me an actual Chicagoan. Add a year in 1984-85 to my three years in law school, living in Wrigleyville in Chicago with my new wife (Volume 2, my friends, Volume 2!) and the four total years makes me a bona fide Chicagoan!

I told you earlier that, in my current hometown of Charleston, I met and know and love Bill Murray, who also spends half of every year out of that dreadful cold that is Chicago. But, I have not had the guts to tell him that I would rewrite their 1978 Saturday Night Live Skit, to thus:

"Cheese? NO. NO CHEESE! Hamburger. No Cheese at Billy Goat! Fries? NO! NO FRIES! Chips. Only Chips at the Billy Goat."

You know how I know that I am a bona fide Chicagoan? Because I know Sam Sianis personally. Yes I do. I spent many nights at the Billy Goat Tavern, way under the bowels of Chicago and the Wrigley Building – oh, remember, I am a Wrigley's Juicyfruit gum, along with my Dad – and I have spent many nights with the actual Chicago Tribune newspaper writers down there at the Billy Goat Bar from 1984-85.

Want more proof that I am a bona fide Chicagoan? Remember when I told you about my actual friendship in my current hometown of Charleston, SC, with Chicago's most famous Actor, Bill Murray, and my going gopher hunting with my Grandfather, Fritz Kuhn, on my family farm, just like the

Bill Murray movie, "***Caddyshack***"? Bill Murray is the ultimate Chicagoan. He cries when our Dear Cubbies lose, just like I used to when I lived in Wrigleyville with my new wife! Second shout out to you, Bill Murray! For the Record, there will be a third shout out to Bill Murray in Volume 2 that he does not even know about, yet!

Because I am now, first and foremost, an Author of my own autobiography – that is what you are reading right now in your hands, stupid! – I am more proud of hanging out with my Chicago writer homies in the Billy Goat Tavern under the Chicago Tribune building than anything else in Chicago! For a little more Chicago humor, it is just like a Chicagoan to call you "stupid," tongue-in-cheek, too! Remember the Chicago restaurant, Ed Debevic's? Chicago humor at its best! By the way, I am delighted to report that Ed Debevic's and its sassy hamburgers (no cheese, please!), is back alive and well in the Streeterville area of Chicago. You cannot keep a good man – or woman – down, can you?

All good Chicago Writers (and I am now, definitively, one – today's pronouncement on my part!) must go to the Billy Goat Tavern, way below Michigan Avenue, in the underpinnings of the City of Chicago, and hobnob with the Chicago Tribune and Chicago Sun-Times newspapers famous daily writers, and pretend we are important, as writers. From May 1984 to August 1985, when I was kicked out of Vanderbilt University for extremely bad grades, I did just that. I moved to Chicago and I did hang out at the Billy Goat Tavern under the Wrigley Building on Michigan Avenue, and drink beer with the Chicago Tribune writers, such as Mike Royko, Clarance Page, and Jerome Holtzman, all of whom I met in the Billy Goat Tavern Bar that year off from Vanderbilt. Mike Royko was my favorite – I read his daily column in the

Chicago Tribune. Boy he could write for the public. And he was a warmhearted, smart, guy.

Why did I fail out of Vanderbilt twice in four years for bad grades? Because we did not have computers or Word Processors anywhere. That would have been a gamechanger for me. Naturally, I was an English major at Vanderbilt and I loved taking all possible English classes, from Milton, to Pope and Johnson, to Shakespeare (both Comedies and Tragedies), American Writers (two semesters), all the way to Modern British Playwrights (for example, Samuel Beckett's **Waiting for Godot**). Consequently, I was required (naturally) to type a couple of 10-Page papers in EVERY English Literature Class. I usually got them written by hand. But then, you must type the papers. I was just too hyperactive and ADD to type the 10-page papers which were due weekly. I would turn in some papers and not turn in some papers. And, when you are an English Major and you do not turn in your papers, you get "Fs" in your classes. That is exactly what I did. I received many F's in my classes. Many, many Fs.

This will provide you, Dear Reader, with much more fun with John Kuhn reading coming along in the next Volume of this Autobiography, next year, where you will find whole chapters on me working on the Chicago Board of Trade in Chicago on my mandatory year off from Vanderbilt. To be honest, my grades were so bad after my Junior year at Vanderbilt, that I was outright dismissed. But, I was allowed to reapply to Vanderbilt if I could show that I had rehabilitated myself. You see, I have lots of fun chapters coming in Volume 2 of my shenanigans in college at Vanderbilt and my being in and out of Nashville in and out of Chicago. I promise, you will not have laughed that hard at a book in a decade when it comes around – just like Arlo

Guthrie's "Alice Restaurant" comes around on the guitar – pun intended, for sure! Lol!

You will also be introduced to my first serious girlfriend, Cricket Jebb from Chicago, at the end of this very Volume. As well, you have lots of fun stories coming in Volume 2 of my visiting my girlfriend in Chicago – lots of Cricket stories coming in Volume 2 that I know you will love! Cricket was as feisty as I was, so we made quite a pair in her hometown of Chicago, we did! All coming, Dear Reader, in Volume 2, just next year!

The upshot of all this, Chicago, is that when this book becomes a million seller, you may completely claim me as one of your own writers and not be lying! Lol!

CHAPTER 25

FARMER'S PRICES VS. FARMER'S COSTS (SADLY, MORE IMPORTANT THAN DODGERS VS. YANKEES!)

As I mentioned earlier in this book (Chapter 17), my father, Fritz Kuhn, Jr., was the most brilliant machinist I have ever been around. He perfected the new-fangled Sugar Beet thinner in 1974, when most Imperial Valley farmers would not even think about standing around in the heat and in the fields for hours watching an electronic sugar beet thinner, let alone buy one! But, my father, Fritz Kuhn, was always trying new things and he had the patience of Job when he was studying machinery in another part of the country or at home in our fields.

After he singlehandedly perfected the Electronic Sugar Beet Thinner in the Autumn of 1973, he made a lot of money in the Summer of 1974 with an unprecedented 3,000 acres of Sugar Beets in 38 fields, when he no longer needed the expensive and time-consuming crews of men with hand hoes going through every Sugar beet plant. This is because in two weeks he spent 224 hours out in our Sugar Beet fields, making thoughtful adjustments to the Sugar Beet Thinning Machine. As well as flying in from Iowa, the Electronic Beet Thinner Engineer who invented the electronic Beet Thinner, making him work on the Beet Thinner we purchased until it worked perfectly! After a mentally and physically exhausting two weeks, my father had the electronic thinner running beautifully though every single long row of sugar beets in every acre of sugar beets.

The United States Congress decided to take the United States off the Price Control they had on actual sugar prices in 1974, for the first time in over 50 years. Nobody really knows why. But, the coincidence left our Sugar beet crop in the best situation on the planet earth. Why? Because, the Sugar price skyrocketed for the first time over 100 years in the United States.

If you are older than 50 years old, do you remember when, as a kid, your Snickers or Baby Ruth Candy bars went from 5 cents in the store to 10 cents in the gas station or grocery store? In just one week? After being 5 cents a candy bar every single day for 10 years! In one day in the summer of 1974 all candy bars in the United States went from 5 cents to 10 cents in the store. That was because US Congress deregulated the US Sugar price in 1973. And, the sugar price in the US market skyrocketed.

The other thing my father did for each of the prior 5 years to 1973 is he worked like crazy meeting with the management of every Sugar Beet processing company in the Imperial Valley and slowly, but surely, got a few more acres of sugar beet contracts from all 3 of the local sugar producers, every year for a decade – Namely: Holly Sugar, Speckels Sugars, and Union Sugar. More work on my father's part.

And we had 3,000 acres of Sugar beets in the ground in Imperial Valley, and because of Sugar price deregulation, we knew that we would get 27 cents per pound of sugar (instead of the prior year's 11 cents per pound) from every pound of sugar we had processed at Holly Sugar and Spreckels Sugar and Union Sugar of our 42,000,000 pounds of actual sugar from our 3,000 acres of sugar beets (3,000 acres x 14,000 pounds of sugar per acre = 42,000,000 pounds of sugar **from Kuhn Farms for Americans to eat in their cakes and bread and candy bars and breakfast cereals!**). YAY!

Better yet, it is 1974 and it is the Hallelujah year of the century because the US government has deregulated sugar price, and we get 27 cents on every pound of those 42,000,000 pounds of sugar. That means that from Holly and Spreckels Sugar and Union Sugar that year we got a total of $11,340,000 for our whole crop. Now, the cost of production per acre of beets for Kuhn Farms in 1974 was $600 per acre of sugar beets. So, $600 x 3,000 acres is $1,800,000 in total costs to produce the 3,000 acres of sugar. Subtracting the total cost for the year of $1,800,000 from the total money we received for all our 42,000,000 pounds of sugar, which was $11,340,000 in the Hallelujah year, we made about $9,540,000 profit in the Hallelujah sugar year of 1974!

Now, don't be that impressed. **As with absolutely every single crop we farmers put in the ground every single year for the past 300 years in the whole United States of America,** *half the time the market is so cruel that* **we lose money on half the crops** we produce every single year. That has been the case in the United States for the past 300 years and is still the case today. Starting in 1690 in little old Charleston in South Carolina, when a cargo sailing ship from Madagascar came into the Charleston Habor to escape a hurricane at sea, and as a big "thank you" to the Charleston Dock Master, the ship Captain of the Madagascar ship gave the Dock Master 5 bags of Madagascar rice. So, notice, this is 1690, and this is another big hurricane. So, forget your global warming. We have had genuine, full-blown (pun intended!) hurricanes on the Florida, Georgia, South Caolina, North Carolina Coast for over 1,000 years and counting, and will have another one before I die.

Back to my story of 300 years of totally unpredictable agriculture market prices for every farm product in every state and every year for over 300 years: Anyway, the Madagascar ship Captain gave the Charleston Dock Master 5 bags of rice as a thank you, and a whole lot of enterprising Englishmen (because that is what they were in Charleson in 1690, before the Revolutionary War) thought: "I bet that rice would grow fantastic here in this miserably hot and rainy, super flat, South Carolina Coastal swamps, with our big rivers." They got some African-American men who were from near Madagascar, and asked, "Do you know how to build grow this rice and do you know how to build irrigation canals to keep the water over the rice in germination?" To which the African Amerian men said, "Yes, we do." With a whole, whole, whole lot of work (work, just like my farmer father 200 years later!), they Rice Planters and the African American slaves built a rice empire in the South Carolina Coast in just 20 years.

And, they immedialy had the same problem, after they had all the money costs, and hard labor and injenity that all farmers put it, and that is: In 1705 you plant the rice in the Spring. Pray for a great rice market in London and Paris and Hamburg in the fall. Fifty percent of the time you have a great price and you make a lot of money. The next year, 1706, you have too much rice in England and Germany from Madagascar itself, so you lose One Half a Million Dollars on rice in 1706. I am not kidding. Look it up. It has been going on every year in the United States with every crop, since the first export USA crop, which was actually South Carolina rice to Europe in 1695.

So, that is really 335 years of farmers not knowing what price their crop would bring the next year in the United States (1690 Charleston rice to 2025 all USA crops), no matter what the crop is: From "safe crops" such as alfalfa hay to unsafe crops, such as broccoli! I do believe that our farming wholesaler and our grocery stores should at least pay 5 cents more for every crop that we farmers produce for you to eat. We would not get rich, but we would stay in business, especially farm to your table! Remember my title of my book: I Tell It Like It Is!

Now, forward to Imperial Valley, California, Farming prices for any of our crops for just the past 25 years – let's just pick random farming years in the 2000s:

Imperial County Farmer plants Sugar beet crop in 2002. We wait one full year and spend $1,500,000 growing it. When you harvest a year later, Sugar beet price is normal, (and in farming, the "normal" price is almost always low – or 5 cents a pound less than it should be, is almost always the normal for us). Harvest your sugar beets a year later, in 2003: 11 cents per pound of sugar. You get $1,300,000 in gross revenue, with $1,500,000 in costs. In 2003 you lost $200,000 and your bank is mad. I am not kidding. All of us farmers do this every year with every crop in this country.

In 2003, farmer plants Sugar beet crop, again. We wait one full year and spend $1,500,000, again, preparing the ground by tiling it, planting it, irrigating it (and praying the plants actually sprout; or, don't get killed in a wind storm). I have seen my father cursing many times when one rain comes and makes half the plants in an 80-acre field fail to sprout. During one germination, here comes a heavy wind. Now the crest of the ground is too hard because the day's strong wind hardens the top one-quarter inch of ground and traps the germinating plants under the crust in the whole 80-acre field. All the plants are living, but dead in three days because they are trapped under the outer layer of crusted dirt.

Three months of hard work planting, and irrigation, and $900 per acre, lost OVERNIGHT, because the crop did not spout, *because of one bad wind*!

If you are lucky enough that your crop sprouts properly, you still have a whole year to go. A full summer of irrigating, weeding, and spraying; then, 10 months later, finally harvesting it.

Oh no. **The price per pound of Sugar beets this year**, 2004 at harvest, is only 8 cents a pound. I am not kidding. And you spent one full year working your butt off, and all your employees working their butt off, and this year, you only get $900,000 total for your crop that cost you $1,500,000 to till, plant, irrigate, spray, fertilize, water, and harvest.

So, you lost $200,000 in 2003 on sugar beets, and you lost $600,000 more in 2004 on sugar beets. Thus, you have lost $800,000 in just the last 2 years on sugar beets. Your bank loan at Bank of America is only 2,000,000 limit. You also lost $1,200,000 on your broccoli and lettuce in the past two years. That means that your $2,000,000 farm loan at Bank of America is tapped out and you cannot farm next year. You cannot pay the $2,000,000 off, so you are, literally, bankrupt in the USA as a farmer. **Happens to 10 percent of the famers every single year in this United States of America.**

Naturally, there are not 10 percent of new farmers going into farming every year. For three reasons: First, all farmers can see this and do math. Second, if you are bankrupt, you are finished as a farmer. Third, our children can see that their parents went bankrupt farming and they will move to the city and work and live a lot more stress-free life! Therefore, you do not have farmers anymore who want to farm in the United States.

It is worse than I am stating above, because, inflation has driven up the cost of farming 1 percent every year (for the past fifty years in a row). That is 50 percent increase in our costs over 50 years. We pay more for irrigators and the irrigation pipes. And, we pay more for the tractor drivers and for fertilizer and for seed every year. But, the price we get for every crop has stayed the same. Or gone down, like the sugar price has in the past 50 years. The cost of growing sugar beets has gone from $400 per acre in 1970 to $2,400 per acre in 2020. The price per pound of sugar is the same in 2020 as it was in 1976. The exact price per pound of sugar in 1976 was 12 cents and the exact price per pound of sugar in 2020 was 13 cents. That is a 1 cent increase in the Sugar Price in 45 years! Remember, cost per acre for production in the same 45 years is from $400 an acre to $2,400 an acre. Mainland US farmers cannot farm sugar beets anymore. Used to be one of the most dependable crops in the United States for the farmer and we loved growing sugar beets.

The inflationary effect of growing Sugar beets in the United States from 1976 to 2020: It cost $400 an acre to produce Sugar beets in the 1970s, it then cost $800 an acre to produce sugar beets in the 1980s, then $1,200 an acre in the 1990s, up to a whopping $1,800 an acre in the 2000s, and finally it is now $2,400 an acre in the 2010s to produce THE SAME Sugar beets. The processing cost at Holly and Spreckels Sugar is not included in that. That is just production costs per acre every decade to plant, grow and harvest sugar beets over the past 50 years in the United States.

So, the cost to grow and harvest sugar beets goes up a little bit every year. But, the price of a pound of sugar does not go up hardly at all!!! **50 years later and the sugar price per pound in the United States is barely up at all. In fact, it is down 10 cents over the past 10 years, from 2010 to 2020.**

Farming costs go up steadily every year. Farming prices do not go up at all, most years. Eventually you cannot grow sugar beets in the United States. Which is why the Holly Sugar factory in the Imperial Valley went absolutely broke in the 2000s. Then, Spreckels Sugar bought it. In April of 2025 (just this year!), the Imperial County Spreckels Sugar plant closed permanently. That is not good for American sugar eaters. No more continental USA sugar. None.

And, worse for Imperial County, California, we just lost the Sugar beet factory that has been in operation in our county for over 70 years. Closed, shuttered, and wasting away. beautiful silos and great sugar mill. Gone. Gone forever from continental America. The farmers' plight and the food buyers' plight (that is you, the eater of the food at home) are also massively the State Government of California's fault. California is way more interested in hundreds of Silicon Valley citizens getting rich in tech than in Imperial Valley farmers getting rich by filling your shelves in your grocery stores all over this USA with outstanding organic and healthy chickens and vegetables. That is backwards on the part of the California Government. I thought government was "of the people and for the people", not of the rich and for the rich.

I thought that the government was to help provide food for its people, first and foremost. If you cannot eat, you cannot live. The California government has forced your Dairy cows out of Los Angeles and your Los Angeles school children must drink pasteurized milk from the State of Texas – pasteurized milk, so it will last long enough to be trucked in huge semi-trucks, 3 days driven halfway across the United States to get to your children in your schools in Los Angeles. Sick, isn't it? Schoolchildren sick because of the Pasteurization of every gallon of milk they drink at all of your schools in the United States. This is real easy to solve: Bring the big Dairy Farms back to California. And, bring the big alfalfa hay (for dairy cows) farmers back to California.

For 150 years the California government was unbelievably great in helping its farmers feed its people, starting with Sacramento Farmer John Sutter in 1845 (that is not a typo – 1845!). California has been helping its farmers for over 150 years, since the 1840s vegetable, milk, and cattle famer Sutter provided milk and beef for the Gold rush people that came to California in 1849!! Sutter had an amazing farm and amazing beef and vegetables all the way back to where the San Francisco 49ers got their name. **Oh, and where do you think farmer Sutter was from? Switzerland, of course! Lol!**

Is there a solution for today's US farmers? Yes! Ironically, simply pay us 5 cents more on every food we grow, and we will never go bankrupt. We will not be rich. But, we won't be plowing up this year's whole onion 2,000-acre crop and failing to bring it to market (because the price is so low it is better to disk up 2,000 acres of onions rather than pay additional $1,000,000 just for harvesting the crop, **when the market is only going to pay us $800,000 for the WHOLE CROP of 2,000 acres.**

Every day this happens in every state in the United States.

In 1974 you get lucky on the Sugar Beet price. The rest of the 49 years you do not. That is not good enough for your farmer, is it? No, Wells Fargo Bank eventually owns the bankrupt farmer and his family and his farm ground.   And, Holly Sugar plant and all it's workers are then gone from California, entirely. Gone. This is exactly what Rock n Roll Singer John Mellencamp sang about on every song on his 1984 album: **Scarecrow.** Looks like we should start paying our farmer 5 cents more for everything and fix the problem. And, stop Pasteurizing our milk so it can be trucked from Texas to California school children every single day. Raw milk is God's answer. Not my answer. Buddha God, Shinto God, Christian God. All have approved of raw milk in the whole world for over 10,000 years. You might as well go back to what truly works for your health and your family. Not what the PhD's are telling you. What you can see works with your own two eyes – unless you are the Greek Cyclops Polyphemus, and your one eye still will not lie to you either!

Probably should have paid us 5 cents more on every dollar for every single crop we grow, from rice, to corn, to beef, to chicken, to broccoli, to cauliflower, to bermuda hay (that I am allergic to), to alfalfa hay, to sugar, to milk. Let us farmers truck our crops directly to the grocery stores and to the restaurants. Let the railroad cars take our broccoli to New York City and Boston with merely ice on the top of the rail cars. Farm to store. Farm to table. It worked for 100 years in this country, folks. It will work way better than pasteurizing your milk at food plants in all 50 states and trucking it for days on end from food plants to school children.

CHAPTER 26

I SIDE WITH ROBERT F. KENNEDY, JR.

Let's be honest, this is not the US Government fault, either. It is the middlemen in the farming community (Archer Daniels Midlands all the way down to Safeway grocery stores and all the rest of them big boys) that could pay us just 5 cents more on every crop we grow.

In fact, let us name the top 10 big boys who could have paid us farmers 5 cents more on every dollar for the past 100 years. In fact, these US Food companies could have also produced and delivered to you at your grocery stores and at your restaurants the **genuinely <u>healthy</u> food** they did deliver to 100 percent of the grocery stores and restaurants in the USA before 1940:

Top 5 Food Manufacturing Companies in the United States Today:

1. PepsiCo.
2. Tyson Foods.
3. Nestle USA
4. Kraft Heinz
5. General Mills.

Top 5 Food Distribution Companies in the United States Today:

1. Sysco
2. US Foods.

I Side with Robert F. Kennedy, Jr.

3. Performance Food Group
4. McLane Company
5. Gordon Food Service.

They are the ones who are greedy and refuse to pay the farmers the five cents extra they need to survive. The farm brokers, and the Food Manufactures, and the Food Distributors, and the grocery stores are ruining American farming with their price controls and Coke products on every shelf everywhere in this county.

Instead of raw milk and fresh eggs from local farms, like we had in EVERY GROCERY STORE in America before the 1960s, *we now have in their place on our shelve Coca-Cola, Pasteurized milk, Preservative-laced cheese products and preservative-laced water!!!!!* Read the label!!

Sadly, your water from your city is even full of chemicals. And, your water at home is full of chemicals, in almost every single city in the USA. What you are drinking from your home nozzle **they call "healthy tap water,"** is, literally, **all laced with Chlorine, Chloramine, Chromium-6, and Floride, at ALL your nozzles in your sinks at home**! You know that cannot be good for you and you know it is causing you cancer. **Make your city stop it immediately**.

Internet and Ph.D. Studies, and podcasts, please stop calling our milk, eggs and chicken bad on every person in the USA's cell phone. And, stop lying about how great Coca-Cola is. Coca-Cola is paying you professional writers and college professors to lie to us about Pasteurized milk and lie to us about almond milk and lie to us about Coca-Cola, all three of which have been proven in Japan, for 50 years and counting, to kill every single person, if you drink these 3 drinks long enough.

Remember, I am going to tell you all about how great Japan in Volume 2 of this Autobiography. When I tried to export USA potato chips and USA cookies to Japan, the Japanese Government Inspectors in all the Ports of Japan informed me, "Mr. Kuhn, you will turn that container around and send it right back to the United States because all of those preservatives and chemicals in all of your foods you sell at the grocery stores in the USA are banned in Japan because they kill 100 percent of human beings over time and they are outlawed from any country into Japan."

Imagine, dear reader, YOUR having a USA government that cared about YOUR health? Imagine having a United States FDA Inspector at every one of your grocery stores, saying NO to all the chemicals and preservatives the US manufactures are putting in your food today (and your food manufacturers have been putting in your food every day at their manufacturing plants for the past 40 years). I hope this book makes you stand up and demand that immediately of your USA government inspectors REJECT, on your behalf, every single preservative in your food and every single Genetically Modified Animal that they have out there. Again, Japan has been doing this for the past 50 years and counting. And, they are the only county that both men and women outlive our USA men and women by a long, long time.

In fact, why do we need Food Manufacturing Plants at all? **Isn't that the Farmer's Job**? Isn't the broccoli plant producing broccoli? Why does it need to go to a manufacturing plant? It does not need to go to a manufacturing plant. It needs to go from farm to field. That is exactly what happened in the United States for the first 200 years, right up until World War II, when every crop in the USA went from the farm to the local store. Up until the 1950s your milk, carrots, and potatoes went right from our fields to your local Mom & Pop store. IT IS ALSO WAY CHEAPER. Plus, they cannot ruin your milk and your health with heated, treated, Pasteurization at the Food Plant. They also cannot ruin your food with preservatives at the Food Plant. And, Coca-Cola will be out of business (just like Budweiser Beer is almost out of business) because Coca-Cola is the unhealthiest drink on the plant earth. Ask your high school biology teacher. He or she will tell you that, too!

Also, demand that your United States Congress immediately ban every food that is banned in Japan. Not that hard is it? **Or die of cancer, instead, like we all are.**

What I learned in Japan with my first gourmet foods that I exported from Atlanta to a huge gourmet food store in Tokyo, was that the products I imported into Japan were banned in Japan for being laced with preservatives. With my little export company that I started myself, I attempted to import 2 containers of USA manufactured potato chips into Japan for their department stores to celebrate the US Olympic Games in Atlanta, of all things.

The Japanese government is AWESOME for its people. Why? They turned away unhealthy foods (that my US food manufactures told me were not tainted with chemicals) and the Japanese import testing labs proved, that every cookie and every potato chip was laced with the preservative TBHQ, and my own manufacturer lied to me that they did not have that in the cookies and the potato chips and they did, testing positive several times at the Japanese ports of entry. My new little export company immediately went bankrupt because I could not survive the misrepresentation by my US manufacturer that there were no preservatives in the potato chips. My Japanese buyers certainly were not going to pay me for food that they purchased from me that could not come into Japan because it was laced with banned preservatives. The Japanese companies would go bankrupt if they paid for food they could not sell because it was not allowed in the Country of Japan. My new company was finished after that. And I lost face in Japan for not telling the truth. Which is legitimate on their part. Do you think my US food manufacturer paid me back after the whole container of potato chips got rejected for deadly preservatives they said were not in there? Heck no.

Thus, **the Japanese Government, is protecting their citizens health and diet**, their people all live longer than we do in the USA, and they have way less Cancer, because the Japanese government will not allow Coke to put all those lethal chemicals in almost all their products they have on our USA shelves, when they are in Japan.

Sick, isn't it? Sick that the US Government continues to allow food manufactures in the United States ruin your health and your bodies pervasive deadly preservatives in your daily food, from your grocery store to your pasteurized milk, to almost every food you eat in your restaurants. That is what is sick.

Actually, in some ways, it is not sick. Far worse than that, almost every food you eat in the USA is making you sick!! (Pun intended – AND lol!). Every one of us Americans is so sick we are dying of cancer because of Coca-Cola Company products that are pervasive everywhere in the USA! Everything the US Government is allowing on the Grocery store shelves is making you sick, right down to their damn Pasteurized Milk, and other chemical laden products they tell you not to drink.

My answer: "Raw Milk, PLLEEEEAASSSEEE!!!" Again, stop the heating God's 10,000-year-old gift to mankind – all milk products – and stop the Pasteurization at every single milk production company in the United States. If it is good enough out of your mother's breast, it is certainly good enough out of a cow's udder!

Oh, on the other side of the coin, please do not use this book to sue the US Food manufacturers and the US Government on this poisoned food issue, that you are buying and consuming. Why? Because you are just as much to blame as your government, are you not? Yes, you are. It is your body. It is your choice every day that you make to put bad, preservative laced, food in your mouth. In your heart, you know better, don't you? So, a lawsuit for your own bad choices is not the answer either, is it? No, the actual answer is what I told you above: From this very moment forward, by not buying one more thing they produce, demand that Coca-Cola Company never sell any unhealthy food ever again. And, from this moment forward, demand (thorough letters and emails) every day to our US Senators and US House members that they immediately pass new food legislation protecting your health, just like they have in Japan. And, demand that your FDA Inspectors start following your demands – not Coca-Cola's demands.

Remember how fast Budweiser Beer had to shape up a couple years ago when they were truly bad, bad people and everyone stopped buying their beer? You can do the exact same thing with your food manufacturers, including Coca-

Cola. No more sodas of any time in your body from this day forward! Today, demand your city stop putting all those chemicals in your God-Given water and leave it alone and we can all drink it like we did all over the WORLD for the past 10,000 years until the 1960s. It is easy to get healthy water and healthy food. Your doctors are all home eating healthy food when you are not. They should be ashamed and stop lying for the big food and drug companies, for their money, too!

CHAPTER 27

JIM KUHN IN ROCK'N'ROLL HEAVEN – FATHER FRITZ KUHN SAVES JOHN FROM THE BEET DIGGER!

I believe you more often get physically killed in the fields as a farmer than you even "make a killing" financially, truthfully. I believe we lose one farmer and one farmworker every year in the Imperial Valley to a farming accident. Because farmers spend so much time in their pickups they do end up dying a lot driving around big farm equipment and getting run over, or flipping the pickup on the sandy, dirt ditchbanks. And, the farmworkers often die on the tractors or the HUGE Caterpillar trucks or graders. Often the most dangerous time is when you are harvesting a crop, because the harvest equipment is often enormous.

My father flipped his Ford F150 pickup on a ditchbank near one of those first eight fields in the 1960s, just after I was born. I believe he was lucky to walk away.

My brother, Jim Kuhn, was not so fortunate. He died at 12:00 noon one day on the farm in 2005, quite near Mrs. Voorting's field, and even closer to Seeley Elementary School. He was stone-cold-sober and coming home for lunch to see his wife, and their 2 little children, for an hour off from work. Rather unusual for Jim, as he rarely came home for lunch. He was multitasking. Another thing we farmers tend to do quite well is multitask. And, nobody in the Imperial Valley was better at multitasking than Jim Kuhn. So, he was driving fast down Old Highway 80 from the Kuhn Hay Double Compress Machine to his home to see his wife for lunch. He was also driving and taking notes on paper and eating an orange. We do this all the time. So, it does not concern me. But, he did not have his seatbelt on.   Old Highway 80 makes a slight veer just before you get to the New River coming East to Seeley. We have driven that road at least 500 times on a tractor and 500 more times in a pickup truck. But, this time he was looking down and did not veer right with the road.

Remember, I told you that all of us farmers and farmworkers in the Imperial Valley go 60 miles per hour on all highways – that is how we get from our home to our shop, 8 miles in 8 minutes! Perfect math. Normally we put our seat belts on. But this time Jim Kuhn did not put his seat belt on because he just did not think about it. This was not the first time Jim Kuhn flipped his pickup truck on the farm. Most Imperial Valley farmers do flip their pickup trucks once or twice during their lifetimes. Remember, my father even flipped his pickup on Derrick Road in the 1960s, without a seat belt (because there were no seat belts in the 1960s) and he walked away unscathed . Exceedingly fortunate.

My brother? Not fortunate. It was simply his time to die. God called him home. It was his day. God decides these things, not us. It was his day and hour. How many times have you just missed another vehicle colliding on the road and by the skin of your teeth, not had a wreck and NOT died? Happens to all of us in the United States all the time. This time, it was simply my brother's time to pin on his Wings. Fly to the Rock'n'Roll section of Heaven, he did! I will meet him there when it is my time! I cannot wait to see Keith Moon and John Lennon hanging out with Jim Kuhn! So far it is not my time to die. But, my name and time are also written in God's book.

It was almost my time to die when I was in the Sugar Beet field with my father at harvest when I was 8 years old. But farmers will always look after their children and protect them from dying, if they can!

This would have been the Summer of 1970 and we were harvesting Sugar Beets for the whole summer and the sugar beets were consistently large that year. My father had Sugar Beet growing down to an art, which is why I spent a few summers when I was a little older and attending high school at Culver Military Academy, which is a Military Boarding school in Indiana, not too far from Chicago, Illinois. By the time I was a freshman at Culver high school, at age 14, I was old enough to drive the IH tractor and the "Beet Topper" I told you about earlier. This was much earlier in 1970 when I was just 8 years old.

When I was 8 years old, my father was still taking me out to the sugar beet fields in his 1960's Ford 1-150 pickup, in that great big, long, seat, that I loved to ride in! Much easier to see out of the truck when you are eight, instead of five, when you are barely high enough to see over the dashboard.

There is lots of activity in a Sugar beet field during harvest time. Most importantly, there is the great big metal beet digger which digs and carries the huge, 10-pound sugar beets, from the ground and empties them into the huge sugar beet dump truck. One HUGE beet digger does all three things: First, it has highspeed spinning metal blades that go down into the dirt and pull up the root of the beet plant, which is the sugar beet itself! Second, the spinning metal disks throw the sugar beet onto a conveyer belt that takes the sugar beet to the right side of the machine to the 12-foot-tall sugar beet chain ladder, that is operating all the time. Third, the 12-foot-tall chain ladder that the 10 pound (average beet weight in Imperial County), huge, sugar beets go up, then plateaus to a six-foot conveyor belt that takes all the sugar beets to the sugar beet harvest truck.

This is very big and dangerous machine. All day long it goes 2 miles per hour and digs thousands of sugar beets. Then, it dumps every single sugar beet into the great big Sugar Beet 18-wheeler trucks, with the HUGE wooden hoppers, that we prepare in the Kuhn Shop every year.   The 18-wheeler trucks drive both 60 miles per hour on the local asphalt highways, empty, out to our fields, and drive for 2 hours in our dirt fields at 2 miles per hour for quarter mile and half mile runs, precisely alongside the sugar beet digger, loading up with sugar beets.   During the 2 hours the huge semi-trucks drive alongside the beet digger in the dirt field, those enormous wooden hoppers are having thousands of sugar beets an hour drop into the huge hoppers from the actual beet digger conveyer belt. Then, our sugar beet trucks, full of beets we harvested, take these sugar beets to the Holly Sugar Beet factory in Brawley to dump in their huge holes for processing that I told you about earlier in this book. Or, our sugar beet trucks take our beets to the Spreckels or Union Sugar train depots in Seeley, near the Kuhn Farms headquarters and shop.

All of this activity takes place in every single sugar beet field in the United States since 1872 when Claus Spreckels started his own sugar beet processing plant in San Francisco. That is over 150 years of sugar beet production in the continental United States, the predominant amount always coming from California since Mr. Spreckels built his first beet plant there! Imagine the incredible growth in fantastic beet sugar for every year over the past 140 years! Awesome for the State and for the U.S. consumer.

Again, too bad all three of the Sugar Beet processers that have been building every year in the United States for the past 150 years, **all went out of business in the past 10 years, due to the California government working full steam ahead against it** and making impossible to grow and process THE NICEST OF FOOD PRODUCTS IN THE WORLD: Good, clean, easy to use, Sugar. Sugar! Really?? Why?!?

In the past 10 years, after Sugar beets growing and growing in production in the United States for the past 150 years (which is awesome!); NOW, in 2010 and onwards, Speckels Sugar and Union Sugar and Holly Sugar (and sugar beets) pretty much left the continental United States. It is not the farmers that are driving them out of your country. It is the U.S. Government under Joe Biden and the State of California and their "Green New Deal" Lie that is, literally, killing all United States local fresh vegetables and huge sugar beet factories. And, California, with their Climate Change Lies, killing Holly Sugar in Brawley, California, only 10 years ago! Killing almost all farming in California in the past 20 years. Stupid. Exceedingly stupid. And, mean.

Your United States climate change lie has a price: Your farmers. Your fresh, locally grown food. That is what you lose to that lie.

Back to the sugar beet field harvest in California the Summer of 1970 with my father as an 8-year-old. He takes me out that Saturday in his pickup and we drive over the big dirt irrigation rows, which are hard to drive over with a pickup. My dad loved to drive over those big dirt sugar beet rows with his pickup truck. He was an expert and would drive just the correct speed and we would get to the beet digger in the middle of the field. I would only be tossed around a little bit on the big canvas pickup truck seat. That means I was merely being tossed around like you would be on a small boat, but not as bad as a pinball! All young boys love that!! Especially with their fathers!

When we got over to the sugar beet digger, my father put me out in the field to sit on an unharvested row of beets, took out his shovel from the back of the pickup and dug up an actual 10-pound sugar beet. Then, took the big juicy green leafy top of the sugar beet off with one strike of his shovel and put the sugar beet in my lap to see how it felt and how much it weighed. Of course, I did what all children do with "sugar beets!" I bit into the sugar beet to see if it tasted sweet. Sure enough, it tasted sweet! Just incredible. And, my father waited for what he knew would happen next – because it has happened with every sugar beet in the world for time in memoriam! About 30 seconds after the deliciously sweet taste that the sugar beet always begins with, the horrible, bitter aftertaste that always takes over from every sugar beet. All over your mouth for about 20 minutes, drying it out and becoming more sour!

Now you know, Dear Reader, why we cannot eat sugar beets like sugar cane out in the fields and why we MUST process the sugar from a sugar beet at a factory. That is to keep the excellent, sweet sugar taste in your granulated sugar and lose the bitter aftertaste in a sugar beet. When California Claus Spreckels invented this beet sugar processing in 1873, he changed California (and U.S. Farming) forever.

Now we can easily grow sugar beets and have the exact same delicious sugar that you used to only have from sugar cane before 1873 and the California sugar beet factories. This gave us a whole new, huge, crop in the continental United States, starting in San Francisco in 1873.

After my father watched me spit out everything in my mouth for 10 minutes straight, after eating the raw sugar beet, he laughed out loud and said, "Now you will remember never to eat a sugar beet in the field again!" He is correct. I have never eaten a raw sugar beet since then. Period.

Another thing I will remember clearly from that hot day in the sugar beet field is that I almost died shortly afterwards. Not from eating a sugar beet. They will not kill you. They are like the beautiful Lorelei on the Rhine River in Germany, who will lure you over with their sweet song and then make you wish you did not try their fruit! Lol!!

No. The way I almost died that day in the sugar beet field was when the gigantic beet harvester started to **come down my row** where I was sitting with my large sugar beet that my father gave me. I was sitting there minding my own business when the beet digger was coming down my row. The beet digger always has one man driving it and 5 more men on the platform overlooking the spinning metal wheels, making sure that the beets cleanly expel onto the resilient conveyor belt from the spinning metal discs and the 10 pound beets then climb up the 12-foot-tall chain ladder the metal link climbing chain to go into the beet semi-truck with the HUGE wooden hoppers that was driving 2 miles per hour alongside the beet digger. I did not see any of this as it was coming to me because, in 80-acre fields, nothing seems that close when you are watching it, until it is upon you and it is too late.

Apparently the driver of the tractor pulling the sugar beet digger did not see me in front of him. But, my father did see me sitting there in front of the beet digger and the huge 18-wheeler semi-truck we owned. And, my father shouted, in the loudest possible voice, to be heard over the meal spinning beet digger and metal belts and chains: ALTO!!!

ALTO means STOP in Spanish. Sometimes you just do not hear it when it is screamed in a farming field with farming equipment. But, the tractor driver did hear the "Alto!" and stopped the beet digger immediately. Which is what you are supposed to do. That day, the tractor driver saved my life because the beet digger stopped 100 feet short of me on the same row that they were digging beets. I remember it like it was yesterday. My father remembered it until the day he died. My mother never knew about that her whole life and died not knowing that incident. I am somewhat certain that my mother would never have let me or Jim back in the sugar beet field if she knew about that one!

I told you that I avoided death in the sugar beet field by the skin of my teeth! As Union Colonel Joshua Chamberlain said, fighting to end slavery in the United States on July 2, 1863 (and in the 1993 movie, "***Gettysburg***"), "It is not our time to die." And, at 8 years old in our sugar beet field, "It was not my time." As I told you earlier. God decides when it is our time. God clearly wants me to at least write Volume 1 of my trilogy in honor of my Kuhn Farms family and in honor of my deceased brother, James Edwin Kuhn, who died instantly, farming on our family farm, on August 28, 2005, at high noon, about half mile from our own Seeley School in Imperial County, California. This Volume 1, of course, is in

Jim's honor. And, these are stories that his daughter and son have not heard at all. Therefore, this book is also for you, my brother's children.

I will always remember my farmer brother, Jim Kuhn, until the day I die. This book is partly about him and I have written it for his two children to get to know their father a little better and respect and love him a little bit more.

By the way, Jim Kuhn is up in Heaven and is very proud of his wife and his two children who are still down here on this earth, doing quite well. He met his wife in College. In fact, Jim and his wife met at Stanford University in California. They got married on the California Big Sur Coast with lots of farmers and Stanford friends at the wedding. They lived happily ever after, just like that Kuhn Swiss Family Fairy Tale back in Chapter 3 of this book! Again, as with all fairy tales, somebody must work like crazy AND slay dragons if you are to have a good ending. Jim's wife did work like crazy to make it still turn into the proverbial "fairy tale" since Jim died at age 41 when their children were six and four years old, and they were only married 11 years when he died prematurely.

Why is Jim Kuhn so proud in Heaven? He is the second of three generations of Kuhn's to graduate from Stanford University. My mother was, in fact, the first generation of Kuhn's to graduate from Stanford. "She-Who-Must-Not-Be-Named," my mother, Madeline Hall Kuhn, graduated in 1948, long before most women were even going to college in the United States! It shows you how impressive and terrific my mother was! Then, Jim Kuhn, graduated in 1986 from Stanford University: A farmer who did, indeed, graduate from "The Farm!" (Pun intended, again – I just cannot leave them alone! Lol!!)

Finally, Jim's daughter graduated from Stanford University in 2020. She is doing quite well in New York City in some sort of pharmaceutical field and is enjoying the energy and great vibe of NYC!

Their son is the most analogous to a farmer on either side of the family. Like his father, one of his God-given talents is managing people and situations. He will do well in the military! He was born on Valentine's Day in 2002 and he is now in the U.S. Army Special Forces basic training in Geogia. **As you probably know, many farmers have done extremely well in the military**, from General Julias Ceaser *before the time of Christ* in Rome, with all his Italian farmer soldiers who beat all of Europe all of the time, for many, many wars thereafter all the way to all those USA farm boys who successfully fought Adolf Hitler and Benito Mussolini in Fascist Germany and Fascist Italy in World War II. In fact, a whole lot of U.S. farm boys freed a whole lot of French and British and Jewish folks at the end of World War II in France and Germany and Italy, not to mention a whole lot more U.S. Farm boys freed a whole lot of Chinese and Filipino folks from Fascist Japan at the end of the same World War, in 1945. My nephew is going to do the same as our boys in World War II.

Therefore, my brother, Jim Kuhn, is, indeed, looking down from Heaven right now and proud as a father can be, with a wife who made the family stay together and worked like crazy to provide for her children, and his daughter graduating from Stanford five years ago and living in New York City, to his son now being a former farmer in the United States Army somewhere making a difference for you and me!

CHAPTER 28

MY FIRST CRUSH AT DON BROCKS ASPARAGUS FARM

We always remember our first crush. Yes we do. Mine was at Don Brock's Asparagus Farm headquarters on Forrester Road outside El Centro a week before Christmas in 1976.

First, I am pleased to report that Don Brock Farms is still there today, and I am besties with all the Brocks: Best friends with Don Brock, best asparagus farmer in the United States – at least his dad was, according to my dad! Best friends with his first wife, Mindy Brock, whom I am still very close to, to this day. And best friends with their three adorable children, who are 10 years behind me and whom I am still close to, to this day: Julie Brock Roggeman, Krissie Brock Kelly, and Matt Brock.

Christmas vacation in 1976 I was 14 years old. I was smitten! First time, ever, for me. Let me set the scene: It is Christmas in El Centro and we love to go out to some farmer's farm headquarters for great big Mariachi band parties. Remember, we are only 10 miles away from Mexicali, Mexico! So, of course, we have real Mariachi bands for the big parties – like Christmas parties! The Brocks had one of the nicest farm headquarters you have ever seen in the Imperial Valley, and they had an asparagus packing shed, so that meant the whole facility was a quarter mile long. And, all dressed up with Christmas lights at Christmas. Plus, my mother loved Don's wife, Mindy Brock, and my father loved Don Brock. So, they took me to my first farming Christmas party that year. I am sure my bother Jim was there, too, but I don't remember. All I remember is "the girl," of course!

Between mariachi band sets on the big stage, they had this great big outdoor sound system – which was pretty cool for those days! And, naturally, they played the song that was the Number One hit the whole Fall of 1976: Rod Stewart's *"Tonight's the Night (Gonna be Alright)"* Still one of the best songs in music history. If you have not heard that song, put it on your Smartphone (right now) and listen to it! **I will wait five minutes for you to listen to it and then get back to this page in my book for the rest of the story**! Five minutes is all it will take!

The Brocks also had a great big fire in a big fire pit in the middle of the entrance to the farming facility. I can see it in my mind, even today. Great big palm trees everywhere, big mesquite tress everywhere, grass as green as Switzerland, and big fire with everyone standing around the fire, with the big black speakers playing Rod Stewart's *"Tonight's the Night."*

Cannot possibly get any better than that for a 14-year-old boy or girl in the United States, right??! Or can it? Well, I had never been smitten before, so I had no idea what that felt like.

But, I did at that very instant! I saw her!! Who? Debbie Ronsevelt (or Debbie R!)! Oh my, oh my. Both sexes know that feeling! She was perfect and she was GORGEOUS!!! And, my mouth hit the floor. Trust me, it was not the song. I had heard the song a thousand times that year. I saw the girl once that year. It was the girl! Debbie Ronsevelt.

I probably should have known more, but you know how it is when you are 14 years old. You don't know much. But, you know when you are smitten!

By that Summer of 1977 I found out from my mother that she was Debbie Rounsavelle and she was a LaBrucherie, another long and outstanding El Centro farming family, like the Brocks. So, of course they were at the Brock's Christmas Party! Everyone loved Matt and Jane LaBrucherie, Debbie Rounsavelle's grandparents – and my parents' best friends! If my mother had been smart, she should have played up this "Debbie R" thing. Why? Because I was smitten! My mother and Jane probably could have orchestrated my remaining in El Centro if Debbie Rounsavelle "had happened to me!!!" By the way, another great song – this song by The Lemonheads from their 1992 album **It's A Shame About Ray** – is my favorite song on that album: *"Alison's Starting to Happen to Me!"* Got to love that Rock'n'Roll music, right!!?

My mother complained bitterly when I married Shea and went all the way across the United States of America to live in Charleston, South Carolina. I told my mother many times that if SHE had been smarter and made me realize Debbie R was a good choice, then I probably would still be in El Centro, farming, to this day. We 14-year-old boys do, indeed, listen to our mother's, even if we do not admit it! Lol!

I even loved Debbie's mother, Suzanne Enis! She is funny and smart and great company, and lives in San Diego County. Her daughter, Debbie Rounsavelle, in fact changed names long before she even got married, to her second father's name, so her named changed to Debbie Enis. I knew her much better as Debbie Enis than Debbie R, in the end. But, since I went off to Boarding School for all four years of high school (Culver Military Academy in Culver, Indiana) I rarely ever saw Debbie Ennis again. Too bad. My loss, of course. She was, and is, beautiful and smart and funny, just like her mother!

There will be several more chapters about the Don Brock family, because I intentionally stayed really close to all of them. Debbie Ennis and Krissie Brock have something in common they probably do not even know about even though they lived blocks apart near McCabe Road, until they read this book. The reason I am certain they do not know what I am about to tell both of them is they are about 10 years apart in age, which is a lot of years when you are young! But, both Debbie Enis and Krissie Brock attended UCLA for college, which was somewhat unusual for El Centro girls, so go Debbie and Krissie!

P.S. Dear Reader, your homework assignment, now that you have finished Author John Kuhn's Chapter 28, titled: "The Crush," is that I order you to download the John Kuhn Top 10 Album of all time (and most people's top 20 album of all time) albums and play it immediately on your music devise, even if it is your smartphone. What is the album you now must listen to, songs in the correct order, just like we used to listen to everything on vinyl: Rod Stewart's album **Night On The Town**. **Every song on the album is amazing**, including my favorite, "The Killing of Georgie, and my wife's favorite, "Tonight's the Night." This album lived on the U.S. Radio all the Summer of 1976. Unbelievable album! Number one in the world all summer long – not sure what beat it in the USA that year, **but it was not what the whole United States of America (all of us!) were buying and listening to at home on the stereo and listening to on the transistor radio the whole Summer and Fall and Winter of**

1976, which was, definitely, Rod Stewart's **Night on the Town**. The proof of that is that is the song that was playing at Don Brock's outdoor Christmas party that year, not Peter Frampton's songs or album. Peter Frampton's album was good; but, song by song, not even in the ballpark with Rod Stewart's **Night on The Town**. Listen to **Night on the Town** right now and *let me know what you think*, Dear Reader! 😊

CHAPTER 29

OFF TO CULVER MILITARY ACADEMY IN THE CORNFIELDS OF INDIANA!

How did I end up going to girls and boys boarding school in the middle of the cornfields of Indiana, **as a freshman in high school** in August 1976? Remember, my mother went to Stanford University in the 1940s and she could see, in her mind, that I was not going to receive an adequate education at the local high school that she taught at years before I was born, Central Union High School. Coupled with my mother's fear that I would not receive an adequate education at our local high school, was that I feared the gangs at the local high school. Well, it turns out there were no gangs at the local high school. However, when you are **an eighth grader** in any school system, don't you always fear the high school gangs at the local high school? I certainly did.

I was a bit of a wimp and sheltered by "She-Who-Must-Not-Be-Named." In fact, my father said I was going to turn out to be a "Mama's Boy" if I stayed home much longer. Thus, my father, Fritz Kuhn, was all for this idea of boarding school without my mother in charge. I did not know that until years later, of course! Lol!

My mother had me take the SSAT test for boarding high schools in the United States. As I told you back in Chapter 5 of this book, I trounced the verbal section of the Secondary School Admissions test because I had read every single chapter of the New Testament in the King James Version of the Bible, out loud, in Keith Macgaffey's Sunday School class every week at St. Peter and St. Paul's Episcopal church in El Centro in 4th though 7th grade.

I also routed the math section of the SSAT as well, because I had been out on my farm so many times with my father, counting bales in haystacks, then multiplying the figures in my head, just like my father did. I assumed that every father in America could do that. I later realized that what my mother said was true: "Your father is way more gifted than I am." That was saying something, because my mother graduated from Stanford and everyone knew she was smart.

Later, I realized I was, also, gifted academically. You do not really know that until years after college when you are in the real world and see every single person is different, physically and academically. Again, God makes us all individuals with each of us having our unique personalities and characteristics. Every single human being belongs on this earth and has something to contribute. Not to mention, become a husband or wife, eventually, for most.

Just so you know, I have never tested higher than a 93rd percentile on any standardized test. I am not a genius. And, I am way too ADD to focus too long to get a perfect score on any test. In fact, I know almost no people with 99th percentile on any standardized tests, let alone perfect scores on standardized tests. Most of us are way more in the middle on almost everything, expect the one thing we love the most. We always excel at what we love, even if we are nowhere near gifted.

Now that I had an excellent test score, time to look at the best boarding schools in California, according to my mother. Let us put this in perspective. This is 1976. According to my

Stanford Republican mother (who graduated with U.S. Supreme Court Justice Sandra Day O'Connor) and Swiss-German farmer father, in 1976, California has a hippie problem. They are correct, of course. Just so you know, I now side with Hippie's in that we need way more pure and healthy foods and get back to organic fruits and vegetables on the land and not in the cities.

Off to California Boarding Schools: Namely, Cate School, Thatcher School and Webb School. We drove to see the boarding schools in California. I loved seeing the boarding schools and could see myself at all three of them. I did not love Thatcher School as much because it as heavily into horses and horsemanship and I knew I had enough animals around us on the farm. My parents were not as impressed. Again, it was the heighth of what my mother called, "Sex, Drugs and Rock'N"Roll," and California was inundated by all of it in the 1970s.

At one school, my mother said, "look at all these girls and guys making out under blankets. This is not okay by me." My father asked every Principal of every school, "What do you do about Drugs?" Answer at all three: "We try to rehabilitate them, of course." To which my father said to me later: "No way."

Now that was a failure, we then went to the closest, excellent, private high school tht my mother knew to El Centro, which was Bishop's School in La Jolla. I would have landed there, but it was all girls at the time.

But, my mother somehow new the Director of Admissions at Bishop's School in San Diego, so we drove over there to talk to him. He listened to our plight. My mother added, "you know, it is getting pretty late in the game, so we need to think of something." To which the Director of Admissions at Bishops said, "Well, you know, you could try Culver Military Academy in Indiana. That might be a much better fit for what you are looking for. It is conservative and it is perfect for what you described." My mother said, "How do you know this?" "Oh," he said, "I used to be on the Admissions staff there years ago, Mrs. Kuhn. Go look at it and see what you think."

Off to Culver we were. Flew straight into Chicago O'Hare and drove down to Culver. Dear Reader, please remember, in the 1970s and earlier in the United States of America, nobody flew anywhere. Surprisingly, you were much more likely to fly to London, England, than to New York City. For all vacations, almost 100 percent of Americans drove to wherever they were going. If living out West, it was to Disneyland or the Grand Canyon. If living out East, it was to New York City of Disneyworld. You certainly did not fly anywhere.

Moreover, you did not fly to boarding school. That was almost unheard of. If you really wanted to go to boarding high school, you drove to whichever one was well known in your area. That is why we drove to Cate, Thatcher and Webb. They were in California. My friends' parents were whispering below their breaths, "Certainly one of those three schools should be good enough for the Kuhn boys."

It was March and we flew into Chicago O'Hare Airport and drove directly to Culver in a rental car. Like almost everyone in the United States in the 1970s, I had never been out of California, my home state, for anything. Only to Yuma, Arizona to swim the breaststroke for my local El Centro Sun Divers Swim team, that we were all on to keep out of the miserable heat in El Centro. Religiously, every year we swam against the Brawley and Imperial and Calexico teams – Holtivlle did not have a pool. Then, the big swim meet of the year, that we loved the most, because it was 50 miles away, was in Yuma, Arizona against the hated Yuma Sidewinders.

At age 14 I could not find Chicago on the map if I had too, let alone find the State of Indiana! We drove the two full hours from Chicago O'Hare to Culver, Indiana. We were an hour away and just crossed into Indiana, and then, it happened. What happened? The whole Interstate turned to corn fields. Corn fields to the left. Corn fields to the right. Corn fields EVERYWHERE! My farmer father said, "now this is more like it!" Lol.

I said, "It sure does not look like our farm desert! I have not seen sand since I have been in Indiana. But those HUGE corn plants seem to be growing in something like sand!" To which my father said, "yes, the soil in Indiana is famous for farming." I could see he was correct.

The closer we got to Culver, the more rural the whole landscape was. Finally, we arrived at Culver. Then, the most unbelievable thing happened in my whole life. We turned into the brick front gate to Culver, and the most beautiful school I had ever seen in my life appeared before us. And, it was HUGE and it was everywhere. Wow! I was impressed!

That turned out to be the appetizers! We came around the stunningly beautiful all-brick Church on the hill, then the road rounded towards the HUGE all-brick athletic center. Then, we went down the hill towards the HUGE LAKE, and pulled up to parking spaces at the ancient, HUGE brick building called, "Sally-Port." Was this little farm boy from

California impressed? I'll say I was! Were my parents impressed? I'll say they were!

We checked into Sally Port. Just for your information, there were very few admissions offices in any boarding school in those days. I do not believe Culver had one, either, in 1976. But, we checked into "Sally-Port" and the first person we ran into was the young cadet Senior, who was, as it turns out, "Officer of the Day." 18 years old, mind you, and in change of the whole school for the WHOLE DAY! Because he was the Officer of the Day, he was dressed in full-dress uniform. To this day, I remember, that he had big yellow wool sashes and had a huge Sabre attached to him. Yes, a real Sabre! Metal and cool and long, used some places for fencing. Looked just like the "**Three Musketeers**," by Andre Dumas, to me!

Sally-Port is a huge, brick building, at the backside entrance to the main campus, near the real dark green U.S. Army howitzer, down near the lake front. When you arrive at Sally-Port, you know that you have arrived at something you have never seen in your life. It is sooooo cool, with the 15,000 square foot brick building, that in the entrance, holds all the: 1. Culver flags for all the military units. 2. All of the offices for the cadet leadership for the school. 3. The actual cannon shells for the howitzer for the cadets to fire every morning of every day at 6:00 am for reveille. 4. Most importantly, Pictures of the 5 Medal-of-Honors winners who graduated high school from Culver, along with two of their actual Metal of Honors, themselves. Right there next to the Officer of the Day's Office on the genuine red-brick corner of the building!

209

My father says to the young man, "We are here to look at the school for our son John for freshman year, next year." The Cadet said, "Where are you in from?" My dad said, "California." The Officer of the Day said, "Wow, that is a long way away." Then he said, "You are at Sally-Port, so this is where the Office of the Commandant is." Would you like to see the Commandant?' My mother said, "What is a Commandant?" To which the Officer of the Day said, "Oh, Army Captain who is in change of the whole military for the whole Culver School." "Perfect, my dad said."

So, we get taken by the young cadet in the yummy yellow wool sashes, with the incredible Sabre, 200 yards inside the building, to the Commandant's Office. We go into the Commandant's Office and we meet Colonel Greene. My father served in Korea in the Army, so he immediately saluted when we went into Col. Greene's Office. It was so impressive, I wanted to salute, too!

Colonel Greene took half an hour and explained the military system at Culver, from the fantastic uniforms, that you get on the first day as a Cadet, to the required Sunday service at the HUGE red brick Culver Memorial Chapel, which was built to honor all the Culver Cadets who died fighting in World War II, to the Saturday morning barracks inspections, to the famous, weekly Sunday (immediately after Services) weekly parades, with the, Black Horse Troup, the Artillery duce-and-halves trucks (driven by the cadets) and the Infantry Battalion. Whatever was "Your thing," they had it. He did not mention the "Plebe System." So, I never heard that part of the military system at Culver until the first day of school when I got to Main Barracks and got my uniform. More funny stories about that, coming up.

Most important moment of the whole trip: My father asked the Commandant, "What do you do about drugs?' To which Colonel Greene immediately replied, "We kick them out, of course!" To which my father, instantly, said, "Well, sign John up, right now! I had seen my father make a lot of quick decisions in my life, but none that quick!!!

After meeting with Commandant Colonel Greene we looked around Sally-Port and found that the Black House Troup barracks were the two floors above the big arched entrance to the campus and that the Officer of the Day was in the Troup, consequently his sashes were yellow wool, since that is Troop's colors and he was an officer so he was required to wear the sashes and the Sabre with his Full-Dress uniform. He told us that Infantry was blue sashes and Artillery was red sashes for officers. He also had on enough military merit stripes to sink a ship. So cool!

We then went to the Mess Hall next because that is what you hit next. The Mess Hall is the largest indoor brick eating facility in the Midwest. Apparently Mr. Lay, of Lay's potato chips, must have graduated from Culver, because it was called the Lay Dining Hall. You think Sally-Port is big? Holy Cow!!! The Mess Hall was the size of two football fields, INSIDE!!! One Cadet there told us that it has been that way since the 1940s because they want to seat the whole Culver Cadet Regiment in the Mess Hall at one seating, every morning for breakfast and every day at 12:00 noon, sharp, for lunch. Whole regiment of 650 high school boy students sitting in one instant motion, when the Cadet Regimental Commander yells, "Seats!" So cool!

We were also told that Mr. Lay was truly nice and going to add another section for the newly opened, in 1971 (5 years

211

earlier than we were there that day), Culver Girls Academy, that was 150 high school girls, *and were not military*, but had to come to all meals with the cadets! Some of the girls were there and they were beautiful and chatty, with their little uniforms on.

The other thing I remember about the Mess Hall (the Dining Hall) was that there were four long food line areas on the far wall to get you food on trays for lunch that was a full football field away from where we were standing in front of the building. I thought they could feed a lot of high schoolers awfully quickly with that set up. That turned out to be correct. Genius.

We then went out of the Mess Hall and crossed a space to another HUGE brick building. Being the next building, we went in the back door. Directly, we realized this was a dormitory. We asked a cadet in there and I he said, "Yes, this four-story brick building is Main Barracks and it houses every cadet in the whole battalion." In my book, that was incredible. I saw a bunch of red banners on the first-floor vestibule, so I asked, "Is this whole barracks just for the Artillery battalion, then?" He immediately turned to me, looked me in the eye, and said, "Yes!" How many high school boys in the United States do that, all the time, every day?

After watching all the commotion for half an hour, we were impressed how every student knew exactly what he was doing, and exactly what to do next. Then, the buzzer rang and the whole barracks stremed down beside us, from all four floors at one time, and within 5 minutes the whole Artilary Batallion was outside forming up in what they called: "Ranks" The buzzer goes off and in 5 minutes there are 200 boys lined up outside the building in perfect order. So cool!

Of course, we went out the front door of Main Barracks to see what was going on. And, then, I saw it. What? Saw what? The Lake!!! Right in front of Main Barracks, 200 high school boys are lining up on the asphalt path immediately in front of Main Barracks, and behind the whole scene is the most beautiful lake you have ever seen. Now remember, I am from the actual desert in California, so there are NO LAKES anywhere where I live. None. So, you need to excuse me for thinking the lake is the most beautiful lake I have ever seen. Lol!

On the other hand, my parents had been all over the world, AND seen lots of beautiful lakes in Switzerland, (homeland to 120 stunningly beautiful lakes) and they were still impressed by this here lake at Culver, too. My mother said, "Oh my gosh, that is a beautiful lake! I cannot believe they have been smart enough to build a gorgeous brick high school on the lake, like that." Then my father chimed in, "Did you see how fast those boys got down here for 'Ranks?'" And I said, "and look how perfectly dressed all 200 of them are? No sloppy anything there! Holy Cow!"

Dear Reader, want to be impressed? Visit Culver Military Academy and Culver Girls Academy any day of the week, every single day, for 9 straight months, in Culver, Indiana, to this very day! Holy Cow. (Yes, that is an advertisement – lol! – but it is true, no matter how you slice it!)

We proceed down this asphalt path to THE LAKE, that is about an eight of a mile down the path. But, on the right there are another two HUGE red brick buildings that we can see are there for something important. This time we ask a girl who is on the path what those two huge buildings are. She says, "Oh, those are CT Barracks and Aragone Dorm. The boys Infantry lives in the CT Barracks and half the girls live in

Aragone Dorm." My farmer father surprises me with his question: My dad asks, "So, that Aragone Dorm, is that named for the World War One battle called "Aragone?" To which the girl beams and say, "Well, yes, that is correct."

We walk on further to the next GORGEOUS Gothic-style red brick building that is the most beautiful building I have ever seen in my whole life. This building red brick, just like all the rest, but this is far more beautiful, for three reasons: First, every single window in the building is not normal wooden white but is actually concrete and exactly like the gothic cathedrals you see in Europe. Second, the building is actually on the lake, and not up from it. Third, we walk up the beautiful cement steps in front of the building and at the top there are two HUGE metal stars imbedded in the cement. This whole thing is the most impressive building I have ever seen, to this day.

As if that is not cool enough: Some Cadet just happens to come out of the big wooden door of the building, then comes to a stone cold stop and salutes the star with the most perfect salute you have ever seen. Up here in the middle of nowhere!

My father asks the Cadet what he is doing. He precisely states:

"This is the Culver Memorial Legion Building and this building is

built in honor of all Americans who died in World War One.

These stars are in the ground here to specifically honor the all the

American soldiers who died in World War One and Culver cadets are required to stand at attention and salute the star every single

time we pass the Star. Sir."

My mother, father, and I were decidedly impressed. We then go inside the gothic red brick building to another world entirely. In the 1970s the Culver library was on the whole right side of the building and the history department was on the left side. We briefly went through the history department with beautiful old wooden teacher's offices for the teachers and big dark carved wooden mahogany classrooms for the students.

But, far more impressive was the Culver Library. These cadets and coeds were all sitting on the main floor with enormous couches and an enormous walnut table in the middle of the room and gorgeous carved mahogany fireplaces all around the room. I will never forget the perfect light blue carpet that made it seem cozy for such a big space. The first-floor ceilings were 16 feet high though the whole room where all the students congregated and talked quietly.

I asked one of the Cadets what all the pipes were all around the rooms of the library, and he said, "It gets really cold here in the Winter so Culver actually has universal steam heating for the whole campus that starts over there at the main quad and you can see all the underground steam heat in the winter when the snow will not stick to the ground where the pipes come to each building." I thought that sounded rather cool, too! Especially the idea that all the rooms stay warm in the winter when you have Lake Michigan snow coming fifty miles from the north with "lake effect snow," which they have at Culver. I also thought I have never seen any snow in my whole life, so that would be so much fun to see snow, alive and in person!

We went up the concrete spiral staircase to the second floor of the library. Someone knew how to pour concrete because that was the most gothic spiral staircase I had ever been in! Second floor turns out to be the books. Books and books and books and more books! I had never seen so many books. Certainly do not have those in El Centro! So cool!!

Back down the solid gothic staircase and out the back of the building. Now we are facing an actual, traditional, boarding school quadrangle. This would have been the highlight of any boarding school or college. My parents and I could see that it was just normal, *around here*.

Nevertheless, the quad in March was stunningly beautiful. Again, grass as green as the school pictures from the East we had all seen. All over the quad and the red brick buildings were perfectly proportioned to look like they had been there forever. There was white wooden trim on every single one of the red brick buildings on the quadrangle. Made them stand out graciously, for sure.

I asked a girl if she knew what the buildings were. She snickered and said, "Well of course! That is the English building on the left, the language building in the middle, and the science building on the right." She snickered that snicker that you make when you think to yourself, "well of course I know what those buildings are – they are the same they have been forever and ALL OF US know them by heart." Boy did I want to go to school here now!

Not to mention, I thought the most beautiful building was essentially the English building. Of course, **it turns out the English building and the Science building are identical.** But,

I love English and I hate science, so the English building is the most beautiful. Period. Beauty is in the eye of the beholder! Lol! Dear Reader, this is also how you can get "A's" on English papers. If your teacher believes your paper is good, you get a good grade. If your math problem is incorrect, you NEVER get a good grade! Lol!

I then asked a Cadet, "Are the students in change of the grass and the grounds?" He laughed and said, "Oh no, the prolees are in charge of the grounds and the school. We are in change of the military and we are in change of the barracks, but not the grounds." I asked, "What are Prolees?" He laughed again and said, "You know, I don't even know why we call them that. They have always been called the 'prolees' at Culver. They are the Culver workers from town who take care of everything, especially the heating system, and the facilities." I was happy to hear that the students were not in charge of the facilities and it made sense that the students were in change of their dorms.

Around the quad we walked, staring starey eyed at everything we saw, especially the buildings, which were breathtaking. Stopping from time to time to see if we could see anything that was less than beautiful. Nothing. Everything was beautiful.

The language building in the middle was quintessential with its bright white wooden clock tower. So, we walked up to it and realized that it was on a little hill. The back side of the quadrangle faced something we had not seen yet, because it was a little lower. But, it turns out it certainly wasn't smaller. Contrarily, it was the biggest building on campus!

From the top of the quadrangle, we could see gigantic Greek-columned building all the way over across the lawn. My mother said, "the statues in the water in front look like Versailles." I thought to myself, "what on earth is Versailles?" I would have that question answered in "The History of the two World Wars" class at Culver, a couple of years later.

The building was enormous and it, too, was all red brick. Except, for the front that looked like the front of the U.S. Capital in Washington, DC, the only other city, besides San Diego, I had been to in my life so far in my young life. Not only was the building beautiful, but it was also framed by a bright green lawn leading all the way up to it from the quadrangle.

Over we walked to the biggest building I had ever seen. We ran into another Cadet. I asked him what that building was. He replied, "That is Eppley. That is where we have our student plays. But, it is so large that we also have our all-school convocations every month there. Sometimes we have movies there," he smiled. Then, turning to a frown, he said, "We also have SAT testing and standardized testing there too." Big frown on that one!

I asked the same Cadet, "How do you get over there?" "Oh," he replied, "we march over there, of course – at least for convocations! But, we have dances there on some Saturday nights and they're fun."

My mother asked him, if there were "girls and guys making out under blankets?" He immediately laughed and said, "No way, that is PDA!" My mother asked, "What is PDA?" To which he replied, "that is short for 'Public Display of Affection,' and that is not allowed at Culver. You have to march five tours for that." I asked, "Five tours, what is that?"

He replied, "You do not even want to know," and he sighed knowingly.

My father said to my mother, "After visiting the Commandant and talking to the Cadets and Coeds, I do not think you are going to have girls and guys making out under blankets." Sadly, I could see he was right. And, I frowned.

We walked all the way back to Sally-Port, which was half a mile back from that Eppley place. Because the campus in the same place since Culver commenced in 1894, it is one whole, contiguous campus. Thus, you never see the town of Culver, except the part of campus that we were on now, that goes from Eppley Auditorium to Sally-Port. Where Beason Hall is, on the back side of the Quadrangle, you do see the back side of the town of Culver.

We would have just passed Beason, so I asked a Coed, "What is this charming red brick building?" She responded, "That is for Seniors only! Do not step on one inch of Beason, or you will be depantzed." I asked her, "What is depantzed?" She said, "That is where the Seniors will take your pants off in front of the whole school if you step on their precious Beason." I asked, "Have you been depantzed?" She laughed and said, "Oh no. Nobody is that stupid! But, the regimental sergeant major was that stupid last year and we all got to see him depantzed in front of the whole school. It was pretty funny!" On other hand, as a high schooler, I was frightened to death of Beason for the next four years and avoided it like the plague!

We walked past Main Barracks and back into Sally-Port. I asked the Officer of the Day if there was any more left of the campus. He laughed and said, "I think you have seen a third of it. You still have the ginormous gym, Culver Memorial

Chapel, the riding hall, and the parade field, in that order, to go." I know that my mother and father, being strong Episcopalians, are going to want to see the Memorial Chapel. We had heard that the Head Rector for the Chapel was an Episcopal Priest. Growing up in Dr. Macgaffey's Episcopal Sunday School in El Centro, I know that I am most interested in the Chapel. I would feel at home there.

But our first stop was the ginormous gym. My mother pointed out that I was a swimmer in local swim league in California and that I was passably good at swimming, so we need to see the Culver indoor pool, that was legitimately famous in the State of Indiana. Why was the Culver pool famous in Indiana? Because it always had heat; moreover, it was always open to the girls swim team and the boys swim team, no matter how bad the blizzard they managed to have at Culver. The statement we heard a lot was, "If the Culver pool ain't open, t'aint no pool in the state open."

Sure enough, the Culver pool was open. I looked around and it was my lucky day! It was girls' swim practice when we got there. After a while, I thought to myself, "Wow, these girls were a lot prettier than the girls I have been swimming with, in El Centro." **Turns out that was untrue for two reasons**: First, it is not fair to compare seventh grade girls with high school girls. Second, now that I think back on it, the only time I regularly saw Debbie Enis in El Centro was when her mother brought her to swim practice, which was quite often, if fact. And no girl in my world was a match for Debbie Enis!

What a spectacular pool it was! Little did I know, but I would be swimming in that pool to John Lennon's **Shaved Fish** album in less than a year, AND Culver would host the Indiana State Championship Boys Swim meet in that very pool my Junior year at Culver. Both of these chapters, Dear Reader, are coming right up in this very Volume!

The three of us could not have expected that Culver had about the oldest, largest, most beautiful old gym of almost any high school in the United States. It was, indeed, ginormous! The hallway in the old gym was a country mile. And, it was covered with old photographs of Culver teams, from the first 75 years of the school's history. Especially football pictures and basketball pictures. So cool!

Then we went into what they called the "new gym." I am guessing they had to build that when they admitted women in 1971. The pool was beautiful, but it was old school. The old gym was beautiful, but it was also old school. Not the new gym! Nicest men's showers and high school lockers I ever saw. Same with the women's showers and high school sports lockers. So new and all working perfectly. Far cry from Central High!

Off to the Church, that we had waited all day to see! It did not disappoint! Wow! Stunningly beautiful newish red brick Church. And I mean, Church. Although it is titled the "Culver Chapel," it is big enough to hold the whole Culver student body of 800 students PLUS all the teachers and faculty and military personal who manage the boy's military school.

Not only that, but **everything at Culver is living**. Living in the present, everyday! The Library is living. The Classrooms are living. The barracks and dorms are living. The Mess Hall is living! The gymnasiums are living! The military is living – training boys to be honorable and men.

And, especially the Culver Memorial Chapel is living! All week long, students come to get away and for peace and quiet. Then, every Sunday all year long, 1,200 students and faculty march up to the Culver Memorial Chapel for the past fifty years. We all march up to the chapel in our Battalions and we file in and listen to the Episcopal Minister and his or her sermons. Mostly sermons designed to help us grow as high schoolers. The Culver Minister giving thoughtful sermons, from being a good person, to being considerate, to being a good neighbor, to loving your neighbor as yourself. Who wouldn't want to go there?

We were getting towards the end of the day and some Cadet said, "You look like a new family. Why don't you go down to the other side of Sally-Port and meet the Head of Schools?" We did not even know there was a Head of Schools. So, my mother asked, "Where is the Superintendent and what is his name?" The reply: "The Superintendent's Office is just across the huge hole that you went through in Sally-Port last time. But the Superintendent's Office is on the left side. Our Superintendent is Dean Mars. He will be there."

My mother was pleased with this, all right. We walked down the hill from Memorial Chapel to Sally-Port, arriving at Sally-Port for the third time that day.   Then we realized our rental car was sitting right there, in one of the ten parking spaces for visitors, just as it was when we parked it six hours ago.

We went into the Superintendent's Office. Of course, there was a nice young lady who was the receptionist. My mother said, "We are the family from California and we would love to meet Dean Mars, if he happens to be in." She said, "Oh, we did not know there was to be a family from

California, but welcome. What are your names?" My mother said, Fritz Kuhn, Madeline Kuhn, and our eighth-grade son, John Kuhn, who is looking at the school."

The secretary said, "I will tell Dean Mars that you are here. He is in, so he will be pleased." In we walked to Dean Mars's office and sat down. The plaque on his desk said, Dean John Mars, Spanish Teacher. I thought, that is different, that the Superintendent would be a Spanish Teacher. He ended up being the nicest man we had ever met. So nice and so attentive.

He asked about my SSAT scores and grades. He was pleased with both. He asked if we were serious about my attending Culver. My mother said, "After talking to Colonel Greene, Fritz is ready to immediately enroll John. Plus, after seeing your policy on PDA, I am ready to enroll John, too!" Dean Mars laughed. I loved him. My parents loved him. The students loved him. And the faculty loved him. So, that was just great.

He also said something in our first meeting that I will never forget. It is not what you might expect, at all. He quipped something about: "Oh, you are from California? You always know we have problems with these California boys. They all have trouble with the Four W's" I asked, "What is the California Four W's?"

"Oh," Dean Mars said, "you know, Wine, Women, Waves, and Weather." And he laughed. I, of couse, did not laugh. The first thing in my mind was that, "I sure do not fit that model!" I thought to myself, little does he know, I am from a farm in the hot desert in California, where there is: 1. No Wine – we are up every morning at 5.30 am to go to school or on weekends to go to work. I could not drink wine if I had to. 2. No Women – all our girls split for San Diego the moment they graduate from high school. 3. No Waves – my county in California **doesn't even have water**, let alone waves! 4. No Weather – OMG, I am from the desert in California that is on the news for being the hottest spot in America almost every single day – sometimes even in the winter! He needs to come to El Centro and see what California is really like! ALL OF THAT crossed my mind in less than 30 seconds after his statement. See, Dear Reader, I still have not forgotten that statement. There are some things in life that you just never forget! Right?

On the other hand, looking back at it, maybe Dean Mars was a lot smarter than I. Why? Because I took that statement seriously. I was determined to prove all that nonsense wrong when I arrived at Culver. Did I accomplish my mission in four years at Culver? Let's put it this way: I was only one of five Cadets in my class to graduate without one of those "Tours things!" No tours for John Kuhn in his four years at Culver, which is rare! However, Dean Mars outsmarted me on that one, for sure! Lol!

At the end of the delightful meeting, with Dean Mars, we all went back out to the rental car and talked for ten minutes. I could not have been more excited about Culver! It was everything any high school boy would want in a school, from some of the best academics in the Untied States, to the best leadership development program in the country (called the military), to the nicest gym and, most importantly to me, the most impressive Church I had ever seen in my life. I also told my parents, "If I go here I want to be in the Artillery and drive around those actual Willy's Jeeps with those actual howitzers behind them and fire those cannons. Plus, ride to Culver parades in a duce-and-a-half dark green truck with a big white star on it! And, I love red, so I hope I can make officer one day and wear that totally cool sash that the Cadet officer was wearing all day, but with those beautiful Battery Battalion red sashes, instead!"

My father said, "He cannot get in much trouble here in the middle of the cornfields of Indiana, that is for sure." My mother said, "Cannot possibly have nicer kids than these high schoolers, nor have I seen a nicer facility in my whole life."

Consequently, we all three walked back into Dean Mars office ten minutes later, and my mother said, "I think John has made the decision that he wants to enroll here immediately and attend in the Fall." Dean Mars asked me, "Is that correct?" To which, I said, "Yes, Sir!" And, he laughed and said, "Well, I see that you learn quickly, Mr. Kuhn."

Just for your information, back in the 1970s there were no Admissions Offices at any high schools anywhere in the Untied States. There were no Admissions Offices for many COLLEGES in the 1970s, either, for that matter. For boarding high schools, you took the SSAT, you mailed your grades and recommendations, and you visited the school, if you wanted to, unannounced, just like we did with Culver. I do not believe Culver even had an Admission's Office as late as the mid-1980s. Culver was always on the cutting edge, taking high school women a full decade before most of the famous New England Boarding schools took any women applicants at all. For Culver to have women when I visited in 1976 was well ahead of the curve! Culver also did not get rid of the military during the Vietnam War, which most military high schools did, for lack of students. Thus, keeping its military for all the boys, making all the students (including girls), attend Church, right up until this day. That is impressive. And makes parents want to send their children there.

Now that Dean Mars got confirmation that I wanted to attend in the Fall, and because there was no admissions office, he simply said, "Well then, you are in." Just like that, I was in! We filled out some paperwork for the next 20 minutes, and I was in. Very happy day for me and my parents!

Culver, here we come!

CHAPTER 30

MY FIRST CROSS-COUNTRY FLIGHT
BY MYSELF

All my prior airplane flights were with my parents. As you know, as a farmer, I was driving a tractor around the farm by myself starting about age 10. And, I was driving my baler jeep at approximately age 11, including on the paved roads and highways around Seeley. Finally, I was driving a Ford F-150 pickup truck everywhere, including to my home in El Centro, around age 12. But, I certainly was not flying in an airplane anywhere without my parents with me. That ended on my first trip as a freshman to high school to Culver Military Academy.

First, I got on a little commercial propeller airplane from El Centro to Los Angeles International Airport – even then called LAX. My parents dopped me off at the tiny El Centro airport with the biggest Sears foot-locker suitcases you ever saw. I got on the "Puddle-Jumper," as my father called it, to LAX. Again, Dear Reader, we did not have airport gates at the airports in those days. You checked into the flight at a desk in the airport, and you received a ticket to go to the next city, in this case, Los Angeles. You paid for the ticket with cash – no credit cards in those days! Then, the desk attendant hand-wrote the airplane ticket for you! And, you took the hand-written ticket with you on the airplane. The propeller airplane would show up on time, and however many of you were going on that flight, went right out to the taxiway, and climbed up the metal ladder, that was part of the airplane, and got in. They closed the metal ladder and you found your seat, and you taxied to the runway and you took off. Just like that.

Then, at the biggest airport on the West Coast, Los Angeles International Airport, you landed, taxied over to a side airplane parking area and they lowered the metal ladder door all the way to the ground and you climbed off the flight to the pavement. Five minutes later, a big bus would pick you up and drive you to the terminal to walk to the next gate. At LAX, biggest airport on the West Coast, of all places!

That is what I did. Without my parents anywhere to be found. Then, I walked though the Terminal to the TWA gate that was my next flight to Chicago O'Hare Airport. That was a very long flight, so that was a HUGE airplane. In fact, it was a Boeing 747 from LAX to Chicago O'Hare, because it was such a popular flight and everyone in the United States wanted to go to the 3 big cities: Los Angeles, Chicago, and New York. Therefore, that was a mammoth airplane – one that would fly regularly from Los Angeles all the way to London. And TWA was a huge airline. Very famous, with gigantic airplanes, like mine, on that trip.

One thing that I did not expect at all happened when I got to my TWA gate to fly the giant airplane to Chicago: Low and behold, several high school students who were also going to Culver on that exact same flight from Los Angeles, were waiting at the gate, too. How did I know? I did not know. But, I made an educated guess because the high school students did not have their parents with them, either!

This is when I was fortunate that Culver had already started taking girls in the Culver Girls Academy! Why? Because two of the prettiest girls I had ever seen were getting on the flight with me! It turns out they were the "Tahse girls." The short-haired blond, older one, Cindy Tahse, was going back to Culver for her Junior year. The younger, long blond hair one, was starting as a Freshman, just like me! And her name was Jackie Tahse. Just to set the record straight, I was an extremely shy, afraid of all girls, farm boy from El Centro, California. Remember, no Wine, Women, Waves, nor Weather for me. I could not even talk to Debbie Enis, and I knew her well, let alone these beautiful, blond, LA chicks! They were so beautiful that I could not possibly talk to them. And I didn't.

God does help me, despite myself, from time to time, and this time God stepped right in. How? There were 325 seats on that Boeing 747 so you know there is only a 1% chance that I am assigned to a seat next to one of them. Low and behold, my seat assignment is exactly next to the older one, Cindy Tahse, and I get to sit next to her on the whole four-hour flight to Chicago. That is exactly what happened. Yay!

Do you think I took advantage of that? Of course not! No matter how hard you try, you cannot take the shyness out of boys around girls they think are pretty. On the other hand, I did not blow my opportunity either. I chatted with Cindy Tahse the whole flight to Chicago and she was the NICEST, prettiest girl I ever met.   Boy, I was impressed. She was cool as a cucumber and just the coolest thing I had ever seen! She was even nice to the incoming Freshman, which is pretty cool!

Believe it or not, the thing I remember the most from my first flight by myself across the Untied States, was not even chatting with Cindy. It was the plug in headphones that TWA had that plugged right into your ears and, more importantly, you could then listen to the funniest comedian on the plant earth, describe how the bus drivers in New York City are paid to make sure that you ALWAWYS fall on the bus when you board the bus, by accelerating at the exact worst moment for every bus passenger. I laughed so hard at that, that I was literally crying. Cindy Tahse probably thought, what on earth could this boy think is so funny that he is crying. Crazy boys! If she thought that, she did not let on. But, I know that in my heart, the real problem for ALL boys is that we are, in fact, crazy stupid when we are around a girl we believe is pretty. Thus, "stupid boy," is right!

By the way, not surprisingly in the end, Cindy and Jackie Tahse, turned out to be exactly the Californians that Dean Mars was talking about with the Four W's! In fact, they embodied all four W's: First, they were fortunate enough to live ON THE BEACH in Huntington Beach, South LA, and they could walk barefoot out of their doors into the actual Waves of the Pacific Ocean! Second, they were, indeed, Women, so that is the embodiment of that claim! Third, Los Angeles does have the second-best Weather in the United States – bingo on that one! But, Number Four, Wine: They were not into Wine, at least not during high school, or their father would have grounded them. So, Dean Mars was 3 for 4 on the Tahse girls! Too bad **it took me 3 of 4 full years to get even one of them interested in me!** Good news for me to come on that one, though! As they used to say on TV: Stay Tuned!

But, they were also fortunate enough to have the nicest parents you could possibly have in California. Thus, to keep them wholesome and nice and considerate, their father sent them to Culver Girls Academy! It worked. They are still the nicest young ladies on the planet earth. They certainly are not pretentious

Californians, which was my mother's only concern about living in California from her native Seattle! My mother also thought they were the nicest girls on the plant earth!

We land at Chicago O'Hare Airport and we get off the airplane. You probably do not know this, Dear Reader, unless you are over the age of 50 right now, then you do know this: Before the World Trade Center Bombing by the Muslims in 2001, in no airport in the United States did you ever have to go though "Security." Before 9/11/2001, there was no security at any airport in the United States. Scouts honor: I am telling the truth. We all flew anywhere in the world, for that matter, without any security. If you were flying to England or Switzerland, you would have to go thru Passport Contril in every county you flew to, including flying back into the USA at LAX or JFK. But, no security whatsoever. None. Anywhere.

That changed in one day. The day of the World Trade Center Bombing by the Muslims in the United States, on September 11, 2001, all the governments of Europe and the United States, overnight, put in Security for every single flight in the world, from that day forward. No radar scanning machines in any airport before that. You might get shot and killed by an Airport Police Man, if you were particularly bad, before 9/11/01, but that was rare. You almost never saw that. And there were no Security checkpoints, anywhere in the USA.

Why do I tell you that? Because, do you realize, that means that anybody in the world could go up to your gate and wait for you as you came off the airplane. They did not even have to have a reason, nor did they have to tell anybody.

What that means is that, Schools like Culver, would have their teachers or faculty come to every single gate at O'Hare Airport and wait for that flight's students until they came off the airplane.

That is exactly what Culver did for the Tahse girls and me when we arrived at Chicago O'Hare. Then the faculty would take you to the Culver bus, where all the incoming Culver students on any airplane would congregate and wait to be taken to Culver itself. The faculty would leave you at the Culver bus and then go into the city of Chicago for an evening of fun. So, that worked out for both sides.

This time the Culver faculty member came all the way into our TWA gate from Los Angeles and got the Tahse girls and me and took us to the Culver bus, parked somewhere at O'Hare Airport.

On the bus we got, with all our remarkably similar stupendous Sears footlockers! This was my first time ever, so I watched with glee out of the window, seeing every inch of the City of Chicago that I could see our of my big clear bus window – which turned out to be way more of Chicago than I expected because the Interstate Freeway goes right through the heart of Chicago, from O'Hare to Culver! So cool!

We could see from the big Culver bus windows, on every trip, in order, in Chicago: The Subway tracks first, the huge Morton Salt factory second, the HUGE Sears Tower third (and for half an hour you could see the Sears tower!), the Big Greek Orthodox Church fourth, the Elevated train tracks going in and out of the Chicago Loop fifth, the big railroad yards sixth.

Then, you hit the South Side of Chicago, and you knew you were on the South Side because you would ALWAYS see White Sox Comisky Park. After that you would leave the city and see endless south side suburbs. For 50 miles. Then, out of nowhere, the biggest mining pit in the history of man – we always thought that was cool! After the mining pit, you immediately left Chicago and hit the Illinois-Indiana border! When you are young, you are amazed how close Chicago truly is to Indiana. Gary, Indiana, with all of its steel mills, in those days! After Gary, nothing. Done with civilization. Corn Fields everywhere. EVERYWHERE, corn fields! As far as you can see! Then, the bus turns off the Interstate onto the smallest country road you have seen in your whole life! So small that in the Winter, with all the snow, you cannot take that road because the bridge crossing the railroad tracks right by the interstate cannot handle the weight of a big bus. But, in August, you definitely take the tiniest road on the planet, 40 miles down to Culver, Indiana.

Did I mention corn fields? Yes, 40 miles more of corn fields. But, now they are right outside the bus – not way over from the Interstate. You can practically touch the cornfields from the bus window they are so close.

Only two memorable items remaining that every Culver student remembers passing on the bus coming South to Culver: First, the massive Union Pacific Railroad Tracks that cross the USA from Los Angeles to New York. Right there we cross them on the tiniest asphalt road in the world in the tiniest town in the world in Indiana. The town is so small that it is just 2 houses on each side of the tracks. And the land is so flat that the asphalt road does not even climb up over the tracks. You just have a railroad gate on either side of the road!

Second item all Culver students remember from that drive is the stop sign where the town of Culver is. If you put this in perspective, the Town of Culver is HUGE compared to everything around it for 40 miles.

Then, Culver Academies itself, which is truly, heaven on earth. Which you will not find **out for the next 1000000000 chapters**!

Thank you for riding with me from El Centro Community Airport to LAX, then on TWA with the Tahse girls to Chicago

O'Hare, then by Culver bus from Chicago, Illinois, to Culver, Indiana, Dear Reader! I enjoyed taking you! Next Chapter we go to the QM and get every single piece of the Culver Uniform that is still required to this day!

CHAPTER 31

THE CULVER UNIFORM – OLD MAN'S JACKETS AND HANDIWIPES!

There did not used to be the Logansport Gate Welcome Ceremony on Arrival Day for new students before Head of Schools John Buxton created that ingenious Culver introduction for new Culverites in the 1990s. Nothing like that when I arrived in August 1976.

However, getting that Culver Uniform on Day One was always soooooo cool, for every Culver student, male or female! I arrived at Culver Academies the night before on the Culver Bus from O'Hare Airport (as you know from the prior chapter!), with my Sears Footlockers in hand. Got to my Battery A Barracks at 9:00 pm and unpacked my footlockers. Before I had even been there 2 hours, I had my first Culver "Orderly Barked Command," which turns out to come from the Commandant's Office. The first command I ever received at Culver was, "You will wake up at 6:00 am tomorrow, dress in comfortable clothes and report to the Uniform Department at exactly 8:00 am to get your uniform." Not get fitted for your uniform. Get your uniform. I had been waiting for my Culver Uniform since I visited Culver in March as a prospective student and fell in love with the Culver uniform.

My high school freshman roommate was Juan Funes from Mexico City and we realized the whole Battery A was going to do the same thing at the same time. We did consume a respectable breakfast in the Mess Hall the following morning and headed over to the Uniform Department for our new Culver Uniforms at precisely 8:00 am. There were only Battery A new students there, so that was nice. **But, you know that you are already at an exceedingly different type of school when there is a WHOLE Uniform Department, and that building is the second biggest on the campus!** The Uniform Department is red-brick Building, of course!

It took me five full hours to obtain the Culver Uniform. Five full hours to proceed with trying on every part of the uniform and purchase the exact same uniform that 650 high school cadets wear every year at Culver.

This is the exact same uniform that 650 cadets have been wearing for over 50 years since then: 2 pairs of blue wool long pants with dark blue stripes, 2 pairs of blue long sleeve shirts, 2 pairs of light blue short sleeve shirts, 2 solid dark blue cotton ties, 2 sets of dark blue cotton sock and 2 sets of dark blue wool socks, one pair of black leather shoes (that you better spit-shine so well that you can see your face in it!), one beautiful blue dress jacket, specifically made for Culver, so that you can look handsome in your dress uniform, especially for Church and Parades.

You receive one pair of your actual company's brass, which is different for every unit (company) but is almost identical and must be shined incessantly by every new Cadet until they finally pass his own Boards and gets new Artillery Brass with your CB's added to the top, making you, officially, an "Old Man." Everyone wants to be an Old Man and not a Plebe. You can go through Boards (similar to the Inquisition – only not any physical hazing) anytime you feel that you are ready, and if you pass you immediately go to the Uniform Department and get your "CBs" added to your brass. Great day for a Culver Cadet! I received my CB's on the first try and raced down to the Uniform Department and got my new brass. So cool to be an "Old Man" and not a Plebe!

Even though the Culver uniform is blue upon blue upon blue, there are, indeed, so many shades of blue that the uniform stands out more than you would think. On the other hand, because the uniform is blue upon blue upon blue, the Cadet Officer full color wool sashes are beautiful and dramatic, not to mention every Battalion has their own full colors: Green for Band, Blue for Infantry, Red for Artillery, and Yellow for Black Horse Troup.

The other reason that we love our dark blue Dress Jackets is they show off our little military merit badges, all with little colors, such as, Expert Marksman, or Passed Federal JROTC inspection that year, very important annually to Culver. When I was there we had never failed to keep our JROTC status, and I am proud to say, that thanks to my best Culver roommate, Mark Holden, covering for me Senior year when I was not ready and he made sure we passed. My Culver hat is off to you, Mark, to this day!

There was another whole section to the Uniform Department that was not dedicated to the Military Dress Uniform, but rather, to the casual Miliary Jackets that we Cadets loved the most: That would be the "Old Man Jacket" which was even cooler than the Dress Uniform. Why? Because it was light weight, casual, easy to throw on anytime, AND most importantly, it had four areas on the front of you, and if you managed to fill in all 4 areas of your casual Culver jacket, you were beyond cool. And, it is all color. Here is what makes your Culver Old Man Jacket beyond compare: The top half, no matter what company or battalion you were in, was the same: Left shoulder was your Class year and your military rank: In my case: 80 (for Class of 1980) AND Officer three stripes plus a Christian Cross for Regimental Aide to the Chaplain. We were always proud of our military rank because we worked the whole entire prior for our exact rank the following year.

The rest of the old man jacket is where we would get the color: Your last name in big black print on your left front and your exact Miliary Company on your left front: Culver Battery A in my Case. We love all this because we are loyal to our Class and we are loyal to our Unit! Once you passed your Boards and became an old man you immediately got your Color Company logo, inn the right front, which meant you worked hard and you belonged at Culver Military Academy. Mine was a bright red "A" (for Battery A). Lastly, if you were beyond cool, you could also get a JV letter, on the fourth empty quadrant of your Old Man jacket, if you earned one, on your right front, bottom half.

The Culver Girls Academy Uniforms were pretty cool, too! Every boys favorite outfit that all the girls got, though, was the "Handiwipe Dress!" Every Cadet fell head over heals for the girls in their "Handiwipes," which only came out at the beginning of the school year and back again in the Spring. The rest of the year was too cold for the "Handiwipe." Why was every boys favorite the "Handiwipe?" Three reasons, in order: First, every girl who came to Culver got fitted for one at the Uniform Shop and they fit every girl PERFECTLY! So, if they wore their "Handiwipe Dress" they would look unbelievably pretty reaching for anything or just walking around. Goddess in motion.

Second, the skirt on the "Handiwipe Dress" was considerably shorter than most other skirts, so they showed off EVERY girls' legs to perfection.

Third, they were seersucker cotton dresses (lightweight cotton known for its alternating smooth and puckered stripes), but, because the alternating stripes were so finely drawn, they looked, at a distance, as one color – in other words, green, or red, or yellow, or blue. But, if you looked up closely, the looked like "Handiwipes," from the grocery store. Most importantly, to us boys were that they were fun, lightweight, and sexy. Plus, you knew Spring was coming when the "Handiwipes" came back out in the girls' school.

Next part of the Culver Girls Academy outfit from the Uniform Department every year was the 2 Scottish blue, green, and white Campbell Dress Tartan wool skirts every Coed received, to this day. Couple that with the light blue wide open summer girl's shirt, and our have another vision entirely beautiful. Even the much more conservative white cotton dress shirts looked beautiful with those Scottish plaid wool skirts. Oh my.

Did I mention jackets? The boys received full length navy blue rain jackets that were perfect in the rain and dark black winter coats for when it was below frezzing – which was at least 20 times every winter.

Again, though, the Coeds had us beat. When they went the first day as a new student to the Uniform Department, they got these stunningly beautiful wool camel's hair long trim, super-warm coats. So nice. So beautiful!

There is one item we all, men and women, that was the same: the heavy wool Varsity Sweater, that you had to earn by winning a Varsity Letter in some Varsity sport. The Culver Varsity sweaters were heavyweight, well made, and are stunning. Couple that with the fact they come in two distinct colors: Bright white (with Maroon lettering) or Bright solid Marron (with white lettering). Last, but not least, every sport you earned a Varsity Letter in would have the coolest patch in that area of the C (for Culver) that was the sport was representing: Tennis racket for tennis, Megaphone for Cheerleading, Hockey stick for hockey, Mercury's winged foot for Track, even a Sabre for the Fencing Varsity letter! Beyond cool. So, Culver to do it all just right! Thank you, very much, Culver Uniform Department!

In 1976, when I arrived at Culver, the Culver Girls Academy was only five years old. But, even then, we could see that Culver was not going to be sexist. The girls had the same LAST NAME ONLY name tags we had. Right from the start. Have to love that about Culver, because it made us Cadets know they would be treated the same, for better or for worse, as we were, just by the last names only, nametags.

And, now, Dear Reader, a note about the most important item on the Culver uniform, for the past 130 years, and counting. Your last name, only.

Name tags. Most important item that you will have at Culver for the next four years. For 85 straight years, same exact nametag. Black name tag with White lettering and your last name only. **For the next four years at Culver, you will be your last name only.**

Kuhn, do this. Kuhn, do that. Kuhn, how did you miss that? Kuhn, do you just not care? Kuhn, what the heck is wrong with you? Kuhn, are you just plain stupid, or just deaf? Kuhn, how did that happen? Please tell us all, KUHN! Kuhn, if you are sick you belong in the infirmary. Kuhn, it is your turn to clean the toilets. Kuhn, it is your turn tomorrow morning as Orderly to give the Dress of the Day! Kuhn, why is that not folded properly? Kuhn, I am throwing everything out of your wardrobe since you have ONE ITEM misfolded. Kuhn, if I had to tell you once, I've had to tell you a thousand times. Kuhn, why are you so damn stupid?

Kuhn, where is your rifle? Kuhn, why did you not clean your rifle? Kuhn, why is your Piece (Rifle) not secure? Kuhn, why is piece not by at attention? Kuhn, why are you not at attention, and at Parade Rest? Kuhn, everyone else seems to have gotten the message! Kuhn, get your butt to Ranks. Kuhn, take your damn

Piece (Rifle) to Ranks! Kuhn, what did you forget this lovely day? KUUUUHHHHHHHNNNN, WHAT IS IT YOU WANT TO HEAR?

Kuhn, if you do not shine that brass properly, I am going to tell your damn Squad Leader! Kuhn, if you do not shine that brass properly, I am going to tell your damn Platoon Leader! Kuhn, if you do not shine that brass properly, I am going to tell your damn Company Commander, Tippy, and he's sure not going to like that! Kuhn, if you do not shine that brass properly, I am going to tell your damn Counsellor, Runkle, and he is so sick and tired of you and your nonsense! Kuhn, for the millionth time, if you do not shine that brass properly, I am going to tell the damn Commandant, that is how bad this has gotten!

Dear Reader, if you have not figured this out yet, at Culver you better not loose that rifle, and you better clean that rifle, and for gosh's sakes, you better shine that damn brass on your lapel or you will be in your Counsellor's Office explaining yourself.

There is a second half of every Culver day that is also truly important because you are back at Barracks after Athletics. Athletics is sports, and is from 2:00 pm to 4:00 pm every day, when you can exercise and compete in intramurals, OR you can join a Varsity team each quarter, from Fencing – yes Fencing! – to Baseball, and about any other sport you want to play. But, everyone's favorite sport is Hockey, that is for sure! After Sport, the whole of Culver goes to dinner, but this time nobody marches in, because they are coming randomly from all various sporting practices all over campus that you participate in, from the tennis courts to the Horse Riding (Equestrian) Arena.

But, after Athletics and dinner, then the most important part of every day comes along, because Culver, brilliantly, requires all 800 students to study from 7:30 pm to 9:30 pm. And, this brings a whole new language and a whole new set of Kuhn Commands:

241

Kuhn, what are you going to study tonight? Kuhn, where are your books? How the hell do you think you are going to study without books? Kuhn, did it occur to you that you need to be in your damn seat at 7:30 when you were down at Holden's room 5 minutes ago? Kuhn, why is your head down on your desk? Kuhn, you know that no one at Culver ever gets tired until 10:00 pm. Kuhn, why are you up before 9:30? Kuhn, where exactly do you think you're going? Kuhn, did you ask permission? Kuhn, did you GET permission?

Kuhn, how many times do I have to tell you that you are not allowed on your bed during CQ (for you uninitiated in book reader land, CQ stands for Closed Quarters). What is Closed Quarters? Look dummy, that is the 2 hours from 7:30 to 9:30 every Sunday through Thursday night that every Culver dorm and barrack is Closed when every Culver student is studying. What if they do not have anything left to study? Then you had better pretend to study or it is not going to go well. And if you say that you are done, and then you fail your math quiz tomorrow, we are going to ask you, Kuhn, all kinds of questions on why you said you had nothing left to study, because clearly that was a lie!

After 9:30 pm when Closed Quarters (studying) are over and before 10:00 pm sharp, which is Taps, is the happiest one-half hour in every Culver student's day because that it the half hour that you can do anything you want and let off steam. It also has the best name at Culver for the past 130 years that you can imagine! That exact one-half hour is called "Tattoo" And gosh knows we love Tattoo!! If you are an upperclassman, this is when you can go see your girlfriend or boyfriend. If you are an underclassman, you can play your stereo as loudly as possible and nobody will care. Most importantly, at exactly 9:30 pm, the whole campus can start talking again!!! And, boy do they ever! Everyone talks from 9:30 pm to 10:00 pm

But, at 10:00 pm it is over. Done. Better not say another word because that is TAPS. Taps is the end of every Culver day, seven days a week, and at Taps you belong in your bed in your pajamas or whatever you wear to bed. I loved my peejays because I could get up in the middle of the night and safely go down to the bathroom. The other reason I loved my peejays is that, after first year, you can start sneaking into your buddies' rooms after Taps for an hour or so and talk, and talk, and talk, and solve the problems of the world. Kind of hard to do that totally naked. So, I loved my peejays!

Because we are at Culver, however, even Tattoo does not end the Kuhn nametag and only last name jargon, whatsoever. Here you go again: Kuhn, where are your peejays – you know you are not allowed out after CQ and before Taps naked in the Hall!!!! Kuhn, peejays, NOW! Kuhn, where do you think you are going 5 minutes before Taps? Kuhn, you know you cannot go up to Holden's room and get back in time for Taps! Kuhn, take that over to Hemming's room. Kuhn, shine your damn brass! Kuhn, take that over to Arquilla's room! Kuhn, take that over to Runkle's Office. KUHN, for God's sake, SHUT UP!

By the way, there are no swear words by the faculty. Not once in four years did I hear one faculty member swear. The Cadets? Yes. All day long. Incessant swear words – we are a MILITARY School, just in case you forgot! But, the faculty never swears.

And, the Coeds never swear – at least not in classes or athletics or anywhere public, I never heard the Coeds swear. We boys tried to be on our best behavior around the Coeds, so we did shape up around them. And, we would not swear in class, either. I think you got DEMERITS for using one swear word in class. No demerits for me. They would eventually lead to those dreaded, TOURS! Lol!

The one reprieve we ALWAYS had from the Military and the discipline was the classroom and the teachers. So, rather quickly, the only place at Culver you truly have a mental reprieve is in the Classrooms and with the teachers. That was first half of every day, Monday through Friday, so that is where every Culver student is, surprisingly, their happiest! In class. In that safe mental environment, from the rest of the Culver world.

The second safe place from the Military system and the Girl's Prefect Leadership system, was in the library every night, studying. Therefore, we all loved to go to the library to study. It was a definite mental break from everything else. Or, looking at the girls in their "Handiwipe" Dresses! That was also a mental break from everything.

CHAPTER 32

PLEBE SYSTEM – IT WAS THE BEST OF TIMES, IT WAS THE WORST OF TIMES!

(AND Murphy's law Is ALWAYS More Reliable than the Weather!)

"I Sir, Am Sir, A Plebe, Sir, and I am Lower than S___, Sir!" That is the Plebe Creed. I memorized it exactly 49 years ago. I can recall it with ease, even though I have not said it to anyone for over a decade, now. We all memorize that our first week of our first year of Culver, which is our Plebe year. Even if your first year at Culver is your Senior year in high school, you are a Plebe, just like everyone else.

I have now written, Dear Reader, 33 pages on Culver, and I have not yet mentioned the Plebe System. That is because I never heard of it until my second day of Culver, in August 1976, when I was sat down on the Battery A first floor Vestibule Steps. It turns out most of the new students knew all about this "Plebe System." But, not this farm boy from California. Until this very moment, second day at Culver, 8:00 am, after I have spent the prior first day at the Culver Uniform Department, getting my awesome Culver Uniform.

God always has a plan. Apparently, it was FANTASTIC that I did not know one single thing about the "Plebe System." Why? For three reasons: First, I did not spend six months at home worrying about the Plebe system – as it turns out all my new first year friends on the steps did – because I did not even know about it!!!

Second, because I had never even heard about it, when the Battery A Sophomore spent 2 full hours hollering at us about it, I was completely open-minded to what he was saying, again, because I have never even heard of the "Plebe System" at Culver. Third, I did not know at all, but coming from the farm, I was way, way, waaaaayyyyyy more ready for the Plebe System than I could have ever imagined.

Here is how the Plebe System went down for John Kuhn on the first-floor stairs in the middle of Battery A Barracks on the second day of school:

Old Man: "Okay boys, you are now going to be introduced to the Plebe System by me. Your whole first year, until February, or much later if you just are dumb, you will now have to immediately do three things, in this order:

"Cadet Kinsey, get down here and sit in this chair. You are going to get the exact same haircut that every single Plebe at this institution has gotten for the past 50 years, and counting." The Culver barber is standing there and immediately, in exactly 10 swoops of the barber's hair shaver, cuts Kinsey's hair to as short over the ears as you can get it (called "white walls") and the rest of the haircut is fairly short all over the top, but still looks, to me, like you have a decent amount of hair on top, to still look like a boy's haircut, on the top, in the real world. But, it is short and all the new Plebes next to me are aghast.

I am watching this for five minutes and immediately think, "Wow, this GREAT!!! I finally get to grow my hair out." Mind you, no other freshman boy is thinking this. But, farmer John Kuhn, is! Why? Because my serious farmer father had me, all the way through eighth grade in Seeley Elementary School, and every day on the farm, in a BUTCH style haircut. What is a "Butch Style

Haircut?" Oh, that is where every single hair on your head is exactly ½ inch long, and no more.

How does one get a Butch Hair Cut? Oh, your father takes you to his El Centro barber shop every 2 weeks and says, "Carl, give these boys the regular." Which means, every two weeks, like clockwork, Jim and I are back at Carl's Barbershop getting our hair back to ½ inch all over, so it does not get too long and unruly and stuck in the spinning grinder on the farm.

I watch Kinsey's haircut and immediate think, "Wow, I have been waiting years to be able to grow my hair out past ½ inch, to RELATIVELY normal boys' haircut! I get to grow my hair out in Military School! Yay!" And, I did! Lol!

Old Man: "From this moment forward, you are all going to wake up at exactly 6:00 am, when the Culver buzzer goes off in the whole school, and you will immediately get up and start getting dressed and come out for Ranks (Formation) at exactly 6:30 pm, completely and properly dressed for the day, seven days a week here at Culver!"

John Kuhn: In my mind: "Oh My Gosh, this is the best thing that has ever happened to me!! I finally get a legitimate SLEEP-IN for every single day for the next four years of my life" How can that be? Remember, Dear Reader, before I stepped foot on Culver Campus, what time did I get up every single day of my life at my house in El Centro, California? Remember, weekdays I was up at 5:30 every morning to go to school. Weekends were worse. I had to be up at 5:00 every weekend day to go out to the Farm as a farmer. And, remember, what my father said, "John and Jim, the cows and the crops do not take Sunday off, so you boys are not taking Sunday off, either." We were up every single weekend day of the past five years at 5:00 am, heading out to the farm to drive the tractor, work in the shop, or irrigate the fields.

John Kuhn: In my mind: So, I get to sleep in one-half hour, every single weekday at Culver, for the rest of my school year, AND I get to sleep in a full one hour on every weekend her at Culver for the next four years! Hallelujah!

Old Man: "Third, every one of you sitting here is now in the Plebe System and from this moment forward will have to walk on the left side of the hall, hugging the wall, and every time you pass an "Old Man" you will turn towards the Old Man and shout "yes, Sir, What can I do, Sir?"

John Kuhn: In my mind: "Wow, to this day, both of my parents require me to say 'Yes Sir' or "Yes Mam," to them and to anyone else we run into, from our teachers at school, to the restaurants in town. In fact, my mother had Jim and I still doing this, in eighth grade, for every woman who comes into "Grasso's Italian Restaurant" in El Centro, and comes over to our table, and my mother, has me and Jim spring to our feet and say "Hello, Mrs. Butcher." Even if the girl is our age, we must spring up and stand, and stay standing AND attentive until Mrs. Butcher says, "You may sit down, boys." No eating, no talking, nothing until the lady says you may sit down. Fortunately, the seventh and eighth grade girls in our town were quite kind, figured this out in short order, and say, "John and Jim, you may sit. No need to stand on my behalf,"

So, when the Old Man said this about bracing for Officers in the Barrack Halls and saying "Yes Sir, Yes Mam" all the time, I thought, well, this is going to certainly be easy for me!

Old Man: "Fourth, one of you Plebes every single day, according to our posted Battery A schedule of 'Orderly of the Day,' will get up early, dress in the uniform of the day, and be in charge of all announcements for that day, but especially you will announce, at EXACTLY 6:00 am, 30 seconds after the Reveille Cannon is fired over the lake, brace at the head of each Battery A hall and holler: 'Culver Dress of the Day is Dress B and you will be fully dressed for Ranks in 30 minutes and outside.' The rest of you will then dress in exactly the same outfit we all wear that day and present yourself for Ranks. Understood?"

Again, I thought to myself, how great is this that for the next four years, I will know exactly what to wear to breakfast, school, and lunch without even having to think at all?

Moreover, no one will judge me for what I am wearing because we will all be wearing the exact same thing! The whole boys' school will be wearing the same exact clothing. Oh, and I will no longer have to embarrass myself, like at Seeley School, with my mother's "Highwater Jeans" she continued to put me in to save money! Awesome!

Within a month or two I began to realize the Coeds must love this to – not being judged for not being fashionable when every girl was wearing the same thing under the Culver Dress of the Day. Of course, they loved that, too!

Consequently, nobody had a better first month in the Culver Plebe System than yours truly, Cadet Kuhn. A lot of my new freshman friends said, "Doesn't this bother you, at all?" and **I thought to myself, I am getting to: 1. Grow my hair out 2. I have a daily sleep in every day over home. 3. I say the same thing I have been saying to my parents for years. 4. No longer have to think for myself what to wear in the morning to school and wear my dreaded, from my "Highwater Blue Jeans" to school!** This is not bothering me in the least!

From late August 1976 to mid-February 1977, I was in the Culver Plebe System. Most of it was truly not that bad. Most importantly, about a year before I arrived at Culver, Head of Schools Dean Mars got rid of all physical hazing at any military unit at Culver. That was a blessing because the academics were so strong at Culver that we did not need physical hazing at Culver. Moreover, the Vietnam war had just ended so we did not need physical hazing at Culver for it to mirror the physical hazing of "basic training" in the miliary.

Another unique aspect of the Culver military training that made it that we did not need physical hazing was that almost all of the Cadets at Culver were so incredibly smart, that they could successfully have mental hazing and it was just as effective as physical hazing. For example, when we were within two weeks of Christmas vacation, we started having to say exactly (every single Ranks) how many Hours and Minutes AND Seconds until Christmas Vacation.

Here is how that worked: Christmas Vacation begins Friday, December 17, 1976, at 5:00 pm. Okay. You now figure out exactly what time Ranks are this moring, and how many days and minutes and seconds until exact Christmas Vacation start time from the exact minute Ranks started that morning or that lunch. Here you go: Ranks start at 6:30 that moring, and it is Monday, December 6, 1976, at exactly 6:30 am that Ranks commence. Since we know Christmas Vacation starts at 5:00 pm on Friday, December 17, 1976, we need to back up from that time, which you can do on your hand. There exactly 10 (24-hour) days between December 6 and December 17.

From this point forward you need a calculator and we all had calculators from math class. We can multiply 24 hours by 11 days, so we have 11 x 24 = 264 hours. Now we have to add exactly how many more hours there are from December 7, backwards to December 6, official Ranks time, which we know is 6:30 am. The last day of Christmas Vacation ends at 5:00 pm, so we just need to back up from 5:00 pm to 6:30 am our same day, so that will be 5:00 pm our same day – so add 5 hours after lunch and 5.5 hours before lunch, which totals 10.5 hours more AND add that to our 264 hours: 264 hours + 10.5 hours = 274.5 hours left until Christmas Vacation. In this case there happens to be no minutes involved, yet. But, remember, every Plebe must state all facts to the Old Men with a Sir!

So, December 6, 1976, 6:30 am, Ranks will go like this: Old Man: "Kuhn, how many hours are there until Christmas Vacation?" Plebe John Kuhn's answer: "274.5 Hours until Christmas Vacation, Sir!!"

Of course that is not good enough! You now have to figure out the same answer in minutes and seconds and MEMORIZE that too, and spit that out at ranks, with the number changing every Ranks, because the number of days and hours until Christmas Vacation goes down every Ranks that you have! But, here you go for 6:30 am on Monday, December 6, 1976: 274.5 hours until Christmas Vacation is actually 274.5 x 60 minutes = 16,470 minutes until Christmas Vacation. The Old Men are not satisfied with that, either. You also must know how many seconds until Christmas Vacation from that exact Ranks start time: So, 16,470 minutes x 60 seconds = 988,200 seconds until Christmas Vacation.

Thus, Old Man: "Kuhn, how many minutes until Christmas Vacation?" Kuhn reply: "16,470 minutes until Christmas Vacation, SIR!" Next to me in ranks that day happens to be my freshman bestie, Mark Holden of Michigan. So, Old Man: "Holden, how many seconds until Christmas Vacation?" Holden's response, as loud as he can holler: "Sir, 988,200 seconds until Christmas Vacation, Sir!!" Obviously, you have no idea for what question you will be called on because it is ALWAYS random with Old Men! So, you must memorize the different time until Christmas Vacation from every Ranks or be screamed at unmercifully!

251

But some ingenious Cadet came up with idea that we Plebes also had to state how many Wiffy-Giffy's there were until Christmas Vacation. Dear Reader, you do not know what a Wiffy-Giffy is? Well, trust me, I did not either. Not surprisingly, there is a unit of time called a Wiffy-Giffy in the real world. It turns out that a Wiffy-Giffy is, indeed, one-sixtieth of a second. So, you must now do that calculation for every Ranks AND memorize that answer, as well, for every Ranks: 988,200 seconds until Christmas Vacation times 1/60th of a second is 988,200 x 60 Wiffy-Giffys = 59,292,000 Wiffy-Giffys until Christmas Vacation. Old Man: "Plebe Kinsey, how many Wiffy-Giffys are there until Christmas Vacation?" Kinsey: "Sir, there are 59 Million, 292 Thousand, Wiffy-Giffys until Christmas Vacation, Sir!!!" "Well done, Plebe Kinsey, well done" Just for the record, Richard Kinsey was a lot better at math than Mark Holden and myself, so we would often go up to his room before every Christmas Ranks and figure this out with him on his calculator. On the other hand, maybe that is why Mark and I got a whole lot better at math Freshman year at Culver! Just another small benefit to the Plebe System!

Of course, the old men could cheat! They would come to ranks with their cheat sheets they hand wrote with exactly how many hours, minutes, seconds AND Wiffy-Giffy's there were until Christmas Break! But, we Plebes? No cheat sheets for us! We had to memorize that ever-changing number every Ranks. Oh, that reminds me of the biggest song that Fall all over the Culver Campus: That would have been David Bowie's "Changes" We certainly LOVED to sing that song as loudly as possible during that one-half that was "Tattoo" every night at Culver, to blow off steam! Lots of "pressure release singing" by we Cadets every night at Culver before bed and almost always whatever was coming on our Transistor Radios from WLS Radio in Chicago!

Fortunately, the Old Men eventually had fun with the Wiffy-Giffys after about a week! They were not all that strict by Christmas time. The first week, you better know everything – every single number – by heart, right up to Wiffy-Giffys. By the second week they were fine with just minutes and hours until Christmas Vacation. Looking back on this, I believe one of the main purposes of the Plebe System was to get your young mind trained to work efficiently and effectively.   It also kept you focused on pleasing others and not being self-centered. Most kids who graduate from Military High School are definitely not self-centered. And, NONE of my Freshman friends in Battery A were. If you came into Culver with lots of money or self-centered, that would not last more than a week and Old Men would have that knocked out of you. Probably, way more high schoolers in the United States should go to miliary high school. It also builds your self-confidence when an Old Man says, "Way to go, Kinsey."

But, you sure better have your Culver Creed and your Culver Cadet Officers memorized by that November and December, or you would me unmercifully mentally harassed by your Squad Leader or your Platoon Leader or your XO at Ranks! The Company Commanders, on the other hand, really would not bother you. I believe it was because they had so much to do every day for their Units that they did not get caught up in the minutia of the Plebe System.

We spent five full months under the Plebe System I told you above, described by our special Battery A Old Man! But, the Plebe System was a lot more than that! The other one item that I alluded to earlier that was imperative to have working perfectly was your assigned Rifle. Every evening that you were a Cadet, you would pull it off your, that year, assigned Barracks room wall and take it apart and clean it. That way if you needed it in combat, it was working perfectly all the time. Thus, the most important time with a rifle for a Cadet was every evening for 15 minutes, when you handled it. Maybe even practiced maneuvers with it.

Every single evening for a Culver Plebe was also spent shining the three most important things in his life: 1. His one pair of black leather shoes, 2. His pair of two Company brass that he wore on both his lapels on EVERY uniform, and 3. His big Culver Eagle brass from his assigned Culver Dress Cap that we wore habitually with our Dress A for Sunday Church and for Sunday Parade.

The two items that you had to shine *every night* as a Plebe were your black leather dress shoes and your exact pair of your Company Brass. These were worn with every single uniform, so you had to shine them every night.   Remember, Closed Quarters was the 2 hours you had to study every night from 7:30 to 9:30 pm, quietly at your desk in your own room. Thus, every night in your room, either before CQ or after CQ, you also must shine your brass and your shoes.

Once a week you would also have to shine your big Culver Dress Cap Eagle Brass for that weekend's General Inspection and Church and Parde. No time to rest, for those Plebes. Most of us would shine them after Sports and before CQ, as a break from everything else.   And, so that we truly had the one-half hour Tattoo free to do whatever we wanted to blow off steam, before bedtime, sharp at 10:00 pm.

Your Rifle was not as important during the week because you did not really need it until the weekend. However, you absolutely must spend every Saturday morning, all Fall, learning to march with the rifle and present the rifles and turn corners as a solid single unit with your rifles.   All kinds of time training with your rifle every Saturday morning, whether you were in Black Horse Troup, the Artillery, or the Infantry. The only exception was the Band, who always learned to march with their instruments.

Saturday afternoons were invariably spent learning our particular Military specialty. For example, if you were in the Artillery (like I was) you learned how to drive your Jeeps and pull your howitzers behind your Army jeeps. Or, you would train for Sunday's parade by learning how to ride in your Army Duce-and-a-Half's that carried your whole platoon in it around the parade field. Thus, we were not required to carry our rifles in the Parade if we were in the Battery.

Likewise, the Black House Troupers did not have to carry their rifles in the Parade because they were mounted, each of them, on their own horse. So, their officers could carry Sabre's, but nobody in the Troup carried their rifles in the weekly Sunday afternoon parade. Same with the Band. Band never carried their rifles anywhere, because they ALWAYS had to carry their musical instruments.

On the other hand, the poor Infantry Battalion always had to carry their rifles everywhere. Why? Because it is their job to fight with their rifles. Thus, the Infantry Companies took their rifles way more seriously than us Artillery Battery men! I was never envious of the Black Horse Troup either. Can you imagine trying to keep all those horses walking in a straight line in parade with all that commotion? Impossible, I'm sure! They trained every Saturday afternoon and had perfected by November every year. So impressive!

The reason your rifle became so important on weekends is you had to have them inspected by true retired Army personnel every Saturday morning for General Inspection (GI) of our barracks and our rooms. Then, the Cadet officers and the Culver military personnel would inspect every Cadets firearm and make sure it was working properly. All 650 of us in the Culver Miliary Boys school would also have our rooms inspected by someone, whether Old Men and officers, or Culver Military Personnel.

Preparing for GIs took about four hours every Friday night. So, the only night you really had off during the Fall semester was Saturday night!! And gosh knows we liked our Saturday nights. The Spring semester was considerably more lenient, because we had all learned how to work together as a Unit and we could enjoy a lot more Friday nights with our friends or girlfriends! Much more time to listen to Rock'n'Roll records in the Spring, too!

Murphy's law is alive and well at Culver. What is Murphy's law? You know. That is the law that says "whatever can go wrong always will go wrong." The most popular derivation of that in the United States is that "whatever could be the worst possible situation for me is, for certain, what will happen." Did that apply to my Freshman year at Culver? Of course it did.

Remember I said that I lived in the very hottest place in the United States, which is El Centro, California, and is in fact, for five days every year the hottest place in the United States. Now, is it a good idea for a young man who grew up in the low desert every day of his life, at age 13 to move to one of the very coldest places in the whole United States, the cornfields on Indiana, just outside of the freezing cold City of Chicago? NO! That is a terrible idea! I decided that luck was with me a little bit because Chicago – and the whole Midwest in general – had one of the warmest five years on record from 1970 to 1975, so I should be okay in that Chicagoland area.

God had other plans. As a farmer and as a person who pays attention to the truth about what happens, I have found that farming – and everything else related to the weather, even in Europe – is based on God's Natural Cycle. And, if you pay attention, no matter where you are, from the United States to Europe, that God's Natural Cycle is weather that is really good for 5 years, and then weather that is really bad for 5 years. We farmers notice these things. But, I was too young at age 13 and going off to Indiana for school to have truly figured out that God's weather cycle is five good years (or dry years) and five bad years (or wet years). This is especially true in Califroina and has been since the Colorado River Compact was formed exactly 100 years ago. Five wet, rainy, snowy years in Calfiorian; then, five extremely dry with no snow or rain for five years in Califoria. Look it up. It is like clockwork.

Well, I am about to find out that the Midwest is no different at all. Even Chicago is no different. Because everyone in Chicago and the Midwest knew that the five years of 1970 to 1975 was almost no snow and fairly warm winters, everyone was talking about how that was the "new normal." Being only 13 years old – and from another part of the USA entirely – of course I believed everyone.

God's Natural Law has been around in full force in the United States since John Locke wrote about it in England and the United States in the early 1700s. All of Locke's treatises on the truthfulness of Natural Law and God's purpose for man, and then United States Founder Thomas Jefferson learned all of the principals and the United States was perfectly built on John Locke's God's Natural Law, straight into the United States Declaration of Independence in 1776 against King George and England, who lost sight of their own brilliant thinkers at the time, namely John Locke in the early 1700's, which Thomas Jefferson draws directly from in writing the Declaration of Independence draws straight from.

250 years later in the United States of America, God's Natural Weather Law of 5 rainy and snowy years, followed by 5 years of drought and little cold, is still very much in effect. For example, let us go to John Kuhn, 13-year-old boy, arriving for Freshman year in August 1976 at Culver Military Academy and hearing that the

freezing cold that Chicago and Lake Michigan are known for are over and don't worry about it. Remember, I have not figured out God's law of five dry years followed by five wet years, nor have I read John Locke, or Henry David Thoreau, **Walden Pond**, for that matter, which is straight up God's Natural Law! I had not even heard of Murphy's law at age 13 and you know Murphy's law is far more accurate and reliable than God's Law! That is intended to be funny and make sure you are paying attention and laugh!

Based upon everything that everyone was saying, we knew that the Winter of 1977 would be mild and nice, just like the last five winters in Chicago and the Midwest. Well, you know what God's Natrual Law has to say about what everyone is saying? God's Natural Law says look at the facts for the area for the past 100 years. Look at God's Five Year Weatther cycle for the past ten years, as well. AND if you are not sure, you know that you can count on Murphy's law to be a much better predictor for your situation that what other people are saying! Lol!

Anyway, God's Chicago and God's Indiana that is close to Lake Michigan (like Culver is) are going to deviate to the norm. And, the norm in Chicago and the norm aloung Lake Michigan is that you will, for certain, have miserable, MISERABLE COLD in Chicago and Northern Indiana. Couple that with God's five year weather Cycles and you just lucking out with way above normal temperature winters in Chicago, and way less snow than normal in Chicago, the years 1970 to 1975, and you better batten down the hatches, because HERE comes five years of MISERABLE COLD and five years of Lake Effect Snow.

And, don't forget, if you are just not sure, take into account Murphy's law, which you know is always reliable (because it is, if fact always reliable). What is the United States version of Murphy's law, that I told you earlier? **Murphy's law is "whatever**

could be the worst possible situation for me is, for certain, what will happen."

What does that mean in my situation as a brand new 13-year-old Plebe in boarding high school in Indiana from the hottest desert city in the United States? Does it mean that I am going to be spared the worst possible weather and have the beautiful weather of the past five years? OR, does it mean that I will, somehow manage to show up in the cornfields in Indiana for the absolute coldest, bitterest, worstest, lowest wind chill in history of the State of Indiana when I get out to Ranks at 6:30 every morning at Main Barracks in Culver, directly across from lovey, frozen over, Lake Maxinkuckee, as a Freshman Plebe from California? Dear Reader, you may answer that question for me, because God certainly did with His normal sense of humor!

If it is going to be the worst case scenario, as a human being – or as a Plebe – you will always take lots of snow and not so much bitter cold. Why? Three reasons: First, bitter blowing cold is the hardest for the human body to take over lots of snow, which invariably comes with slightly warmer temperatures. Second, bitter cold usually does not come with much snow and lots of snow can at least be pretty. Third, if you are standing in ranks, everything is pretty all covered in snow, but brutal blowing cold will frost bite your ears and make them hurt so bad that you cannot stand it!

So, what does Murphy's law say happened in Culver, Indiana, the months of January and February 1976? Well, of course, we Plebes (and Old Men, for that matter) were subjected to the bitterest, coldest winter in the whole recorded history of Northern Indiana! In fact, standing out there in Ranks, the whole Culver Artillery Battalion had the most below-negative-40-degree days in the history of Northern Indiana, for 6:30 am AND 12-noon Ranks.

We had a whopping 22 days of negative 40 Wind Chill Factor! 22 days of NEGATIVE 40 Windchill and **Negative 30 degrees bitter cold**. 22 days of that miserable, bitter, biting, blasphemous cold!!! 40 minutes of that each Ranks that winter! Of my Gosh – yes I will not call on his name. God knows. We don't know. Just like God knew that 2 years later we would have the Blizzard of 1979, that came with the most Snow in Chicago history (same five-year cycle of 1976 to 1980 with the coldest, snowest winters in Midwest USA history!)

Dear Reader, what did I tell you about nice five-year weather cycles, followed by miserable five year miserable weather cycles, all over this World. I Tell It Like It Is! God's plan. Not mine. However, as your day turns blue every morning, **wherever you live in this world**, you can thank God for making it so reliable! Oh, and all of us farmers all over the world, from China to Australia to Japan, know that we can count on God's Natural World, because we truly can. Which is also helpful for you Northern Tourists, because you know that Spain will be nice and warm every single Summer so you can go there and thaw out from Berlin and London every Summer!!

What did Culver Academies do about it? They had committee meetings and decided that NEXT YEAR they would issue wool knit caps as a new part of the Culver Uniform, for both Cadets and Coeds. To be honest with you, that turned out to be incredibly helpful, because the next 4 years were the five-year God's cycle of cold and snow, and those black wool knit caps were a Godsend, especially in the worst Snow Year in Northern Indiana history, which was the Blizzard of 1979! Thank you Dean Mars and faculty. All of you attending Culver right now may write a thank you note to all four of our classes at Culver in 1977 for getting you those black wool knit caps you all have now! Lol!

I am saving my best for last! As I said earlier, Culver Academies, has kept it's tradition of requiring all Cadets and Coeds go to Church, like almost every single famous barding high school in this country. This is still paying HUGE DIVIDENDS for Culver, by making sure that the honesty of the Christian Culture, and the encouragement of the boarding school teachers, still extends to the Sunday Church service. Plus, as high school students, we all know at ages 13 to 18, that we need a Sunday escape from the pressures of the academic world, and the leadership world. The famous New England boarding schools, such as St. Paul's School in Concord, New Hampsire, were founded as Episcopal Schools. Now St. Paul's and Groutou and Phillip's Exeter, where my son went, have banished the Bibles and crosses from the on-campus churches. That is not smart.   That makes your Church holy, not holy!! (Pun intended!) But, it also tells all of your boarding school high schoolers from all over the United States that God is not important. That having a Rock in your life is not important. Like I said earlier, the Japanese would not do that with their Buddist or Shinto Gods. That is absurd. How are your high school students able to make chices for their life without your providing those choices, St. Paul's Episcopal School and Phillip's Exeter School, founded by a Unitarian Minister. Again, this is a mistake. And most parents will begin to shun these schools for getting rid of the bedrocks of our society, like our Chruches and our King James Version of the Bible, like you did 20 years ago at Phillips Exeter Academy. Big mistake.

How do I know? Becusse the Culver Episcopal Serives was requreid for every student at Culverr that did not attend another service, and we all learned to Read the Old Testament and New Testament Lesson's for every service, loudly, in front of all of our friends. How great is that training for a high school gril or boy? Want to give your students confidence? I will repeat that: Do you

261

want to give your students confidence? Then have them start reading the lessons from the Lectors at all the oncampus chapels that you have inexpicably closed to all students of faith. That is counterproductive. Bad idea at a high school.

Culver's huge Memorial Chapel is stunningly beautiful! What student would not want to go there and at least learn about the people in your school who died in World War Two fighting Nazi Germany and Facist Japan. Again, what 13 to 18 year old would not want to learn about that? Why would you not want to teach them at all of your boarding schools in the United States, when you have the same Chruchss and Chapels just sitting there. Teach. Train. Instruct. It is just waiting there for you, every school in this United States of America. It is not healthy to ignore it. Your students see that and it is the wrong message. Just the wrong message.

Also, in our fantastic public schools all over the United States, ask yourselves as teachers why you continue to teach to the SAT tests and the AP tests? Why don't you go back to teaching for the pure joy of learning. It is not that hard. The public high schools in the United States in the 1950s, when my parents attended them, were amazing. That was because they taught courses that you needed to know for real life. And, ALL of the teachers were interested in nothing more than their students learning everything they could. From my little farm public schools in Imperial County, California, where my father attended schools, to big fancy public schools in Seattle, Washington, where my mother attended schools. Fantastic education all over this United States in ALL the public schools in the 1950s. All of them everywhere. Please, Mr. and Mrs. Teacher, lets go back to that. You can make it happen if you want to, teachers. You can even teach your favorite subjects, again, if you want to.

What we all learned by heart as Plebes in every single unit (or company or battery or troup or band) was the Culver Creed, and more importantly, the Culver song! We even found that all the Coeds were required to lean both the Culver Creed and the Culver Song in their Prefect Leadership system, which is based on the English Boarding School System and is incredibly effective, as well.

We have the Creed and the Song so well memorized, that we can all say (and sing) both to this day, anytime we see another Culver alumni anywhere, anytime. That is fun for ALL OF US! Just to make sure that I can, I will do both from heart, right here, right now, to end this Chapter:

By the way, how fantastic is this Culver Creed? It is genius! And, motivational,

especially for high school students!!

The Culver Creed

The hope to win, the zeal to dare
Contempt for what is base and mean
Pride in Achievement that is fair
And high regard for what is clean
The strength that lies in brotherhood
And the Courage that Proclaims Success,
And First and always, manliness!

Now, the Culver Song"

Back, back to Culver Days
The Song My Heart Sings Ever
No matter where I roam,
'tis Culver, Culver, Culver
To hear the Bugle Call
Oh, memories how they thrill me

And Proud am I of Culver
And to be a Culver grad!

CHAPTER 33

PASSING BOARDS WITH FLYING COLORS

A Cadet spends his whole first year at Culver Military Academy attempting to pass out of the Plebe System and become an "Old Man." The ultimate goal, for all of us, was to pass our Boards within our Unit, and become an Old Man. Culver Boards were basically the same for every year and for most Cadets. But, the best Plebes truly were able to take their Boards before the rest of the Plebes. On the other hand, there was no correlation between how well you performed as a Plebe and whether you passed your Boards. Boards were a completely different animal, so to speak, than being a Plebe. The reason for that was when you appeared before your Unit's Officers and Counselor, you had to be excellent on your feet. You also had to be mentally tough and be able to handle being grilled by the whole team of your Officers and Counselor, or you just simply failed Boards. Then you had to retake them as many times as was needed for you to toughen up and be ready for the onslaught of questions and inuendo and mental hazing.

Because I grew up on a farm with farmworkers and tough parents, I was well equipped for Culver Boards. First, they did not rattle me. That is super helpful for passing. Second, I was born with a God given trait of being good on my feet. Another huge help. Third, the more pressure that comes upon me the more clearly I see the correct route and invariably act upon that methodically.

Fortunately, my best friend was prepared to take his Boards first, just like I was. Thus, we had Boards the same evening. I know that Mark Holden is not one who thrives under pressure so I knew this would be more difficult for him. Thus, when he went just before me and Passed his Boards the first time, I was utterly delighted for him! You know, you are always pleased when your friends do well. Mark Holden ended up being my only Culver groomsman in my Wedding – so that shows you how close we were and how close we remained!

How early you were allowed to take your Boards was also a factor of how good your grades were, so that was another reason Mark Holden got to take his Boards the first round, with me. He had excellent grades all four years at Culver, which was saying something at a very strong academic institution, where we sent 5 students every year to the Ivys and another 25 every year to the top 20 Colleges in the USA.   I certainly had excellent grades in my freshman year, which was when it counted for Culver Boards. Mark Holden's grades would stay abstemiously high all four years at Culver.

My grades, on the other hand, went down every year as I took on more responsibilities every year at the 80-year-old Culver Student Newspaper, **The Culver Vedette.** Just for the record, those increased responsibilities at the Culver Vedette were: Freshman Year, Photo editor. Sophomore Year, Sports Editor and Photo Editor. Junior Year, News Editor and Photo Editor. Senior Year, Sole Editor-in-Chief. Obviously, when you are taking lots of black and white photos every year and writing endless articles for publication every two weeks you end up suffering in your schoolwork and grades. I spent all four years at Culver "Living in the Culver Darkroom" every night after Taps, especially Sophomore through Senior year.

I believe that it was my freshman year at Culver when I began to prepare for Boards that I began to realize that I was gifted on my feet and gifted to not let anything worry me. Everyone else in my Battery A was all worried about Boards and they did not even phase me. Consequently, I begin to realize that God had designed me to work incredibly well under pressure. Another trait which, unexpectedly, came in very handy with **The Vedette** Newspaper deadlines, which did not seem to bother me either.

This is another situation in life when sending a gifted boy or girl to boarding high school can really hone their talents long before the real world. I sincerely believe that we should immediately change in the United States the high school education system to mirror Europe, where High School is the last schooling for most children before they go into the real world. In Europe, most 18-year-olds finish all schooling and go into the real world, with their special talent. Not in the United States. Like Europe, most 18-year-olds in the USA are fully ready, educationally and mentally for the real world. Like Europe, they would already thrive in the real world with their special talent. But, oh no. In the United States our parents and our educational system tells the students they need to get a college education. That is not true in Europe. That is not true in the United States. But our 18-year-olds are being lied to and told to waste 4 full more years in college they do not need. Worse yet, **those college 4 more years put way more stress on every student**, when they could have been gaining confidence every day in the real world.

This extra 4 years of schooling, called college, is exorbitantly expensive. You leave college with $85,000 in debt! Instead of going to work and spending $85,000 on a downpayment on a house and marrying the love of your life! You know what is even worse than the four years lost and the money lost? Genuinely, the fact that almost every college graduate in the United States, after they graduate, has no confidence, whatsoever! Four more years of school, $85,000 of debt and NO COFIDENCE at all!

Wouldn't you think that after four extra years wasted in college for most students, the professors would at least boost their students' confidence level? Oh no. Conversely, college professors expound for four more years how "scary the real world is" to their students. So, that makes almost all college students even less mentally tough for the real world when they graduate. Worse yet, most college students now come out of college afraid of the real world they were just spending four more years in college preparing for! This is insane!

Get rid of college for everyone who does not need it and start teaching basic trades in high school, such as electrician, and food and beverage worker, mother, or even secretary. Also, We need to give our high school students the exact same confidence my father and mother had coming out of high school in the 1940s. Confidence is the name of the game, for students in school and employees in the workforce. **Let's go back to giving children confidence in school.**

Also, in the 1940s and 1950s in ALL high schools in the United States, you could learn everything as diverse as becoming a farmer – to becoming a mother – as my mother did in Seattle in high school. Did I say "farmer?" Yes! Cannot get a more useful profession than that, can you? Did I say "mother?" Yes! Again, cannot get more useful profession than that! **Then why is our United States education system always putting down "farmers" and "mothers" when those are the two most useful professions in the world?** You cannot do better than Mother. You cannot do better than Farmer.

You need high school to start teaching both professions again, **just like in the 1950s in every high school in the United States!** I know this because my mother, after graduating from Stanford University in 1948, came out of college and taught "Home Economics" in high school. And it was her favorite class to teach because she knew she helped so many young women become great mothers! My mother would be so pleased if she saw us go back to that!

Back to Culver Boards: I knew I would flourish in my Boards because I heard all the rumors that the Battery A Senior Officers and Sword Bearing Sergeants, and Battery A Counselor, Mr. Fred Lintner were in change of grilling you. I thought to myself, if all these Cadets end up becoming Old Men every year at Culver, it could not be that hard! By the way, I also thought the exact same thing when I took the State of South Carolina Bar Examination in 1994. I psyched myself up for the S.C. Bar Exam by saying to myself, if all these men and women can pass the Bar exam in South Carlina every year, certainly I can, too. I passed both examinations on the first time with flying colors: My Culver Boards in February 1977 and my South Carolina 3-day written Bar Examination in February 1994. I do wish South Carolina would go back to the 3 days of Special Essays on every major South Carolina topic like they used to do. Obviously it is quite helpful when you are a born writer, like my wife and I both are, when taking an almost fully Essay Bar Exam. But, anyone can pass the older, harder, Bar Exam. I do know that. Because many, many folks passed the old Bar Exam when it was almost all essays. It is like everything else in life. You simply must study hard and be prepared and get yourself in the correct state of mind. **If you cannot get yourself in the correct state of mind for the Bar Exam, then you probably should not be a lawyer, right?** Right, to that, too! Otherwise, we have way too many lawyers in this country. As my youngest daughter says, "Things that make you go huuuummmmmm."

I was still 13 years old when I took the Culver Battery A Boards and got one full hour of non-stop grilling from unbelievably brilliant Seniors, the two Battery A, Four-Year-Running Gold A, and

Cum Laude senior year, Cadet Officers, Jon Agne and David Hemmings. Couple that with the other end of the spectrum on the street smarts side, with my Battery A Company Commander, Tom Tippy, who made the State Finals in the State of Indiana in Wrestling one year at Culver. Captain Tippy loved to sneak questions in that you just did not see coming. I knew our Counsellor Fred Linter, who was also brilliant, would not grill me with questions because I knew that was just not his nature. Don't worry, Cadet Officers Flickinger and Denisar made up for it, that is for sure! But, I survived my one-hour of non-stop questions and gave enough great answers to pass my Boards on the first time!

There is genuinely a second aspect of Culver Boards that takes way, way more time for a Plebe than the actual one- or two-hour grilling part of Boards! That is the part that takes the whole year to prepare for. Now that I rewrote the Culver Creed, above, from memory, it reminds me of the one thing that Culver takes sooooooo seriously. That would be "High Regard for what is Clean." For Boards, you must spend the whole six months hand-shining that stupid Battery A brass with a cloth and Brasso, week after week, so that it is almost flat on the top. All semblance of the welts on the battery cannon that are part of the original brass must be shined off entirely, with daily manual labor with that hand towel. You also must have your black oxford leather shoes so shined with several hours of manual labor with your little glass of water and your little can of shoe polish and your making little rounded motions for about 120 straight minutes, with the water and the cotton ball, that your black shoes eventually have a perfectly reflective surface on the toes that can reflect a man in them from any distance! Incredible, what Military School can come up with as perfection. But, every Plebe, for 80 years, knows what perfection in our brass and in our shoes is. Just look around and realize that everyone is doing it every day. If you want to be part of the A-Team, you better get to work. (Pun intended on that A-Team, of course!)

One of the biggest benefits of shining brass as a 13-year-old Freshman in high school was that I got to learn, and totally love, the Beach Boys <u>**Endless Summer**</u> greatest hits Double-Vinyl Album, inside and out. Another huge, awesome thing that came along in 1976 that nobody in the USA had ever seen before was **this new-fangled contraption called the Cassette Tape!** What that meant was that you did not have to get up and go over the record player every 20 minutes and turn the record over again!

From the 1940s to the 1970s in the whole world, with the old-fashioned record player everyone had, you had to play 4 sides of any Double Vinyl Album by putting one vinyl record on the record player. Then, sit down and listen to the first 5 songs on the first side. Get up, flip the record over and play the second side, another 5 songs and 22 minutes. Later, you had to do it again for side three. Finally, you had to get up 20 minutes after that and turn the record over again and play five more songs. Not with the newfangled Cassette Tape! You put the tape in your little Motorola cassette player and pushed play and the tape would play ALL THE WAY THROUGH, with your music coming out of the little speaker on the top of your cassette player!

My Freshman roommate, Juan Funes, and my Freshman best friend Mark Holden, had ***never even heard of the Beach Boys***, or heard their songs, so, while we polished brass every day and polished shoes every day as Plebes, we listened to our new Motorola cassette player play the **Beach Boys' <u>Endless Summer</u>, endlessly!!** (Dear Reader, I am proud of that alliteration!)

Do you want to know why guys know every word and every note to every song? Because once we start listening to a record, we listen to it again, and again, and again. And, again. Moreover, in the 1970s and 1980s, when you bought music it was either a vinyl record or a cassette tape, and it cost you $8.00. Thus, you could only afford one piece of music a month. Therefore, you played the cassette tape so incessantly, like the Beach Boys **Endless Summer**, that you could sing along perfectly AND know the vocals, guitar, bass and drums like the back of your hand. Truly, better than the back of your hand, if you are a guy. Not better than the back of your hand if you are a girl! Lol!

You want to know why most girls do not know every song by heart and all the instruments by heart, and the name of the record by heart? Because girls did not buy albums! Guys bought albums. Girls bought Singles!!! To be precise, girls love 45 rpm SINGLES, instead of albums. Three reasons: First, girls like one thing at a time and they like one song at a time. Second, girls like to dance to the one song they love that month. So, in their rooms at home, they will practice dancing until they are blue in the face, their own particular dance to that particular hit single! Third, all the 45 rpm Singles were pop songs and danceable, as opposed to albums, like Elton John's **Goodbye Yellow Brick Road** double album, which has the most varied music you will ever hear. But, again, girls like the Singles off the **Goodbye Yellow Brick Road** album, right to now in 2025: *"Bennie and the Jets"* and *"Goodbye Norma Jean!!"* Nothing wrong with that! God made us all different! And, if you want to date a girl, you better dance to the Singles, or forget it!!!! (YOU ALL KNOW I AM RIGHT!)

Therefore, we all spend two weeks getting ready for Boards by shining our shoes and all our brass to perfection. While spending two weeks shining our brass and shoes to perfection, we also re-memorize every little thing we have been required to learn all year by heart, that is required by the Culver Military Academy Old Men for decades: Namely the name and rank of every Cadet Officer, at Culver our Plebe year, all the way down to the Regimental Mess

Hall Officer that year. Second, we must make sure we can say the culver Creed and the Culver Song with alacrity. Third, we must be able to state the Year of the founding of the school and every little piece of history that is on our CMA history sheet, from the year of the Logansport Indiana Flood and how many lives we saved their, to every Head of School and Commandant, who has served Culver well – and all of them have served Culer well! Lol! I know there were other things we had to memorize, but that was all I remember right now.

When our name was called, we went into the Basement of Main Barracks, had a huge spotlight shining into our eyes by the Sword Bearing Sergeants (oh, better know their names, too!), step into position, come to attending, and present our Rifle for inspection. If your Rifle is not shiny and in perfect order, you leave immediately, because you have already failed Boards. Captain Tippy was big on that one!

If you pass your rifle inspection, then Sword Bearing Sergeants inspect your Plebe Battery A brass to see if it shined down enough, inspect the beautiful Culver Eagle Brass on your beautiful Culver Dress A Cap and make sure it is also shined down enough. Finally, they inspect your black leather shoes and make sure that the top is so glossy that it reflects everything in the room. If you do not pass your shinning brass and shoes inspection, again, you are sent home immediately to try another day.

I passed both. So now the "real fun" begins! Now we come to The Inquisition, especially from brilliant officers, like Officer Agne, and Officer Hemmings. Even though they were roommates at the end of my Battery A hall, but did not have remotely similar personalities. Jon Agne was quite stern and did not put up with anything. David Hemmings was low key, nice, and easy going and delightful. One thing they both had in common: they were both brilliant! So, I got grilled by both with rapid fire questions, such as: "Kuhn, why did you end up in the Battery A Dumpster last week??" My immediate response, "Officer Agne, I accidently threw out my brass and that was not going to work for Boards." Agne: "So I heard, Kuhn. Too bad you are that clumsy and stupid." My response: "You are correct, Sir, I should not be so stupid and clumsy, Sir!"

I did not expect Cadet Officers Flickinger and Denisar to be so difficult, but they were! They had a great time at my expense. The item I remember the most from them is they said, "We all know that all Plebes can recite the Culver song by heart, because you are required to, but, really, Kuhn, you need to sing it for us. Don't you realize that once you graduate you will be singing the Culver song, not reciting it for gosh sakes." So, I had to sing the Culver song. Being nervous and not decent at carrying a tune, I did not do too well at that. They certainly laughed at my attempt to sing the Culver song! They were all laughing at me by the end of Boards, which is always a good thing!

Battery A Commander Tippy tells you if you passed right at the end of the inquisition, so I knew right away! So rewarding to pass your Culver Boards and immediately cease being a Plebe and immediately become an Old Man. That means the very next day you can go to the Culver Uniform Department, with your little Culver Order in hand, and get your band new collar brass for the rest of your Culver career, with the new C.B. on the top half – above the Artillery Cannons and the A (for Battery A) on the bottom half. Mark Holden and I raced over to the Uniform department right after class ended the next day and got our "CBs!" Proud little freshmen, we were! (Again, thank you Yoda, for the language!)

After you finally become an Old Man, and everyone does by the end of Plebe year, you do not have nearly so much to do for the military that year. So, that is great time to focus on your special organization that you love the most, whether it be rifle shooting, or sports, or theatre, or in my case, the Student Newspaper, **The Culver Vedette**! Another item that you can focus on is your girlfriend; however, most of us freshmen and sophomore boys were waaaayyyy too scared to have a girlfriend! **From Saturday Night Live: Jane Curtin's: <u>"And that's the truth!"</u> Lol!**

It took me two full years to even start THINKING ABOUT girls, I was so shy and so scared! Therefore, considerably easier, mentally, to focus on school and the <u>**Vedette**</u> Newspaper than worry about girls. And, yes, all boys worry about girls, whether we admit it or not! Why? Because they move the world! And, they do move the world. In fact, all girls move the world, and always in a good way, too!

After you are an Old Man in the military system at Culver Military Academy, you now are ready for actual Rank, as opposed to Ranks! Pun intended – lol! So, what is the difference? Ranks are where you form as a Company to march somewhere. This is why we drill like crazy in the Miliary. If you want to get from your Barracks to the Mess Hall, you need to march there. Thus, you need to practice marching all the time. That way you can get to Church on time on Sunday, as well! **Oh, that reminds of a fantastic song, "Get Me to the Church On Time," from the Broadway musical <u>My Fair Lady</u>!** Eliza Dolittle's father, Alfred Doolittle, is a drunk and knows **he will not get to the Church on time for his daughter's wedding**, so he turns it into one of the funniest songs in all Musical history!! My favorite musical of all time! Why? **Because, what English major would not LOVE a musical about English??!!**

In fact, another hilarious song from the same musical is "Why Can't the English – Teach their children how to Speak English?" Cannot get better than that! Plus, the premise of the whole musical is that, if you can teach an English girl how to speak properly, she can go ANYWHERE!! **Including vising The Queen at Ascot** – another hilarious song where Eliza Doolittle gets so excited at the races that she completely loses her poise – AND completely loses her English!! Lol!

Dear Reader, time for you to take another music break! Go listen to the Lerner and Loewe musical, **My Fair Lady** on your iPhone, NOW!!! You are missing out on the best Julie Andrews singing of your whole life, AND the funniest musical of all time. **Do not take my word for it. LISTEN TO IT!** Oh, and remember, those pronouncements of mine, like this one, really come from She-Who-Must-Not-Be-Named!   Thus, it is not my fault that I am turning into my mother! On the other hand, everyone always leaned around my mother, from how to speak properly to her favorite countries (England) to her favorite musicals (My Fair Lady!), to how to be a great Mother in her high school class she taught every year, called "Home Economics."

Where was I? Oh, I was telling you the difference between Ranks and Rank. I explained that Ranks are where you form up as a unit and in front of your Barracks march to the Church on time on Sundays. That was always important to me, because my Senior Rank was Regimental Aide to the Chaplain. See! There is the difference! Where? Where is the difference? Oh, you missed it? I will repeat it. So, at all military organizations, from high school to the Marines, you form up in Ranks to get organized as a military unit to march as a perfectly cadenced unit to wherever your Company Commander wants you to march.

Rank is the actual miliary assigned job you get, personally, as a human being in your organization. Rank is personal and you work like crazy, personally, to achieve your rank. Ranks, with an "s" at the end, on the other hand, are where you form up as a group people and march somewhere. Or maybe even form up as a group and go nowhere. Rather, stand at Parade Rest and listen to your Executive Officer blab endlessly about something you just do not care about. Lol!

So, here we go: Executive Officer ("XO") in a miliary unit is the second in command just behind the company commander. The Executive Officer – that is his job and NOT his Rank – and he is always terrific at detail work and making his company commandeer look good and getting his unit informed and on time. His Rank (in other words his position as opposed to his job) in both the United States Army AND at Culver Military Academy, is First Lieutenant. **That is the Executive Officer's Rank: First Lieutenant.** His job is executive officer (we just call him the "XO") and everyone knows what the XO's job is.

Everyone has their own personality and strengths. Consequently, some people want to be XO. Mark Holden wanted to be XO and a First Lieutenant Rank that goes with it. Actually, he would have been perfect for it!

Not me! I have a large, outgoing, personality, so I want to be Commander – Company Commander. That is a job. And, the Rank for that job in the Army (and at Culver) is Captain. I wanted to be a Cadet Captain my Senior year (naturally, who wouldn't, right?) and be Battery A Commander – which is the job for the Rank of Captain. That was my goal all four years and I am proud to say that I came extremely close to Company Commander.

But, remember, I told you, God also has a plan. And the military also has a say in this. In fact, the military has ALL the say in it! And my Battery A Counselor said to me at the end of my Junior year, "John, we need you to be Editor-In-Chief of the

Vedette." By the way, notice by Junior and Senior year it is no longer Kuhn – now it is John! Yay!

My same Unit Counselor went on to say: "Being Editor-In-Chief of the **Vedette** is far more important to the kids *and* to the school. The faculty wants you to continue to take the **Vedette** to new levels it has not seen in years. So, we are going to come close as possible to Commander with your rank and make you Regimental Aide to the Chaplain, which immediately makes you on Regimental Staff, the highest ranking First Lieutenants in the Crops. However, as Aide to the Chaplain, you will have almost no military duties, compared to company commander, except to run your beloved Sunday Culver Memorial Chapel and hang out with your favorite person, Chaplain Martin. Most importantly to everyone, you can continue to work tirelessly at the **Vedette** as the new as Editor-in-Chief, your first love, and you know it." That was God's plan. That was Culver Military Academy plan. That was my Counsellor's plan and it was perfect. More on that, Dear Reader, my full year in charge of my three favorite places in the world (**The Vedette**, the darkroom, and the Culver Memorial Chapel) and the Men who were so instrumental in my joy and success (Reverand Chaplain Martin and my new Battery A Counselor, starting Sophomore year, Major Runkle) a few chapters from now in this same Volume 1, for my Senior year at Culver.

Oh, and now, Dear Reader, I have edjamacated you on the difference between Ranks and Rank. My mother always thought the mispronunciation 'educated' to 'edjamacated' was hilarious and she did it all the time. I believe it was to make sure she did not come across as stuffy or self-important. So, I now use it myself. Like mother, like son, in the end! Lol!

Now that taught you the difference between all the jobs and Rank in the military AND told you if you want to "*Get Me to the Church On Time*," (thank you again, Alfred Doolittle from **My Fair**

Lady!); then, form up in Ranks and march there (thank you my Freshman year Cadet Captain, Battery A Commander Thomas Tippy!). Culver will always make sure you are not late, Mr. Doolittle and Mr. Kuhn!

And, if Culver was not there for me, my Swiss-watch Farmer Father, Fritz Kuhn, would make sure I was on time! (Again, all puns intended!)

CHAPTER 34

THE CULVER VEDETTE – FRESHMAN YEAR

God has so many plans for your life that you do not even know about. She-Who-Must-Not-Be-Named decided that I would benefit tremendously by learning how to use a film camera at the local 4-H Club in El Centro, California, when I was in the sixth grade at Seeley Elementary School. That would be 1973 and I was 11 years old. I took the course called "Camera" at the local 4-H Club from a nice teacher named Mrs. Hurley. I dove in and studied and precited with a normal Kodak camera. I learned all that I could about photography for the whole 9 months of my sixth-grade year, in a class at night near my home at the 4-H Club. I read the whole little 4-H Manuel about taking photographs and practiced everything that year with my Kodak color film camera. I was decent at taking photographs at the end of the year.

Just like most Americans all over the whole United States, I would take a roll of 24 pictures over a 2-week period, then my mother would drive me to the local drug store and they would ship our roll of film to Kodak Company in Rochester, New York, for processing. Everywhere, everyone, all over the United States would do this. Then, a week later your 24 prints would come back to your local drug store to pick up, with your name handwritten on the envelope of pictures. That happened all the way through the 1980s in the whole United States!

I am not sure if you realize it or not, but there were no cell phone cameras in the USA in the 1970s when I started taking photographs. **In the 1970s all the way through the 1990s we all used film cameras, with 36 pictures in each roll of film. Film**

cameras. That was it. The year 2000 changed everything for photopapers. That is when Nikon started making legitimate Digital Cameras and almost all of us switched to digital photography from 2000 to 2005. All photographers only took film pictures until the year 2000. **If you were born before 2000, you were born in the age of film cameras only.**

But, what I believe is even more amazing is that a camera did not even come in your Apple iPhone until 2007. Think of that! No cameras in your cell phone until 2007. Before 2007 you just had digital cameras and very few people used digital cameras because they were too big and clumsy and hard to use. Plus, digital software was too complicated. Only professional photographers used Digital Cameras. Nobody else used them. So, that iPhone that came out in 2007 was a gamechanger for photography! Before 2007, most Americans were still using film cameras – with just 36 pictures each – to take pictures!

I am fully convinced that in 2010 when Apple improved the cell phone camera so much that instantly you could use your cell phone for pictures, that was the biggest gamechanger for ALL photographers in America, both professional and amateur. In 2010 you no longer had to use your digital camera that was too big and clumsy and complicated, with unfriendly software! Suddenly, in 2010 the iPhone Camera definitively, faster and easier to use. Moreover, the iPhone 6 finally had great quality photographs, which meant you could now only use your iPhone for pictures. That is just 15 years ago, that you could finally begin fully relying on your portable electronic device for pictures.

The great thing about photography and taking fantastic photographs is that not much has changed since I took my 4-H course on Photography as an 11-year-old in 1973. What I learned then is still, to this day, fully applicable now. The cameras have changed dramatically. However, taking great photographs has not changed at all. It still has absolutely everything to do with getting the lighting behind you. That was true in the 1950s and 1960s with simple Kodak cameras. That was true in the 1970s with fancy Nikon F1 and Nikon F2 Cameras, that took 36 pictures on a color Kodak film roll, or 36 pictures on a black and white Kodak film roll. Get the lighting behind you and you win!!! Every single time. Still true today with your iPhone 13 Camera, isn't it? In the 1970s and 1980s we had the exact same "Golden Hour" that you use with your iPhone, with our professional Nikon cameras in the 1970s and 1980s.

So, when I joined the **Culver Vedette** Newspaper in 1976 with my Vivitar 35mm SLR Film Camera, Fall of Freshman year at Culver Academies, I was fully prepared to take lots and lots of pictures for the Vedette the whole year. That is exactly what I did.

As with all matches made in heaven, if both sides come out way ahead, that is truly a match made in heaven. That is exactly what happened when I joined the Vedette as a staff photographer in Fall 1976. I did not even realize how good a photographer I already was until I joined the newspaper and could see I was better than I thought. But, the true reason it was also a match made in heaven was that Culver had all the money anyone could want for its Vedette Newspaper. I did not know it at the time, but money at your student newspaper means that your photographers can take as many pictures as they want, develop as many pictures as possible, and most importantly, learn from every single mistake you make on every picture you print.

An endless photography budget is priceless. And, that is exactly what Culver academies had. An endless student newspaper budget is also priceless and that is also what Culver had. I am extremely thankful to Culver Academies for that budget and for their emotional and financial support they gave me and the **Vedette** Newspaper all four years. I would not be the person I am today without it. Plus, the great stories from the four years on the Culver newspaper are so fun and varied that I can spend the next 20 pages telling you, Dear Reader, all about it.

The first fun story was when I received my first Vedette at my desk in my Freshman Battery A room about the second week that I was at school. In comes **The Vedette** and my roommate, Juan Funes, and I sit down to read it and see what this is all about. Well, what it was all about was that it was hilarious! I mean absolutely hilarious! I was a brand-new Plebe and a brand-new Freshman, so I may have been gullible, but looking back on it, it was one of the funniest newspapers that you would read anywhere. The first article was about "Dust Bunnies" uninvited, rapidly racing across the floor just in time for Culver General Inspection, which would be a HUGE uh-ho, and a HUGE oh no! The whole article continued along the same theme in General Inspection and by the time I finished the article, my sides split from laughing and I was crying from laughing. I thought, "oh boy, this newspaper is hilarious!" Just hilarious! Then, I decided to look and see what cadet could possibly have written such a side-splittingly funny story. Low and behold, it is my Battery A hallmates, Daivd Hemmings and Jon Agne! Yes! The very same Cadet Officers that were down my very hall that I was having to be instructed by John Agne, "Kuhn, take whatever is at the front desk to Officer Hemmings room down the hall." I'm thinking, "Wow, I did not know these guys could be sooooo funnyyyyyy!!"

But, I also read thought the whole newspaper and thought to myself it is only 4 pages. I sure wish it was more pages, especially since it was sooooo funny! I will tell you, John Agne and David Hemmings, if I never told you before, looking back on it, you had the funniest newspaper on planet earth! I am not kidding!

283

I also noticed that the newspaper had black and white photographs and a lot of them. Way more than I would have expected. I thought somebody is having a lot of fun taking all those photographs! Not only that, they look really good. Better than my hometown newspaper, as a matter of fact! So, I decided to go to the next Vedette student meeting and sign up to take pictures for the paper. I KNEW I could at least do a good job of taking pictures and that looked like fun – having your own photographs printed for your fellow students!

Next week, off to the Vedette office, in the basement of the English Building, to join as a Staff Photographer. I get there at 5:00 pm. I guess I was not thinking at all, but, low and behold, there are Jon Agne and David Hemmings, in the flesh, sitting at the tables, looking at me and saying "wow, you here to join the newspaper, Kuhn? What do you want to do?"

I was dumbfounded for two reasons: First, I already idolized these guys from their utterly hilarious articles AND newspaper cartoons, about Dust Bunnies invading General Inspection. Second, they were so nice and relaxed and fun and I could see that it was going to be fun being part of a student newspaper. I had never even thought of that!

 Hemmings asks me what I think I can do on the newspaper and I tell him about my Vivitar 35mm camera and that I was taking eighth grade football team action photos at Seeley School with that camera. That got his attention. Hemmings said, "We definitely need a sprots photographer, so welcome aboard!" Just like that, I was a Sports Photographer as a Freshman on the Vedette. Jon Agne then explained that Culver paid for the Vedette film and we had an endless supply if we needed it. Remember, Agne is the detail guy. Not surprisingly, he was XO (detail man) of Battery A my Freshman year – that very year. Perfect fit.

Jon Agne was incredibly helpful. He also explained to me in quite some detail about how the Culver Vedette also has a Darkroom in the top of the Music Building near the Uniform Shop, and we can use it anytime we want! "Best of all," Agne said, "there is an unlimited budget to the Vedette darkroom, too!" Then, he introduced me to the Photo Editor, then he said, "Go with Dave Bourland to the Darkroom next week and get start learning from him how to develop your film and learn how to print pictures on that old-fashioned printer's easel." Boy, I was into the sound of that!

Into the Darkroom of the **Culver Vedette** I went and started to learn from the **Vedette** photographers how to develop a full roll of 36 black and white pictures from each roll of Ilford film! Apparently someone was in the know at Culver because they had Ilford Black and White film long before anyone else. Everyone was using Kodak black and white film. But, not the Culver **Roll Call** Yearbook, nor the Culver **Vedette** Newspaper. **But, the best Color film in the 1960s, 1970s and all the way through today, is Kodak Color film**. Cannot beat the Kodak color film, for sure. But, we only developed black and white film in the Culver Darkroom. Way too hard to develop color film in those days. It is even more difficult to print Color Photographs in a Darkroom. Way too many steps.   Plus, your timing of pulling the paper out of the liquid solutions in the old days had to be perfect or you ruined your Color prints. We would send all our Color film to Kodak Company in Rochester, NY, for processing. Every package would come back in three days with cut negatives and beautiful color prints. Black and White was considerably more forgiving so we did it all in house, at the Culver Darkroom.

I am guessing that I developed over 300 rolls of film my Freshman year, over 1,000 rolls of film my Sophomore year, over 400 rolls of film my Junior year and over 100 rolls of film my

Senior year. Right there in that same Culver Darkroom directly above the Quarter Master Store on campus. That would be over 1,800 rolls of black and white film that I personally developed in just four years at Culver. That is a lot of film! Half was Kodak and half was Ilford film.

Ironically, developing the film was the easy part! The painstakingly difficult, time-consuming, part was hand printing every single black and white print that you wanted or needed. But, that was also the creative part. For me, it was a blast slowly but surely improving one of my prints in the Darkroom to perfection. An absolute art, assuredly! I was an artist in the Darkroom, almost overnight. More about that in later chapters.

 Most of the black and white were for my **Vedette** Newspaper, so I loved that part. I took a lot more pictures for the **Roll Call** Yearbook, especially my Sophomore year as Sports Editor AND Sports Photographer for the newspaper, that led to hundreds of my sports photos being printed in the Culver Yearbook my Sophomore year.

Starting as early as my Freshman year, I also printed lots of black and white photos for friends and even for the Culver administration, and all Culver Publications, even the Culver Alumni Magazine. I did all of that in black and white. In fact, I also did most of the Color photography from 1977 to 1980 for the Culver Administration and the Culver Publications and most of the Color photography for my Senior Roll Call 1980.

In fact, shout out right here to our Senior year **Roll Call** 1980 Yearbook Editor-in-Chief, and one of my very best friends, Jim Martin, for coming to see me beginning of Senior year and personally asking me to take most of the Color photographs in the 1980 Yearbook! I am most appreciative because those are some of the best Color photographs I have ever taken and my mother was incredibly pleased to show off my Color photographs in the 1980 **Roll Call** for the next 35 years to her friends until she died. Truly, Jim Martin, to this day, I cannot thank you enough for thinking to ask me and for printing all those color photos.

What does a boy who sneaks a cassette boom box onto his Caterpillar Tractor his Junior Year to listen to The Who, knowing he will get busted and chewed out by his father, do when he has a quiet, dark, Darkroom to himself his whole Freshman year of high school as a 13-year-old boy? Night Moves! By Bob Seger!! That is what he does!! Lol!! (That really is funny if I do say so, myself!)

To be more precise, John Kuhn listens to the three top songs on Bob Seger's **Night Moves** album, incessantly on the transistor Radio in the Culver **Vedette** Darkroom. As luck would have it – and luck has a lot to do with it – Culver, in the Cornfields of Indiana, was just close enough to Chicago to receive a strong signal from WLS AM, Rock'n"Roll radio with all the current rock and roll music hits every month, without fail. For the whole nine months of Freshman year, we had three of the best singles in Rock'n'Roll history released off Bob Seger's **Night Moves** Album in this order, while I listened to them nonstop in the Darkroom at Culver: *"Night Moves"* itself, released November 1976, right when I probably started listening to the radio in the darkroom. *"Mainstreet"* Top 100 song of all time in my book, Released April 1977 and *"Rock and Roll Never Forgets,"* released in June 1977, just in time for my brother and I to listen to it ALL SUMMER on the farm at home on our Transistor Radio.

Cut to the chase, every girl in America loved the Song *"Night Moves"* because they could sing it and dance to it and picture themselves in the 60s Chevy. Every boy in America loved the song *"Night Moves"* because they could immediately picture themselves with "a black-haired beauty with big dark eyes...out past the cornfields where the woods got heavy, out in the back seat of my '60s Chevy" Does the song say "Cornfields?" Oh, yes it does!

By the way, Dear Reader, this is where Vinyl record albums downright destroy cassette tapes. From 1976 when the album was released, and all the way unwaveringly up to today, if you listen to the whole album of **Night Moves** on any excellent vinal record player and decent stereo, it is munificently recorded. Every instrument, every voice, every intuition on *"Mainstreet"* and every insinuation on *"Night Moves,"* comes right into your listening room on this shockingly incredible album! Moreover, with vinyl records you do not have the flimsy, unbelievably long thin tape spilling out of the Cassette itself and self-imploding, which they ALWAYS do within several years of buying them. I have over 1,000 Vinyl records on my shelves at home, each one I bought the year they came out (from 1971 to 2025) and not one single Vinyl record (of over 1,000) has ever self-imploded. **Even more importantly, ALL the Vinyl records have the exact same amazing sound they had the day you bought them.** Not true for cassette tapes, at all. If you are keeping score at home: 1,000 for the Vinyl Records. 0 for the Cassette Tapes. Lol!

I already told you that the **Culver Vedette** student newspaper under Co-Editor-in-Chiefs Jon Agne and Dave Hemmings was hilarious, all the way from the articles to the cartoons, to the opinion section. Apparently they also got a beautiful, modern, clean new Masthead that I just loved. In fact, everyone loved the new Nameplate!

I also told you that God has a plan. God certainly had a plan for me anyway. As a Freshman, I already knew that I wanted to administer the **Vedette** by my Senior year. I also thought that I could write hilarious articles, like the Culver **Vedette** my Freshman year. I came to the realization that I was half correct, and half incorrect. Turns out I was destined to manage the Vedette already by my Junior year because of my Swiss work ethic. But, it turns out that I was not anywhere nearly as funny as Agne and Hemmings and their staff of Vedette writers.

The Godwink my Freshman year was when I managed to receive terrific grades my first semester and found out after Christmas that came with terrific privileges! Mainly, that for my whole second semester, even though I was a Plebe, I was permitted to go to the Culver Library for the two hours of Closed Quarters (study hall) from 7:30 to 9:30 every night. I did not realize what a true benefit this was until I went the first time and found that I was not required to keep my nose in my books for two straight hours and could even talk in a whisper!! Wow! How great is that?

The very first week I was in the Culver Library, supposedly studying, I STUMBLED upon the old Culver **Vedettes** from every single year. Even better, apparently Culver was not shy about them because they were front and center at the top of the stairs when you arrived on the second floor. That is why I say that I stumbled upon them; they were lined up in rows and rows of shelves directly in front of the stairs.

Of course, I started to browse through them because they were right there and there was a big table and couch to look at them. Pretty soon I could see why Culver was proud of them! They were AMAZING! Every single year was amazing, from 1894 onwards. It took me the whole CQ to get through most of them. Naturally, I found that some decades were better than others. Honestly, what I truly found was that every Editor-in-Chief had his own style and that some years they would put out 10 full pages of newsprint every two weeks, and some years, they would only put out 4 pages every two weeks. Some months they might not even put out an issue. Quite varied. I also found that when they were putting out 8 to 12 to 16 pages of newsprint, invariably they had a bigger staff of writers. I could see that if you wanted to consistently put out 12 pages every 2 weeks, you needed at least 20 students on the staff. I thought we easily could be doing that since we have an unlimited budget and at least 800 students, which should be enough to recruit from!

The second thing I found in the **Vedette** newspapers was that the 1950s and 1960s Vedettes were so almost professional in nature. I looked at the staff listing for those two decades and found that they were all just Culver students – no faculty writing anything. I thought, "That is truly incredible!" The third thing I found in the Masthead in the 1950s and the 1960s Vedettes was that about every 2 years they would win the National Scholastic Press Association All-American Newspaper Awards, as the number one high school newspaper in the United States. I was shocked. I was delighted! I thought, if the Vedette student newspaper could do that a recently as 1968, certainly we could be doing that 8 years later!!

Two weeks later I went into the basement of the English Building to find **Vedette** Faculty Advisor John Walters and ask him who this National Scholastic Press Association (NSPA) was and why we were nowhere near the quality of the 1960s **Vedettes** and if we could somehow get to top student newspaper in the United States by my Senior year. Of course, he was delighted with these questions because he could see that we might be heading that direction again.

Mr. Walters was considerably more knowledgeable than I expected on the NSPA and told me that, fortunately, they had broke all student newspapers in the United States down by size of high school, so we would be in the 800-1,000 student sized high school. More importantly, we just needed to be the top newspaper I our high school size to win the Award "Top High School Newspaper in the United States" by the National Scholastic Press Association. That made it doable. But it also meant we would be up against Andover boarding school in Boston. Of course, the first thing I did was order full subscription to the Andover High School newspaper the next week to see what our competition was doing. When the first Andover newspaper came a few weeks later, I was delighted, because I could see they were not at their strongest in the late 1970s either. The Kent School student newspaper in Connecticut in the late 1970s was another matter. It was outstanding! So, that was the one we would have to beat!

The other thing I could immediately see was that our current high school newspaper was truly funny and well-read, which is the most important thing for any student newspaper. You want the students to **Not Be Able To Wait** until the next issue comes out and be asking for it. And, if nothing else, it needs to be funny. That can make up for a lot of shortcomings. Under Agne and Hemmings we had both things going for us!

Because I put myself in the Culver Library with my excellent grades first semester at Culver, God led me to the **Culver Vedette** Newspapers on the second floor the very first day I was there. Plus, back then, Culver was proud of it's student newspapers because the faculty had them front and center at the top of the stairs. I am not pleased to report that by the time I came back for my 10th reunion, Culver no longer had their student newspapers ANYWHRE available to the students. You need to know, Culver, that makes me mad. As former Editor-in-Chief who took thousands of photographs for that **Vedette** newspaper, and creating one of the biggest staffs in three years that then produced the top High school Newspaper in the United States in 1979-80, chosen NSPA number one high school student newspaper in the USA my senior year, you should be ashamed for not having OUR **Vedettes** out for there past 30 years.

Moreover, you should also be ashamed that you don't have ALL the **Culver Vedettes** out and fully available all the time for all the Culver students. Look how inspirational they were to me, as a 13-year-old Culver Freshman in 1976, when I first read them. That was a gamechanger to have all the **Vedettes,** front and center, at the top of the Library stairs, with a big table to read them all. **This is your 125 years of your students' work**. Please stop hiding them you're your students. Please stop hiding them from me, former Editor, and stop hiding them from my **Vedette** newspaper award-winning staff, when they come in the library. We cannot even show our own children our high school pride and joy – our own newspapers!

And, please stop hiding your **Culver Vedettes** from your own students who are attending Culver now! I met my best Culver female friend on that **Vedette** staff my Freshman year, Mary Ivory Smith. She came to Culver just 6 years after you opened to girls, in 1971. Culver, you were smart enough to give Coeds the exact same opportunities as the boys, having them on the Culver newspaper, as well. Shouldn't you put their student newspapers back out. The women want to see them too!

Secretly, I am most disappointed to not be able to read November 1976 issue with Dave Hemmings and Jon Agne's hysterical articles about Dust Bunnies running across your Barrack room floors right when General Inspection commences! I miss those. Please get all the student newspapers back out for everyone to read anytime.

Those student newspapers at the top of the stairs in the Culver Library in 1976 led to one of the best Culver **Vedette** staffs and best newspapers in the Untied States three years later. That is what the Library should be doing for its students.

CHAPTER 35

I FOUND REVEREND MARTIN'S BIBLE STUDY
IN THE MESS HALL

One of the first organizations I joined as a Freshman at Culver was the Reverend's Bible Study/Youth Group. It turns out that Reverend Chaplain William Martin had a Bible Study that met in the Mess Hall every other Tuesday for Lunch. As soon as I found out about it, I joined.

Reverend Martin was an Episcopal Minister, originally from the State of Virginia. When I joined his Bible Study I did not know that he was an Episcopalian, like I was.   That makes this another God Thing! As you know from way back in this book in Chapter 5, that I was brought up in Dr. Macgaffey's Episcopal Sunday school class at St. Peter & St. Paul's Episcopal Church in El Centro. No surprise, then, that God would have virtually the same education going on at Culver when I arrived for high school. I was quite pleased, because I had some semblance of an idea of what was going on in the Main Culver Memorial Chapel and in Chaplain Martin's Bible Study.

This was indeed the first place I met Mary Ivory Smith, another Culver Freshman from farming country in California, although from the other end of the State. It turned out that Mary Ivory was also brought up Episcopalian, so we had that in common. A couple of months later I met her on the **Vedette** Newspaper. The second meeting was a strong indication to me that we must have a lot in common! It turns out over the next four years we became much closer on the Vedette Newspaper than in Bible Study.

For now, Bible Study every other week at lunch in the Mess Hall Small Dining Room was a nice diversion from the Plebe system and classes. Plus, this was the first time I began to feel smart at Culver, because I had read a lot of the King James Version of The Bible at home, so I was able to understand it and talk intelligently about it. When you are 13 years old and begin to feel smart, no matter where that might be, from the sports fields to the Cadet Military system, to Bible study, you begin to gain some confidence. As we all know, confidence can take you a long way! I was not feeling smart at the newspaper or the military system quite yet, so this early confidence boost at the King James Version of the Bible Study, under Reverend Martin, was just what I needed Freshman year.

It also led me to be close to Chaplain Martin for my whole four years at Culver. Nice to have that constant rock and someone looking out for me. He did the same for Mary Ivory, too! Again, parents in the United States and other countries, is that not what you want for your children? No better place to get confidence, learning, and moral values than at your Church, whether it is Protestant, Catholic, Orthodox Christian, Buddhist, Hindu, Sikhism, Judaism, Bahai, Shinto, or Jainism?

CHAPTER 36

BOSTON'S FIRST ALBUM – SUMMER OF 1977
GREATEST ALBUM OF ALL TIME, BAR NONE!

Opening lines to Boston's Rock'n'Roll song, *"More Than a Feeling,"* off the rock band Boston's first album, titled, **Boston**:

I looked out this morning and the sun was gone
Turned on some music to start my day
I lost myself in a familiar song
I closed my eyes and I slipped away
It's more than a feeling
(More than a feeling)
When I hear that song they used to play.

Every girl and boy in the United States born in the 1950s and 1960s knows every single word to that song and will instantaneously recall the melody in his or her mind, when he or she reads those words I just typed.

Furthermore, we will ALL remember exactly where we were when we first heard that song on our radios in our homes or at our friends' homes. That song was the greatest song of the 1977s decade. Don't take my word for it. Take your parents word for it! The Album was released in August 1976. The first single, *"More Than a Feeling,"* was released the next month, September 1976. By the end of 1976, every middle schooler and every single high schooler, even young couples in their 30's dating, all knew that song by heart.

By the Summer of 1977, the kids in every basement in America were listening to that exact album, and only that album, the whole summer of 1977. I know this because my brother and I built a Lionel Train set in our basement, just listening to that album, day and night, day after day, the whole summer of 1977. If we went over to any friend's house, male or female, they were playing that album – and only that album – the whole Summer of '77. That had never happened before in America and it has never happened since in America: The whole country was listening to that **Boston** album and only that album, day and night.

Why? Because it is the greatest Rock'n'"Roll album of all time. The Who, **Who's Next** is number two – and you know how much I love The Who and **Who's Next**! The Beatles **Sergeant Pepper's Lonely Hearts Club Band** is number three. Fleetwood Mac, **Rumors**, is number four. And those are my three all-time favorite bands: The Beatles, The Who and Fleetwood Mac are unbelievably awesome bands. I believe that the Beatles are, far and away, the greatest rock band of all time. And, those 3 albums by those 3 bands are unbelievably awesome albums. But, those three albums cannot hold a candle to Boston's first album, **Boston**. Don't worry, I will explain myself right here and right now!

How do I know? First, every kid in the world bought Boston's first album. **Every single kid in the world played Boston's first album non-stop** from issue date in August 1976 to the end of Summer 1977 and virtually no other album.

Second, listen to Boston's first album all the way through. Right now. Listen to Boston's **Boston**, every song without stopping. Then, listen to the other top 3 albums of all time I listed above. Plus, **even listen to your own favorite album of all time** that you love the most, all the way though. If you don't have an all-time favorite album, then I recommend my number five favorite album of all time: The Beach Boy's **Pet Sounds**. When you listen to the top five albums of all time, and especially your favorite album of all time, all the way through, for example, Beatles **Sgt. Pepper's**, is admittedly, phenomenal! But, it has some weak songs.

Is **Sgt. Pepper's**, all the way though, truly song after song, as great, as Boston's **Boston**? My wife does not like half of **Sgt. Peppers** because it is too hard and too crazy for her to even listen all the way to the end. Not Boston's **Boston**! My wife LOVES all the songs on that Boston album and she has listened to it all the way through many, many times when she was younger and even now. By the way, you may rate your favorite album of all time, ahead of my favorite album of all time. That is perfectly fine! That is what makes being a human so great! We do get to decide what our favorite is! And, in America we always get to vote on the radio in the old days! And we all get to vote with our pocketbook, by purchasing the albums we love.

After you have listened to all five of your favorite albums all time, then listen to Boston's first album, **Boston**, again, all the way though. **I promise: You will not be able to stop listening to it.** Just like all the rest of us in the whole world when it came out in 1976-77! It is the only album I have ever heard where EVERY SINGLE SONG is 5-Star fantastic! When the worst song on the album, *"We're Just Another Band out of Boston"* is 5-Star AMAZING, and it is the worst song on the album, what does that tell you? It tells you that it is the greatest album of all time.

Finally, when I was out on the farm in El Centro, in 1986, just finished college at Vanderbilt, and was sitting with my brother, Jim Kuhn, and some friends, we asked ourselves the age-old question,

"What is the best rock album of all time?" My friends knew I would say one of those other three albums from the other three great bands, because I love those three bands the best and their albums are iconic. But, I immediately said "Boston's first album is the best album of all time and my number one." My brother and my friends were dumbfounded.

So, I said to them all, "I have an actual test as to what is the best album of all time." They said, "What is your test?" I said, "It is easy and after you hear the test, you will all agree with me." They said, "John, what is your test?"

I said, "Okay, imagine someone puts a gun against your head and says you can only take one album with you to a deserted island and only play the one album the rest of your life. If you take two albums you are shot, by the gun against your head, and killed because you cheated. **You can only take one album to the deserted island for the rest of your life.** And, you cannot take a greatest hits album because that is cheating – greatest hits albums are not the rock band's actual album, rather, the band's greatest songs."

My friends and my brother said, "Ohhhh, I see where you are going with this! And, you are correct, you might have a different choice of album if it is the only album you could play the rest of your life. So, when you think about it, the album you would want to hear the rest of your life, is your all-time favorite album, isn't it?"

I said, "Exactly!! That is your favorite album." Then, I went on to exclaim: "And, if I were told I could only take one album and listen to it the rest of MY life, **I would take Boston's first album because EVERY SONG makes you feel happy and makes you want to sing to it!** Every song is upbeat and amazingly melodic and the guitars are mind-blowing!! ALL THE SONGS on the album are astonishing. Plus, the songs are fun, beautiful, and upbeat. If I can take only one album with me and can only listen to one album the rest of my life, it will, indeed, be Boston's First Album, **Boston**."

Just for you readers, even though Fleetwood Mac is my **third favorite band** of all time, way ahead of Boston which is probably number 15 all-time favorite band for me, I would be hesitant to take Fleetwood Mac's album, **Rumors**, to a deserted island, because I just do not love Stevie Nicks' nasal voice. She has a number one single on that album that I do not even like – and I did not buy it as a single – because it is too nasally. I only give the song by Stevie Nicks on the album *"Dreams"* 3-Stars. Plus, I only give *"The Chain"* song 4-Stars, which brings the album down a touch, in my book. Although, Mick Fleetwood's drumming on "The Chain is phenomenal, so that is one of the best Fleetwood Mac songs in concert, bar none.   If you are one who loves Stevie Nicks' voice, you probably take **Rumors** and that will be your Number One album, which is fine and that is why we all get a vote! However, most of America already voted with me in the 1970s when they never took the needle off Boston's first album for 13 straight months. All of us loved it and played it, every day, for a whole year. Nothing nasally on Boston's first album. Their lead singer, Brad Delp, has one of the greatest, smoothest, rock voices of all time. Brad Delp's voice is lightyears better than Robert Plant's voice in Led Zeppelin, who my wife does not like because he is way too nasally on every song. However, my wife does love Stevie Nicks' voice, but she would also take Boston's first album, **Boston**, first to a deserted island because she LOVES all the songs on the album.

Here is why the Beatles' **Sergeant Pepper's Lonely Hearts Club Band** is number 3 all time and not number 1: I do not love every song on the album, like I do EVERY SONG on Boston, **Boston**. Off **Sgt. Peppers**, I do not even remotely care for "Within You, Without You." Way too whiny for me and too much Sitar guitar. Nothing whiny on Boston's first album. If George Harrison's *"Here Comes the Sun"* had happened in time for **Sgt. Peppers**, instead of his whiny *"Within You, Without You,"* that would move Sgt. Peppers to number one. But, you cannot play that game. And you only get to take ONE ALBUM with you on the deserted island for the rest of your life. Again, most of us Rock'n'Roll fans, if pressed would pick Boston, **Boston.**

And, I already told you that I do not love lead singer Stevie Nicks nasally voice most of the time, especially on Fleetwood Mac's **Rumors**. But, her voice is AMAZING on the song *"Landslide,"* but that is a different album. On the other hand, I believe Lindsey Buckingham is the greatest guitarist of all time, and top 5 songwriters in Rock history, and he has *"Go Your Own Way"* on **Rumors** to prove it. If there was more Lindsey and less Stevie, I would be happy! Without Lindsey Buckingham's absolute musical genius – putting him right up there with his beloved Brian Wilson of the Beach Boys – Fleetwood Mac was decent, but not amazing. All of Lindsey Buckingham's music is AMAZING, right down to *"What Makes You Think You're the One,"* on the album **Tusk,** and Buckingham's guitar playing, over the past 40 years and still counting, is still second to none. Even my beloved Who guitarist, Peter Townshend – who in my book is the second greatest guitarist of all time – but he is well behind my all-time favorite guitarist, Lindsey Buckingham!

The other incredibly close second greatest album of all time is The Who's **Who's Next**. But, like the Beatles' **Sergeant Pepper's Lonely Hearts Club Band**, it has one 3-star song amongst all those 5-Star songs, and that is John Entwistle's *"My Wife."* However, that is one star better than George Harrison's whiny *"Within You, Without You,"* and, to Entwistle's credit, *"My Wife"* is an outstanding straight-forward Rock'n'"Roll song, and Entwistle is not one bit nasally, and the lyrics are funny, even to women! So, I will place **Who's Next** number 2 all-time, and one ahead of **Sgt. Pepper's**, which, for me is Number 3 all time.

That still makes Fleetwood Mac's **Rumors** Number 4 all-time, despite Stevie Nicks nasally voice! The star female singer on **Rumors**, for most of us, is candidly, Christine McVie! Shout out to probably the most underrated song writer in Rock'n'Roll history, who just died, and that would be Fleetwood Mac's Christine McVie. She maybe has the best female voice in rock history and she has *"Songbird"* on **Rumors** to prove it! I would take her all day, any day, over Stevie Nicks! Plus, Christine McVie's *"Dreams"* was a legitimate number one song off **Rumors** that every girl in America danced to for years! Fleetwood Mac had Christine McVie sing *"Songbird"* as the encore for every Fleetwood Mac concert for 20 years and all the fans would raise their lighters and close their eyes and sing along with Christine and her *"Songbird!"* Cannot do better than that!!

Dear Reader, this is the last chapter of Volume 1 of my Trilogy, Autobiography. That means next year you can buy Volume 2 of *I Tell It Like It Is!* which will not disappoint on the music front! Why? Oh, because, next volume you are going to find out that I ended up at Vanderbilt University for college and you will immediately find out three "rock-star" musicalicious (there, I created a new word for the Oxford English Dictionary (OED) – one of my long-time goals!) things coming in Volume 2:

First, I was elected as the youngest Social Chairman in the history of the 100-year-old Sigma Chi, Alpha Psi Chapter at Vanderbilt and introduced black music to the girls and boys of Vanderbilt, putting Grand Master Flash's *"Don't Push Me I'm Close to the Edge"* first on my unbelievably awesome Mixed Cassette Tapes "Playlists" that I made for Sigma Chi on my Nakamichi Dragon tape deck. Second, I also signed the alternative rock band R.E.M. my Freshman year at Vanderbilt, end of 1980, for our Sigma Chi fraternity parties the next Fall, only to get a call from Micheal Stipe that summer of 1981 saying they got too big over the summer to play fraternities – and my telling him it was "all cool." I told Michael Stipe I was just delighted that I obtained all their signatures at "Cantrels Music Bar" when I saw them in Nashville with only 50 other folks, Spring of 1981 before they made it. That R.E.M. report will be a fantastic narrative in the next volume of this book, Dear Reader. Third, you will learn that I love all music, so long as it has a melody, especially Beethoven's sixth symphony, and I will give you a deep dive in Volume 2 as to what that means!

The beginning of Volume 2 we will go back to Culver Academies for 15 Chapters, my Sophomore to my Senior year, that I have not covered, and how I was hired by Sports Illustrated out of High School as an 18-Year-Old Sports photographer. You will love that story! Plus, I will fill you in with many stories about the **Vedette** and how we climbed to top high school student newspaper in the United States by my Senior year. Oh, and I will tell you fully about the HUGE fire my sophomore year that completely destroyed the beautiful "Old Gym" in one night **and how my black and white photographs of that fire were printed nationally**. Plus, how I met actual owner of the New York Yankees, Culver Graduate, George Steinbrenner, several times when he came to Culver to replace the "Old Gym" in one year with the Yankees gym straight from Yankee Stadium. I took lots of black and white photographs of the Steinbrenner New Gym, including the new weight room equipment and lockers and mailed them to George Steinbrenner. Five chapters on that are coming in the second volume!

I will tell you another Godwink for this (as you already know from this Volume) huge Los Angeles Dodgers fan, when I found out another actual graduate of Culver Military Academy, in 1922, was Los Angeles Dodger's owner, Walter O'Malley. Almost all New Yorkers know Walter O'Malley as the baseball Owner who hired the first black man in baseball, Jackie Robinson – yes Walter O'Malley, of Culver, broke the color barriers when he was owner and they were still the Brooklyn Dodgers. I will give you 5 more Chapters on Walter O'Malley in the next Volume about how I LOVED Walter O'Malley for moving The Dodgers from NYC to Los Angeles, and how my favorite pitcher was Sandy Koufax, most accurate fastball pitcher ever! I will cover how Walter O'Malley allowed me to interview third-baseman Ron Cey on Opening Day at Dodger Stadium, for the Culver Vedette! Yes, lots for me to cover in Volume 2, coming out next year!

I did not even mention that about one-half of Volume 2, as you know from prior chapters of this Volume, will be my taking you with me, Dear Reader, to Japan, to start a dairy cow hay businesses from nothing at all, saving my family farm in the process. So many funny stories, from my not knowing what a Freight Forwarder was, to establishing that whole department on our farm, or going to Japan port and asking the Japanese what a 40-foot container was! You will be taken to lots of Japanese business meetings in downtown Tokyo, with the cutest Japanese girls ever serving me green tea, to lots of Japanese business meetings on the Dairy farms, with the cutest Japanese dairy daughters serving me green tea. Dear Reader, you are going to love learning the Japanese hard-working mentality and Samurai-sword culture from me, who loves all Japanese people.

You will also learn how my father got Huntington's Disease, and then how my brother got Huntington's Disease, and how you learn how to cope with whatever God throws your way! Huntington's Disease is the cruelest disease in the world. I will not dwell on that in any of my books, because I am a born cheerleader, especially in business with the Japanese and with my tax advice business that I will introduce you to in Volume 3. But, for our children, I will tell you how my wife and I negated Huntington's Disease for our children by using the information and technology from the best medical researchers in the United States, which helped us stop the disease with our generation. I will even talk about **meeting the Indiana Rock Singer John Cougar Mellencamp at the incredible Hereditary Disease Concert** at the Waldorf Asteria Hotel in New York City with my mother.

Oh, and I will tell you in the next Volume how, in the 1980s, my mother discovered Bauman Rare Books in that same Waldorf Astoria Hotel in NYC, on the same trip. How my mother purchased for me my Great-Grandfathers (Winfred Embury of Canada) Centennial Edition of his favorite poet, Robert Burns of Scotland and bought me my first literary books in her Grandfather's memory and put them under the Christmas tree for me that year!

In fact, that is how I got so interested in Writing! My Mother's Christmas gift of Robert Burns Complete Works inspired me, for certain. I figured if Robert Burns, from the Countryside in Scotland, can write half crazy, then certainly I, from the Countryside in California, can write half crazy, too! That Christmas Gift from She-Who-Must-Not-Be-Named, was the impetus for this very John Kuhn Autobiography! Don't forget, my mother was "the hand that rocked my cradle," so I do owe every instance of my inspiration to her. I cannot thank Madeline Hall Kuhn enough, that is for sure. Everything in my life started with her (pun intended, lol, since she gave birth to me!) My mother started me on my God-given path in this life in El Centro Memorial Hospital on July 31, 1962!

Want to keep keeping up with the Kardashians; **ohhhh, I meant**, want to keep keeping up with the Kuhns? Be sure to buy Volume 2 when it comes out next year!

www.ingramcontent.com/pod-product-compliance
Lightning Source LLC
Chambersburg PA
CBHW071712120626
46550CB00001B/194